W9-BIR-264

All About Christmas

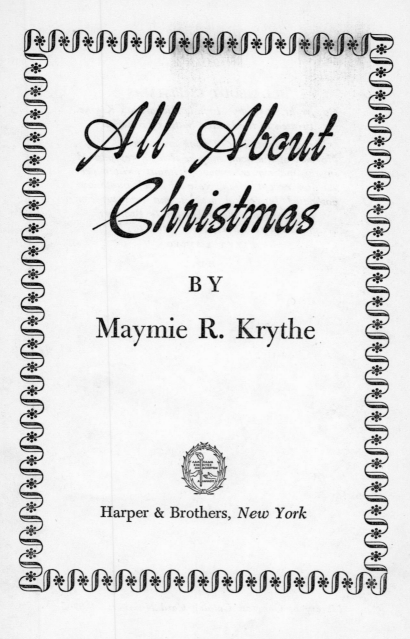

All About Christmas

BY

Maymie R. Krythe

Harper & Brothers, *New York*

To Carol Jean Kirschbaum

Contents

1. "It Came Upon the Midnight Clear"   1
   The origin and development of our modern Christmas

2. "We Three Kings . . ."   13
   The story of the Wise Men or Magi

3. "Good Saint Nick"   24
   The Evolution of Santa Claus

4. "Bearing Gifts . . ."   36
   Christmas gifts and gift bearers

5. "Deck the Halls . . ."   45
   The origin, types, and legends of Christmas greenery

6. "O Christmas Tree! O Christmas Tree!"   61
   The origin and spread of the custom of decorating Christmas trees

7. "Kindle the Christmas Brand . . ."   76
   Customs and beliefs associated with the Yule log

8. "Away in a Manger . . ."   85
   Nativity scenes, the Putz

9. "The Boar's Head in Hand Bring I"   97
   Christmas feasts and foods

CONTENTS

10. "No Candle Was There . . ."   113
    Christmas uses of candles and other lights

11. "There's a Star in the Sky"   120
    The origin and uses of the Christmas star

12. "I Heard the Bells on Christmas Day"   125
    The history and traditions of Christmas bells

13. "Joy to the World"   131
    *The history, types, and purpose of Christmas
    cards*

14. "Christmas Voices"   138
    *The history, uses, and purpose of Christmas
    seals*

15. "Shout the Glad Tidings"   144
    A general history of carols

16. "Good Christian Men, Rejoice"   155
    Stories about certain Christmas carols

17. "There's a Song in the Air"   165
    More stories about carols

18. "O Come, All Ye Faithful"   177
    *Unusual ways, places, and circumstances of
    carol singing*

Bibliography   193

Index   201

All About Christmas

1

"It Came Upon the Midnight Clear"

WHEN THE ANGELS appeared to the wondering shepherds, as they kept watch over their sheep, in the fields near Bethlehem, the celestial chorus sang "that glorious song of old"—"Glory to God in the highest, and on earth peace, good will toward men." So began our most beloved religious festival—Christmas, or *Christes Mass*. Now, all over the world, this holiday is celebrated in various ways, under such names as *Kerst-Misse* in Holland; *Noël* in France; *Il Natale* in Italy; *Weihnachten* in Germany; and *El Natal* in Spain.

A celebration, at the time of the winter solstice, when all were looking forward to the coming of spring, was not an original idea with the Christians. For, many years before Christ's birth, other religious groups had held festivals (connected with the earth's fertility) at this same season. The Romans, for example, observed the lavish Saturnalia—honoring Saturn, their god of agriculture—from the middle of December to the beginning of the new year. They exchanged gifts, and indulged in much eating, drinking, gaming, and visiting. Masked revelers on the streets often went to great excess during this riotous celebration.

Since primitive peoples realized their dependence upon the sun as the source of light and life, sun worship was prevalent among them. In Persia at the winter solstice, they observed a notable feast to show their reverence for the sun, and they kindled great fires in homage to Mithra, their deity of light.

In Northern Europe, the pagan Teutonic tribes (whose new year began at the time of the winter solstice) met at that period, to honor their "All-Father," Woden (or Odin). After gathering their harvests, they slaughtered animals for meat during the following months. This was the natural time for feasting and general rejoicing. By the light of bonfires, they consumed quantities of food and drink during their "Yuletide" season, the rebirth of the sun.

When Emperor Constantine established Christianity as the state religion of the Roman Empire, the persecution of the Christians came to an end. At first, Christ's birthday was not observed by His followers, for the Church fathers did not want this sacred occasion put on a par with pagan carnivals. One official, Origen, especially declared against such a practice, asserting that it was sinful to keep Christ's birthday "as though He were a King Pharaoh."

Although in the early centuries of the Christian era the exact date of the nativity was not known, by the third century some had been observing the event on these varying dates: January 6, February 2, March 25, April 19, May 20, and November 17. (At this period there were five different systems of reckoning time.)

Finally—according to St. Chrysostom—at the request of St. Cyril of Jerusalem, Julius I (Pope or Bishop of Rome from A.D. 337 to 352) made an investigation into the matter of the date. In A.D. 350, December 25 was set as the most probable time. The Feast of the Nativity was first observed on this day at Rome, perhaps in 353; and from then on the custom spread eastward.

About a century later (440) the Pope at Jerusalem also accepted this ruling, as did most of the other Christians, except the Armenians, who still observe Christmas on January 6. Various scholars had wanted the date established as January 1, March 21, March 29, April 9, or September 29. Although authorities did not agree—and this time may not be the correct one—the world will no doubt continue to celebrate the holy festival on December 25.

It is interesting to note that different sources have suggested reasons why the early Church officials selected this particular date. Many of the Roman soldiers were adherents of Mithraism, a religion that for a time was a strong rival to Christianity in the Empire. Its most important feast day, *Dies Solis Invicti Nati* (Birth of the

2

Unconquered Sun), occurred on December 25. Also, the Roman Saturnalia came at this time, as did the Jewish Feast of Dedication of the Temple. The latter, one of their most important sacred days, commemorated the cleansing of the temple after its profanation by Antiochus Epiphanes in the second century.

The Church authorities *may* have set the date of Christ's birth to correspond to celebrations already in vogue through earlier beliefs. Perhaps they thought it wise to give a sacred meaning to pagan observances, rather than antagonize new converts by doing away completely with old customs. For instance, instead of thanking a heathen deity for the rebirth of the year, the Christians were inspired to show their gratitude to the one and only true God.

Pope Gregory once wrote St. Augustine, advising him about the wisest way of converting the Anglo-Saxons. The prelate was in favor of allowing them to continue their heathen practice of slaughtering oxen, but to do so to the glory of God, rather than to Woden, as had formerly been their practice.

But attempts to combine pagan and Christian events led to difficulties. In Rome, for example, where the Saturnalian ideas still were strong at this season, many Christians were guilty of conduct frowned upon by the Church. St. Gregory (who died in 389) urged his people to celebrate Christmas "after a heavenly and not an earthly manner"; and he warned them against excessive indulgence in gluttony, dancing, etc. Taking part in plays and other secular spectacles, dressing in grotesque costumes, such as animals' skins, were also forbidden.

The actions of some unruly converts in Rome had a strong influence, even on the distant Teutonic tribes. St. Boniface, "The Apostle to Germany," wrote to the Pope, complaining that his efforts were frustrated by the conduct some northern visitors had witnessed near the great Church of St. Peter at Rome.

This caused embarrassment to the prelate; and by repeated bans he tried to restrain Roman Christians from going to excess at the winter festival. And, as the early Church found itself unable to abolish former customs entirely, it did the next best thing; it took over certain ones, "christianized" them after purging them of their

3

worst features, and incorporated them into the Christian observance of Christmas.

Such traditions as using greenery and candles, or other lights, for decorating homes and churches, bringing in and burning the Yule log, singing carols, giving presents, feasting happily together, amid general rejoicing—all these have become integral parts of our Yule-tide festivities. Although, at first, Christians were supposed to observe the day of the nativity only as a religious holiday, gradually secular elements were added. Therefore, our modern Christmas, in which varied elements are successfully combined, is indeed "the feast of all mankind."

In the United States we now have an unusually complicated celebration, one that is truly "a strange medley of Christian and pagan rites." For our land was settled by men of differing religious ideas, men from various countries, each of which had its own characteristic customs and traditions.

Before reviewing the influence of other lands on our holiday festival, it may be interesting to note how the first Christmas was spent here in the New World by a white man—its discoverer, Christopher Columbus. This has been described by Vincent Edwards, who tells us the explorer had planned to spend the feast day in 1492 with an Indian chief, ruler of the island of Haiti. But on Christmas Eve, Columbus's flagship, the *Santa Maria,* was wrecked on a coral reef, so he and his men had to go aboard the *Niña.*

At once the chief sent natives to remove all the valuables from the wreck. Then on Christmas the Spaniards dined with the Indian ruler. Columbus had planned to start the first Spanish colony here, so he built a small fortress on the island naming it *La Navidad* (the nativity) as they had been wrecked at this season.

Since so many early American settlers came here from "Merrie England," we are naturally greatly indebted to her for many of our cherished Yuletide traditions.

In England—so the story goes—Christmas was first observed as a holiday in A.D. 521, when King Arthur celebrated his victory in re-taking York. Many guests sat at his famous Round Table, and enjoyed a bounteous meal. They were entertained by wandering minstrels, who sang of the mighty deeds of their national heroes. Jugglers, harpists, and pipe players added to the enjoyment; also such pastimes as gambling, playing dice or backgammon, along with hunting, hawking, and jousting, were popular when the Anglo-Saxons got together for their winter celebrations. At this season, the council, or Witenagemot met to attend to affairs of state, wherever the king and his courtiers happened to be.

During the ninth century, seven petty kingdoms in Britain were united under Alfred the Great, who annually set aside twelve days for Yule festivities. In 878, while he and his court were feasting in lavish style, their enemies, the Danes, suddenly rode through the land of the West Saxons and made a surprise attack. Alfred's army was scattered; and the King, with a small band, fled to the forest. According to one account, Alfred, in order to discover the Danish strength, disguised himself as a Christmas minstrel. He spent several days in their camp, where he pleased them with his ability as an entertainer, and left without their learning his identity.

After the Normans had conquered England in 1066, they built great castles and introduced their feudal system with its strict division of people into various classes, from the king and his luxury-loving nobles, down to the meanest serf. Christmas became gayer than ever before; each great lord kept open house; and food and drink were given to all who entered his walls during the holy season. This entertaining and revelry continued until Twelfth Night, January 6.

In the spacious manor halls, great fires blazed on wide hearths, lighting the walls, high ceilings, and decorations of holiday greenery. The "Lord of Misrule," a person who was well paid for his services, presided over his subjects during the Yule period with absolute power. He planned the entertainment with the assistance of jesters, mummers, and musicians, who played on their bagpipes, harps, drums, fiddles, or flageolets. Games, such as snapdragon, dancing, and caroling were the order of the time.

During the Middle Ages, Christmas was England's most popular holiday with everyone, from the king to beggars, taking part. All who could do so quit work, and gave themselves entirely to pleasure. And no people ever entered more heartily into the joys of the Yule season than the Britons did.

Christmas was elaborately observed by English monarchs of this epoch; and several outstanding events occurred on the holiday. On Christmas, 1085, William the Conqueror met with his Great Council, when they decided to make that noted survey of England contained in the *Domesday Book*. Henry II was crowned on Christmas, 1154; and on the same date in 1214, the barons forced King John to sign the Magna Carta. During the Yule of 1346, Edward III established the senior order of chivalry, that of the famous Garter. A few years later, this same ruler had, as his Christmas guests, the kings of Scotland and Cyprus.

Tournaments, staged at the winter holidays, such as Richard II gave for his visitor, the king of Armenia, were lavish and expensive affairs. Holiday entertainment also included the presentation of sumptuous pageants and masques, put on by actors, dancers, and tumblers. Some of the productions were of religious origin; but the performers often added bits of comic relief. In one popular play, the shepherd Mak stole a sheep and hid it in a child's bed in his home. When his fellow shepherds discovered his deceit, they tossed Mak in a canvas; this horseplay, of course, delighted the audiences of that period.

The English stage owes much to early holiday customs, for the first British comedy was written for a Yuletide performance. Also the earliest tragedy, *Gorbuduc,* was performed at Christmas, 1561. During the reigns of the Tudors, holiday productions reached their zenith. Since Henry VIII loved buffoonery, he furnished the actors with expensive costumes, paid them well, and encouraged his subjects in their fondness for theatrical entertainments.

His daughter, Queen Elizabeth, organized companies of actors, and sponsored Christmas plays at Greenwich and at Hampton Court; thus the modern English stage got its start. In addition to court productions, it had, for some time, been customary for the lawyers (members of the Inns of Court) to put on expensive stage performances at Christmas time.

Similar celebrations continued under the Stuart Kings; but the

Reformation was having its effect. The Calvinists declared that observing Christ's birthday was a human invention. They disapproved of it, not only because of its pagan origin, but because of the excesses to which too many Christmas celebrants went. In some places, groups of holiday revelers, under their "Lord of Misrule," even took possession of towns and caused much trouble for the authorities.

When the Civil War broke out (1642) and the Puritans came into power under Oliver Cromwell, their ministers preached strongly against Christmas observance as a "heathen" practice. They asserted that Christ would not have approved of it, for it merely furnished excuse for wrong-doing.

As soon as the new regime felt secure in its position, Parliament passed an act forbidding the celebration of Christ's nativity and other religious festivals, including Whitsuntide and Easter. Everyone was ordered to go on with his work as usual; shops were to stay open on Christmas Day; and no one was allowed to light Christmas candles or to eat holiday cakes. In many places on Christmas Eve the town criers went around and called out loudly so that all might hear, "No Christmas! No Christmas!"

This edict caused rioting on the streets between the two factions —in Ealing and Canterbury, for example. But many Englishmen continued to observe the day in spite of the Puritanic law. Some ministers, with members of their congregations, were actually arrested for attending services on Christmas. The Puritans went about their daily business on former Church holidays; and their Parliament met on Christmas Day as usual.

With the Restoration of the monarchy under Charles II (1660), old Yuletide customs "emerged from hiding." However, from this time on, holiday observance never reached its former extravagance. During his exile, Charles had known poverty, so he discouraged his lords from putting on the expensive pre-Cromwellian masques. Gradually the "Lord of Misrule" disappeared from the scene; the "Age of Cards" arrived; and this became a favorite holiday pastime. Some of the nobles still kept open house for their tenants; people of the middle class enjoyed their Christmas dinners; and in remote rural districts many of the old customs continued in use.

7

ALL ABOUT CHRISTMAS

A characteristically British holiday tradition that survives today came into existence during the eighteenth century—the Christmas pantomime. In December, 1717, Edmund Rich, who held the license for the theater at Lincoln's Inn Fields, put on *Harlequin Executed,* the first English pantomime. During the next forty-five years—until his death in 1761—Rich kept producing these annual performances with their fantastic stories, spectacular stage effects, singing, and dancing.

In the Victorian period Charles Dickens, who reveled in Christmas lore and traditions of his native England, revived former customs, and many of his countrymen joined him. Dickens's influence, through his incomparable *Christmas Carol* and other holiday classics, was also felt strongly here in the United States.

With the settlement of America by both Puritan and Cavalier types, naturally the attitudes of each group in regard to Yuletide traditions and observances had their effects upon the development of our chief holiday.

The Puritans, of course, brought their hatred of such festivities with them. That first Christmas on the bleak New England shore must have been a gloomy one, with all merriment banned. The men went ashore from the *Mayflower* to fell and carry lumber, and worked the entire day. Governor Bradford reported in his diary that on "ye 25th day begane to erect ye first house for comone use to receive them and their goods."

Next year, 1621, the governor again insisted that work be continued as usual, and permitted no religious observance. That Christmas Day, some young men who had come on the *Fortune* (after the arrival of the *Mayflower*) excused themselves from work for religious reasons. Later that day, when the governor found them on the street, playing ball, he became very angry and stopped their sport, declaring it went against *his* conscience to see them at play while others were laboring. He added that if it were "a matter of devotion," they should stay indoors. (Even though the Pilgrims did not take any notice of Christmas, their Thanksgiving Day, with its feasting and sports, really took its place, when they joined in festive celebrations with friendly Indian neighbors.)

In 1659, because of their continued enmity toward holiday joys, the Pilgrims passed this law:

> Whosoever shall be found observing any such day as Christmas and the like, either by forbearing labor, feasting, or any other way upon such account as aforesaid, every such person so offending shall pay for each offense five shillings as a fine to the country.

Despite this decree, there was some celebrating in Massachusetts, for members of the Church of England were also settling there. After a long struggle the law was repealed in 1681. Five years later Governor Andros conducted a service in the Boston Town Hall; and this may have been the first legal Christmas held in the colony. However, the holiday did not become lawful in Massachusetts until 1856; and New England did not enter wholeheartedly into Christmas celebrations until late in the nineteenth century.

In marked contrast to these stern Puritans was the attitude of the jolly Dutch settlers in near-by New Amsterdam, later New York. They loved Yuletide feasting and merriment; and from their "Sant Nikolass" evolved our modern Santa Claus.

Christmas has been properly observed in Virginia from the time of Captain John Smith, when he and his men feasted on fish, oysters, and game they had caught. As the colony grew and prospered, visiting and gay festivities went on at the stately colonial mansions. Many of the settlers in Virginia were descendants of the pleasure-loving Cavaliers. So from "Merrie England" they brought with them such holiday customs as ringing bells, burning a Yule log, dining elaborately, dancing, playing games, and singing carols. Their homes and churches were lavishly decorated with garlands of evergreens, while hundreds of candles furnished illumination for long-remembered holiday balls, where handsomely dressed ladies and gentlemen danced the stately minuet.

(During the Revolution, General Washington knew that the German mercenary soldiers, the Hessians, whom George III had sent across the Atlantic to fight his rebellious colonists, would be celebrating Christmas as they had done at their homes in the Old World. So he took advantage of this fact, crossed the Delaware in

1776, and attacked the redcoats while they were sleeping off the effects of too much holiday food and drink.)

Today, in beautifully restored Williamsburg, Virginia, the gracious eighteenth-century customs have been revived. Many visitors join with the townspeople in Yule log ceremonies, candlelight concerts, square dancing, and caroling. And on Christmas Day open house is held at the old Raleigh Tavern; and at other hotels in this unique city, delicious Southern dishes are served with the same grace that distinguished the Christmas dinners of colonial days.

In the South many persons continue the characteristic Yule habit of shooting firearms or firecrackers. Some sources say this custom originated in early days when settlers wished to send Christmas greetings to distant neighbors. Others believe the idea goes back to the ancient habit of making noises to frighten away evil spirits.

In Theriot, Louisiana, the holiday is kept in the middle of February, for during the regular Christmas season the men are away on the marshes trapping. In some parts of the South, "Old Christmas" is celebrated on January 5, or 7, a date related to the visit of the Magi, or Wise Men, to the Holy Babe.

During the holidays, Florida becomes closely connected with all the other states through the mails. Near Orlando there is a small town, Christmas, with about 250 inhabitants. It was formerly a fort and was so named because it was completed on Christmas, 1835. For the past twenty or more years its postmistress, Mrs. Juanita Tucker, has been kept busy stamping cards, letters, and packages (sent from all parts of our country) with "Christmas, Florida," and remailing them. In one year alone, her small post office handled more than 300,000 pieces of mail. And to live up to its name, the town has a permanent Christmas tree set up, with weatherproof ornaments.

In Pennsylvania, many persons observe the old holiday traditions of their Moravian ancestors, while, at various places in the Middle West, Scandinavian customs still prevail. They usually begin on St. Lucia's Day—December 13—and the same special dishes are enjoyed that were served generations ago by their European ancestors.

The Spanish influence in our great Southwest has strongly affected Christmas celebrations. An ancient Spanish nativity play, *Los Pastores,* reached this section from Spain, by way of Old Mexico. In its complete form, it took about five hours for one performance, and was usually given out of doors. It has been played in Texas; and in December, 1950, was revived in Los Angeles. Several of the episodes were staged by members of *Los Fiesteros,* a group made up of descendants of early families and others who are interested in preserving California customs, music, and traditions.

Los Pastores (The Shepherds) is an old miracle play with its theme the eternal struggle between Good and Evil. One of its chief features is the attempt of the Devil (*El Diablo*) to prevent the shepherds' going to Bethlehem to worship the Christ Child. But with the aid of the Archangel, St. Michael, the Devil is put to rout; and the shepherds reach the stable, kneel devoutly before *El Niño,* and present Him their gifts.

Before the American conquest of California, *Los Pastores* was very popular in the pueblo of Los Angeles. Men and boys from a near-by *rancho* practiced their parts for weeks before Christmas. Then, on Christmas Eve, they came into town, stopped at various homes around the Plaza, and gave their play, often adding some humor to the speeches. These performances continued until Twelfth Night in town and at outlying *ranchos.*

Las Posadas (The Lodgings) is one episode of *Los Pastores,* depicting the journey of Mary and Joseph from Nazareth to Bethlehem, and their fruitless search for an inn in the crowded town. In recent years this play has been a special feature of the holidays on Olvera Street in Los Angeles, beginning on December 16 and continuing until Christmas Eve. Each evening four Mexicans carry a small cart, containing wax figures of Joseph and Mary. They are followed by a procession of men, women, and children in colorful garb with lighted candles and gaily decorated shepherds' crooks.

When they knock at a door, they chant "The Litany of Loretto," and ask for admission, which at first is refused. When the owner finally relents, all enter and kneel before the manger, or *nacimiento.* This pageant is repeated at a different home each night; after the religious ceremony, the evening is spent playing games, dancing, and feasting together. On Christmas Eve the climax is reached when an image of the Christ Child is gently placed in the empty cradle.

At Mexican Christmas parties in our Southwest a popular feature is the *pinata,* a large earthenware jug, filled with candy and nuts. It hangs on a rope from the ceiling; and a blindfolded child is given a bat, and allowed three "tries" at breaking the *pinata.* As the jug can be pulled up and down by the rope, the game often continues for some time, before the youngster succeeds in breaking it. There is a wild scramble when the children get down on the floor to gather the goodies scattered over it.

So, today, wherever you travel over this great country, you'll find interesting, varied customs and ways of celebrating our modern Christmas. All these traditions are a valuable heritage from different periods of time and from faraway places; and they combine to make our Yuletide unique. Here in the United States all kinds of individuals from widely diverse backgrounds join in homage to the Christ Child.

2

"We Three Kings . . ."

> They laid their offerings at his feet;
>   The gold was their tribute to a King,
> The frankincense, with its odor sweet,
> Was for the Priest, the Paraclete,
> The myrrh for the body's burying.
>
> —from Longfellow's "The Three Kings"

ONE OF THE most highly cherished traditions connected with our Christmas celebration is the story of the coming of the Wise Men (Magi, or the Three Kings, as they are variously called) from the East to pay homage to the Infant Jesus in the manger at Bethlehem. A popular and stately Christmas hymn, "We Three Kings of Orient Are," reminds us of this famous incident, the "Adoration of the Magi." The scene has been depicted by some of the world's finest artists, including Botticelli, Veronese, Leonardo da Vinci, Rubens and Dürer. This incident was a popular one with painters during the Renaissance and following periods.

These Oriental visitors are shown in splendid, colorful robes, and make a strong contrast to the roughly clad shepherds, who kneel near by. This strange visit of the Magi is reported in the New Testament only by St. Matthew, who called them "Wise Men from the East." As early as the sixth century, they were spoken of as "kings"; but artists did not picture them with crowns and regal dress until after the eleventh century. Then they were shown with a large number of attendants; and some of the faces were portraits of contemporary persons.

As time passed, many legends grew up around the mysterious

13

travelers, who have been identified by some historians—Bede, for instance—as Melchior (ruler of Nubia and Arabia); Balthasar, of Ethiopia; and Kaspar (or Caspar), of Tarsus. The trio represents three stages of life, with Melchior depicted as a small, venerable man with a long beard; Balthasar, swarthy and bearded, is about forty; while Kaspar, a tall, ruddy, beardless youth, is perhaps twenty years of age.

"Magi," a word meaning "august," was the name given to the priestly caste among the ancient Medes and Persians. These men were, in addition to "the keepers of the sacred things, the learned of the people, the philosophers and servants of God," also highly esteemed as diviners and astrologists. No matter of importance took place without their being consulted; they were closely associated with the reigning monarchs and in charge of the princes' education. However, when in later centuries their influence lessened, they became, in some cases, merely wandering fortunetellers and quacks.

According to tradition, the three Wise Men who journeyed to Bethlehem had had contacts with Jews and had heard the prophecy that a bright new star would arise to announce the coming of salvation to the world. Therefore, they watched the sky patiently for years; and when the star finally appeared, the Magi set out to find and worship the One who was to redeem mankind.

Babylon—so legends tell—was their starting point. The food and drink they carried with them never diminished in amount. After the star had led them to Jerusalem, it wavered and disappeared. The Jews in the capital of Judea were astonished to see this cavalcade of strangers on camels making their way through the city and asking, "Where is he that is born King of the Jews? for we have seen his star in the east, and are come to worship him."

Immediately Herod, greatly troubled by this unusual turn of events, gathered the members of his council together. He demanded to know where their prophets had foretold that Christ would be born. When he learned that Bethlehem was the chosen place, Herod pretended an interest in the Wise Men's story, and told them, "Go and search diligently for the young child; and when ye have found him, bring me word again, that I may come and worship him also."

As soon as the Magi left Jerusalem, they again saw the star, shining more brightly than before. ". . . they rejoiced with exceeding great joy"; and it led them to the place where the Child lay. It is said that when the trampling of the camels' feet sounded in the narrow street Mary, frightened, held the Baby Jesus more closely to her breast. (Some authorities assert that the visit of the Three Kings occurred on January 6, when Christ was about two weeks old, while others maintain the event happened one or two years later, in Egypt.)

"And when they were come into the house, they saw the young child with Mary his mother, and fell down, and worshipped him: and when they had opened their treasures, they presented him gifts; gold, and frankincense, and myrrh." The gold, carried in a shrine-shaped casket, signified acceptance of Him as their King; the frankincense was symbolic of His Deity; while the myrrh, in a golden horn, was prophetic of His death. Mary, it is said, in return gave the Wise Men the white linen bands in which she had wrapped the Holy Infant.

The Magi, warned by God not to return to Herod, left for their own homes by another route. Joseph, too, was told in a vision to flee with Mary and Jesus to Egypt. According to tradition, when the Magi reached their kingdoms, they gave up their high positions, distributed their property to the poor, and went out to preach the gospel of the Prince of Peace. Forty years later in India, St. Thomas, one of the Apostles, met them, baptized the trio, and ordained them as priests of the Christian Church. As bishops, they were persecuted for their faith, and suffered martyrdom together.

Three hundred years later, Empress Helena, mother of Constantine I, ordered the bones of the Three Kings placed in the great mosque of St. Sophia in Constantinople, where they were held in veneration. At the time of the First Crusade, they were transferred to the Cathedral of Milan.

When Emperor Barbarossa conquered Milan in 1164, he bequeathed the relics to Raynaldus, Archbishop of Cologne, who at first placed them in a small chapel. Then "with much pomp and joy" they were moved to the magnificent cathedral of Cologne that rose on the bank of the Rhine River. In this way, the Wise Men became known as the "Three Kings of Cologne." There Philip von Heinsburg furnished a beautiful and costly marble shrine, "a mass of gilded and jeweled sculpture" to hold the sacred remains. When the doors of this shrine were opened, the tops of three skulls ("reputed to be those of the Magi"), draped in velvet and adorned with jewels and embroidery, could be seen. The ability to perform miracles has been attached to these famous relics.

The memory of the visit of the Wise Men to the Holy Land is preserved by the fact that a well named for them is still used today. It is located on the road from Jerusalem to Bethlehem. A legend relates that, after they had lost their guiding star, they stopped at this well to refresh themselves and the camels. Looking down into it, they saw the star reflected in its waters.

Another story, associated with the Three Kings, is that of Befana, the woman Santa Claus of Italian children (known as Babouschka in Russia). When the three strangers were on their search for the Child, they passed Befana's home as she was busy sweeping. They told her of their quest; and she wanted to go with them. Although she begged them to wait until she had finished her work, they continued their journey.

Later, when Befana tried to overtake the Magi, they had gone too far; so she failed to find them and worship the Holy Babe with them. Now the children in Italy believe she rides through the air on a broomstick on January 6 (the Feast of the Three Kings) in her unending search for the Christ Child. Befana, hoping that one of the babies may be the Infant Jesus, goes down all the chimneys and leaves her gifts near the manger scenes the boys and girls have set up.

The reputed date of the visit of the Three Kings to the Manger, January 6, is an important Church feast day, and has several names, including "Epiphany," "Little Christmas," "Old Christmas," "Day of the Three Kings," and "Twelfth Night."

Its official name, "Epiphany," means "manifestation" and was given the holiday because on this date there had been three important manifestations of Christ's deity: the adoration of the Wise Men; Christ's baptism with the voice from Heaven confirming His divinity; and His first miracle at the wedding feast in Cana of Galilee.

Epiphany, one of the earliest Christian celebrations, was first mentioned by Clement of Alexandria in the second century. As a feast of high significance, it is observed both in the Greek and Roman Catholic churches, as well as the Anglican. This celebration is also symbolic of the divine purpose of extending the gospel to the gentiles as well as the Jews.

In early times, Epiphany rites were a rather strange combination of heathen and Christian customs, and seem to have had some connection with the pagan observance of the spring festival, when offerings were made to streams. This may have been related to Christ's baptism in the River Jordan.

On Epiphany in such lands as Russia, Yugoslavia, and Bulgaria, the "Blessing of the Waters" was performed as a solemn service by officials of the Greek Church. In St. Petersburg, in the days of the Czars, these important rites occurred on the bank of the river, just in front of the imperial palace. Then the Czar appeared with his court and Church dignitaries for the impressive ceremonies.

In smaller places, the village priest, clad in his full vestments, led a procession of his parishioners, carrying banners and ikons; and all chanted a litany as they marched to the river. After a hole had been dug in the ice, the priest threw a crucifix into the water. At once, young men vied with each other in trying to recover the cross. The successful contestant received a special blessing from the officiating priest. After the rites, all the townspeople filled large vessels with this sacred water, carried them home, and placed the jars near their ikons. St. Chrysostom asserted that water drawn from streams on this feast day could be preserved much longer than ordinary water.

This custom, brought to the United States years ago, is still observed at Tarpon Springs, Florida (just north of Tampa), the sponge capital of the country. There Greek fishermen have charge of the ceremony which attracts thousands of visitors on each annual "Greek Cross Day" in January.

Beginning at dawn, Masses are said in the church of St. Nicholas, which is brilliantly lighted with innumerable candles. At noon the procession leaves the sanctuary. The Archbishop, wearing a jeweled crown and carrying a scepter, is attended by priests all in ceremonial robes. The altar boys—bearing various insignia—officials, members of the choir, and thousands of spectators go to Spring Bayou at the end of Tarpon Avenue. Selections from the Bible are read both in Greek and English, and a white dove, symbolic of the Holy Spirit, is released over the waters. Then the Archbishop hurls the cross, significant of Christ's baptism, into the waters.

Sometimes as many as thirty young divers try to recover it, for success is said to bring good fortune to the lucky youth. When he presents the cross to the Archbishop, the official blesses him, and the young man considers this a great honor.

In January, 1952, this ancient, colorful ceremony was introduced to the Pacific Coast at Long Beach, California. Thousands of visitors, many of Greek ancestry, gathered at the Municipal Auditorium, where the Reverend Bishop Demetrios of New York, assisted by priests from various Greek churches in the West, conducted the Divine Liturgy Mass of St. Basil.

After the service, the procession went to a near-by park. There on the quay was a font of holy water with the Holy Cross and some olive branches. The bishop dipped the latter in the font, then touched the foreheads of the persons who filed past him to kiss the cross and to receive vials of the water. When the prelate threw a small cross into the lagoon, twelve young Greek divers plunged into the waters. Then the one who brought up the cross returned it to the bishop and received a blessing.

Again, in January, 1953, the beautiful ritual of the Greek Orthodox Church was carried out at Long Beach. Bishop Athenagoras, head of the Fourth Diocese embracing eleven Western states, was in charge. After the Feast of Light on the lawn, fifteen hundred persons watched the traditional rites that commemorate Christ's baptism. California youths who braved the cold waters were defeated by a Navy man from the *U.S.S. Matthews* (whose home is at Tarpon Springs). This was his fifth attempt and first success.

For many years at Epiphany, Milan, Italy has held an outstanding celebration of the Feast of the Three Kings. The monarchs, dressed in rich costumes and attended by their pages, ride on horseback through the streets. A man carries before them a large golden star on a tall pole, representing the Star of Bethlehem. Along the way, the Kings are stopped by a man, in the role of Herod, who tries to prevent their going to the church services. But the Magi reach the church and present gifts to an image of the Holy Child in a manger.

During the Middle Ages, European priests staged simple plays to explain Biblical stories to their followers. And in Portugal, at Epiphany, dramas honoring the Wise Men were given. In Sweden, "Star Boys" went around singing carols, and gave a little pageant about the Magi. Such groups were also welcomed at homes in Germany, Poland, and Lithuania. It was the custom for these boys to mark the houses they visited with three crosses, and the initials, K, M, and B for the monarchs, so no harm would come near the dwellings. Since Epiphany ended the Yule season, French and Italian children carefully put away their manger scenes for use again next Christmas.

Spanish parents told their boys and girls that the Wise Men, each year, passed through Spain on their way to Bethlehem and that they would leave presents for children who had been good. Therefore, on Epiphany Eve, the young Spaniards would place carrots or hay in their shoes for the camels to enjoy. Of course, the next morning the food was gone, and they found presents. At night, some Spanish parents blackened their children's faces with charcoal; early next day the youngsters would rush to a mirror to see whether the Black King, Balthasar, had kissed them on his way to Bethlehem.

The Syrians have a legend that the youngest camel of the Three Kings was so weary that it fell down; and, in pity, the Christ Child blessed it. So the children in Syria believe this animal brings their presents on January 6.

ALL ABOUT CHRISTMAS

Rome, at Epiphany, was crowded with people buying gifts for boys and girls at various open-air markets, while men dressed as the Magi went about asking for alms. At St. Peter's on this day, Mass was said at three altars, with one of the officiating priests, a Negro, for during the Renaissance the idea had evolved, in connection with the Three Kings, of "racial symbolism—Asiatic, European and African."

In Belgium and France, *Le Jour des Rois* (Feast of the Three Kings), has long had a special feature, a cake called *La Galette des Rois* (Cake of the Kings). This goes back to the thirteenth century when the monks of St. Michel used to choose their Epiphany "king" by means of a cake. This elaborate piece of cookery is "plentifully daubed with almond paste," and is cut into pieces, one more than there are members of the family. The extra slice, "God's share," is given to the first needy person who knocks at the door.

The cake contains one bean; and the finder becomes the "king" or "queen" and can choose his or her partner for the day. The ruler is lifted onto the shoulders of four men, and makes a cross on the ceiling to frighten away evil spirits. That day everyone must obey all the royal commands, and it is a time of gaiety, with dancing and games.

At Epiphany in England there was also a special cake, such as the French used, called the "Twelfth Cake." The English custom of choosing a "king" (akin to the "Boy Bishop" idea) is mentioned as early as the reign of Edward, who ascended the throne in 1327.

Although Shakespeare wrote his play, *Twelfth Night,* for use at this holiday, it does not deal with Epiphany legends. There was a play, however, for the occasion, based on the custom of the king's giving gifts of gold, frankincense, and myrrh, at this season. Horace Walpole once wrote to George Montague:

> Monday, being Twelfth Day, His Majesty, according to annual custom offered myrrh, frankincense, and a small bit of gold; and at midnight in commemoration of the Three Kings, or Wise Men, the King and Royal Family played at hazard, for the benefit of a prince of the blood.

The present sovereign still carries out this ancient tradition by proxy in the Royal Chapel of St. James.

Twelfth Night was a time in Britain of much revelry; and everyone had as much fun as possible on this date, for it marked the close of the holiday season and its merriment; and all the Christmas greenery was taken down and burned in the wide fireplaces.

On Christmas Eve (on Epiphany Eve in some districts of rural England) men went out to their orchards to "wassail" the trees. They believed that if they failed to follow this old custom their trees would bear little fruit. A farmer and his helpers carried out a great pitcher of cider, encircled a tree, and drank a toast to it three times. One old chant began, "Here's to thee, old apple tree"; and the main idea of their wassailing was to beg the trees to be fruitful in the coming season.

Sometimes they dipped a branch in the cider and sprinkled the trees or poured the drink around their roots. In Devonshire it was an old custom to place a cake in the fork of a tree, and pour cider over it. The men, at times, drank part of the contents of the pitcher, then threw the rest on the branches.

In West Sussex, this pastime was called "worsling." Singers, with a man holding a cow's horn, would ask a farmer if he wanted his trees "worsled." Then they sang their doggerel, beat the trunks to insure fertility, and even discharged firearms through the bare branches. Of course, this Epiphany custom was accompanied with much noise and merriment. When they had finished the job, they went into the farmer's home to feast in his kitchen.

Twelfth Night parties are still popular affairs in some South American countries, and in Europe, where they have several Halloween aspects such as witches and fortune-telling. In some farming regions in Greece, the people used to save their old shoes to burn between Christmas and Twelfth Night. They believed that harmful elves disliked the smell of burning leather, so this act was supposed to save the villagers being bothered by these spirits.

In Mexico, the Magi, or Three Kings, still play an important part in the holiday celebration, which lasts for two weeks. In recent years, on this feast day, *La Fiesta de los Tres Reyes,"* an unusual ceremony has been taking place in Los Angeles. Three modern Mexico City businessmen, carrying a large star, and dressed in the costumes of the Wise Men, arrive by airplane, bringing greetings from their president to the mayor. In addition, they have an elaborate *pinata* of giant size filled with candy and other gifts for the children. (It is said that the *pinata* used on these occasions is in memory of the crude containers in which the Holy Family were given food and drink on their way to Bethlehem.)

After the exchange of greetings between the Mexican envoys of good will and the Angelenos, children are asked to help the mayor break the great *pinata*. There is much excitement as the gifts scatter on the platform, and the boys and girls try to get their share. This visit is another expression of the close friendship existing between our country and our neighbor, "south of the border," and also reveals that the spirit of the Wise Men is still alive today.

Many churches have Epiphany Eve services which attract visitors. In Williamsburg, Virginia, stately "Old Bruton" Church on the Eve of Epiphany—January 5—has a traditional "Feast of Lights" that is very impressive and inspiring.

In recent years cities and towns all over the United States have revived the ancient Twelfth Night custom of burning Christmas trees and other greenery. Now city recreation departments plan such festivities at public parks for neighborhood groups. The children bring in great numbers of trees; they are also collected by the town for this big event.

After dark the gigantic pile is set afire; soon the dry trees are burning brightly and lighting the sky. Sometimes chemicals are added for beautiful, colorful effects. Everyone, old and young, joins in a circle and sings Christmas carols; and they bring the festive holidays to a fitting close. Besides affording community entertainment for countless families, this custom eliminates fire hazards.

One of the finest modern contributions to our Christmas traditions here in the United States is Gian Carlo Menotti's opera, *Amahl and the Night Visitors*. The story of the Three Kings provided the composer with the subject for this, the first, and very successful opera written for television production. It was first produced, with a magnificent cast, on Christmas Eve, 1951, repeated the following Easter, and again at Christmas, in 1952 and 1953.

Amahl and the Night Visitors is the story of a crippled shepherd boy and his mother who give shelter to the Wise Men. A miracle happens, and Amahl can walk again. This production has already become a modern classic; and it will no doubt continue as an American tradition, making the story of the Magi more real to all who see it.

Thus, even in our modern world, we are thrilled to hear, or join with others in singing "We Three Kings of Orient Are"; and this story inspires us each Christmas, like the Magi of old, to "follow the star" and pay homage to the Baby Jesus in the stable in far-off Palestine.

3

"Good Saint Nick"

FOR MANY CENTURIES, "Good Saint Nick"—Saint Nicholas or Santa Claus to American children—the patron saint of young people, has been associated with Christmas and gifts. His name, originally from the Latin, *Sanctus Nicolaus,* has had various forms, including the German, *Sankt Nikolaus,* Dutch *Sinter Klaas,* finally becoming our modern "Santa Claus." Although it is customary to regard him as a myth, there actually was a real St. Nicholas, an early Christian bishop, who lived during the fourth century. It was because of his unusual generosity that our ideas of the modern saint have developed.

Nicholas, the only child of wealthy Christian parents, was born at the close of the third century, perhaps about 280, at Patara, a port in the province of Lycia in Asia Minor. Early in his childhood, his devout mother taught him the Scriptures. When both parents died during an epidemic, they left the young boy in possession of all their wealth.

Young Nicholas dedicated his life to God's service and moved to Myra, chief city of his province. There, after the death of their bishop, members of the Council balloted unsuccessfully, for some time, trying to choose a successor. Finally, in a dream, the oldest official was told to stand next day at the cathedral door and select as the new bishop the first man named Nicholas who entered.

When the young Christian went to the church as usual for morning prayers, he was asked his name; and soon afterward he was selected by the Council and consecrated to the high office. Nicholas, because of his youth, tried to refuse the position, but he was over-ruled.

Early in his new career, during a visit to the Holy Land, he was so impressed by the places connected with Christ's life that he decided to resign from his bishopric at Myra and remain in Palestine. But God commanded him to return to Asia Minor. During the reign of Emperor Diocletian, when many Christians were persecuted, the young bishop was imprisoned, in the year 303. Later he was freed, when Constantine the Great "proclaimed an imperial toleration of all religions."

Nicholas was very popular as bishop, and several stories of his ability to perform miracles have come down to us. On his return from the Holy Land, it is said that a mighty storm arose, and the ship was almost wrecked. Nicholas calmly prayed to God; and the sailors were astonished when the wind suddenly abated, and their lives and ship were saved.

Also there is a legend that he restored to life a sailor who had died as a result of falling from a high mast. On this voyage it was revealed to Nicholas that the ship's master was planning not to return him to Patara, but to sell him as a slave. Again Nicholas was successful through his prayers, for a heavy wind forced the vessel back to Asia Minor.

During a famine St. Nicholas saved his province from starvation by persuading captains of imperial grain ships to let him have part of their cargo. They were not willing, at first, to do this, for the grain had been weighed carefully for delivery to the Emperor's officials. But finally they yielded to his pleas; and the starving populace was fed. Then, when the masters delivered the grain to the authorities at Constantinople, they found to their astonishment, that they still had the original amount. Also, the supply they had furnished to Nicholas miraculously increased, and fed the people of Asia Minor for two years.

Another miracle attributed to him happened in 325, when the sons of a rich Asiatic, on their way to study at Athens, were killed and robbed by a wicked innkeeper, who had previously been guilty of similar offenses. This man hid the boys' dismembered bodies in

67915

casks of brine, or as one source said, "salted them down for pork." St. Nicholas, on his way to the Council of Nicaea, stopped at this inn, and that night in a dream the crime was revealed to him. He forced the wicked man to confess; then Nicholas made the sign of the cross over the casks, prayed earnestly to God, and immediately the three boys were restored to life. Therefore, it is not surprising that the good saint became the patron of children.

One of Nicholas's chief characteristics was his unsurpassed generosity. In his youth he had learned, by going around among the people, how many were oppressed by poverty. As a result, he often went out in disguise and distributed presents, especially to children.

The most popular story of the saint's good deeds concerned the three daughters of a nobleman who had lost his fortune in unsuccessful business ventures. As a result, there was no money for dowries; and in those days, a daughter without a dowry had little chance for marriage.

The bishop decided to remedy this; and when the oldest girl was of marriageable age, he went to their home one night and secretly threw a bag of gold through the window. Not long afterward, the girl married well; and at the proper time for the second, Nicholas repeated his kind deed.

But when the third was grown, her father decided to keep a close watch to find out who their benefactor was. When he caught the bishop in the very act of throwing in the bag of money, the grateful father could not keep the secret, even though the donor begged him not to reveal his name. So the three daughters were happily married, all through the kindness and generosity of St. Nicholas, who is consequently regarded as the patron of marriageable girls.

One version of this story is that one of the purses or bags fell into a stocking hung near the chimney to dry and that, from this incident, the Christmas custom of hanging stockings in anticipation of receiving presents originated. Stories of the bishop's liberality soon spread; and, thereafter, when unexpected gifts were received, he was given credit as the donor.

After the bishop's death in 341 (or near that date) there was sincere mourning for him. Stories of his generosity and miracles were told far and wide; and pilgrims came from long distances to visit his burial place. Although this rich shrine was raided by Saracens in the ninth century, they were driven off. By the eleventh, St. Nicholas's was one of the most visited tombs. But after the Saracens overran Asia Minor, they took Myra in 1034, and made it difficult for Christians to go to the shrine.

About 1085 some sailors and merchants of the Italian city of Bari, at the heel of the Italian "boot," decided to remove St. Nicholas's remains to their town for safekeeping. Three ships went on the expedition; and several men landed secretly at Myra, and carried off the sacred relics. One story is that on the return voyage there was a heavy storm; and the sea did not become calm until certain sailors replaced some small bones they had stolen from the casket.

The expedition reached Bari on May 9, 1087; and within a few years the bishop's remains were placed in their permanent resting place, a great basilica, named to honor him. Soon Bari had become the mecca for religious pilgrims, including those of the First Crusade, on their way to Palestine. These devotees carried back to their own countries stories of St. Nicholas and his generous deeds and miracles.

Each year on May 9, the inhabitants of Bari celebrate his arrival from Myra. They carry a statue of this saint far out to sea in a boat, accompanied by other craft. When night comes, all return to Bari, where the streets are thronged with quaintly dressed pilgrims. Immense bonfires, torches, and fireworks welcome the return of St. Nicholas. Before replacing the image in the church of his name, they carry it from one church to another; and the entire day and night are filled with happiness and rejoicing.

Because of the bishop's remarkable childhood and his selection while still a youth as a high Church official, he was sometimes called the "Boy Bishop." An unusual custom, in vogue for centuries, had its origin in this fact.

In medieval times in some lands, especially Germany and England, at such great cathedrals as York, Winchester, St. Paul's and Westminster, "Boy Bishops" were selected each year on St. Nicholas's feast day, December 6 (which is the date of his death, not his birth). At schools connected with monasteries, the students of such institutions chose one of their fellows to rule over them on this date. They were obliged to obey his canonical commands; sometimes he exercised the privileges of this office until December 28, "Holy Innocents' Day."

Early in the tenth century, King Conrad of Germany visited a monastery, and told of seeing boys engaged in such ceremonies. The young "Bishop" wore a mitre, carried a crosier; and he and his retainers were dressed in colorful garments. They solemnly entered the chancel, and took part in the service, where the "Boy Bishop" preached the sermon. When they marched in a procession through the streets, they were allowed to collect money called the "Bishop's Subsidy." That same evening the youthful group was entertained at supper by high church officials.

"Boy Bishops" were elected in many English parishes: for example, one said vespers before Edward I when that monarch was en route to Scotland; and the king gave him money as a present. Edward III once paid nineteen shillings to such a young ruler, which was said to be a large sum for that time.

Henry VIII, after breaking away from the Catholic Church, abolished the "Boy Bishop" idea, but his Catholic daughter, Mary, restored the tradition in 1554 by ordering one "Boy Bishop" to be chosen in each parish. That same year the "Boy Bishop" of St. Paul's, London, and his retinue sang before the queen. Soon after Elizabeth's accession to the throne, the custom was discontinued. However, just a few years ago in Kent, it was revived, when a youth named Nicholas Smith was selected as "Boy Bishop."

In his pictures and statues, St. Nicholas is usually shown carrying three bags or balls of gold, reminiscent of his gifts to the three dowryless sisters. To show their regard for him, bankers of Lombardy in Northern Italy took him as their patron, and placed three balls over their places of business. Since they lent money to clients, this sign became associated with pawnbrokers; and ever since it has been used by the latter. A custom also gradually came into vogue of paying rents, mortgages, and various bills on the saint's feast day.

Because the bishop had been famed for his ability to calm the sea in times of storm, he became the patron of all sea-faring men. Along seacoasts many chapels have been dedicated to his memory. Shipowners, too, placed the insignia of the three balls on their vessels. It is said that Dutch seamen were the first to carry to western Europe tales of the bishop's generosity; as a result, children in Holland got their presents on December 6.

St. Nicholas had spent some years in prison because of his religious faith, and so had become acquainted with thieves and other criminals. They, also, prayed to him; but when robbers placed goods under his protection, he made them return the plunder to the lawful owners. In England thieves were often spoken of as "St. Nicholas's clerks."

More than six hundred years after his death, Vladimir of Russia went to Constantinople to be baptized. Back in his native land, he told so many stories of St. Nicholas that Russia took him as her patron, as did Greece, where even today many boys are named for him. St. Nicholas is popular elsewhere as the saint of such cities as Liége in Belgium, Lucerne in Switzerland, and Freiburg in Germany. More churches have been named for him than for any of the apostles. In Belgium alone, three hundred bear his name; Rome has sixty; while there are almost four hundred in England.

When the Dutch settled *Nieuw Amsterdam*—now New York— they brought along their traditions of St. Nicholas, and named their first church for him. In fact, a figurehead of the saint adorned the vessel, the *Goede Vrouw,* which brought them to these shores in 1630. The image wore a broad-brimmed hat, and had a long Dutch pipe. In the New World, the bishop laid aside his official, churchly robe, and was transformed from a pale ascetic into a tubby character in short breeches.

On his feast day in December the Dutch were accustomed to parade down their main street, carrying his statue with them. The children, of course, were on hand for this festive occasion, for this was the day he brought them presents. In New York, through the English influence, by the beginning of the nineteenth century, the St. Nicholas Day celebration had merged with that of Christmas, although many persons there of Dutch extraction continued to observe it on the earlier date.

In New York on February 22, 1835, a society was organized to honor the bishop by the famous writer, Washington Irving, who served as its first secretary. Anyone who had lived in the state in 1785, or who was descended from a settler of that time, was eligible for membership. Each year on December 6 the members met, smoked long pipes, and observed other early Dutch customs.

Our well-known and popular Christmas poem honoring the saint, "A Visit from St. Nicholas," was written by Dr. Clement C. Moore, who taught in a theological seminary in New York. His verses popularized the new conception of Santa Claus driving his eight reindeer over the housetops.

It is said that Dr. Moore had heard a Dutch friend, a short, chubby man with a long white beard, telling stories about the saint. No doubt, the author drew inspiration for his noted description of St. Nicholas from him. On December 22, 1822, Dr. Moore read the poem to his children for the first time. A visitor in the home was so delighted with the stanzas that she copied them; and next year she had the poem published in the Troy, New York, *Sentinel*.

At once it became very popular; but the author apparently thought it somewhat beneath his dignity, for he did not include the verses among his printed works until years later. After his death, on several occasions, Dr. Moore was honored on Christmas Eve at a chapel near his burial place. At these memorial services, there was a Bible reading, followed by tableaux and carols. Then a procession of children carrying lighted candles made its way to his grave.

Clement C. Moore's description of St. Nicholas was read in all parts of our country. And our modern Santa Claus was further developed when the well-known cartoonist, Thomas Nast, pictured him in *Harper's Illustrated Weekly* in 1863 in a red, fur-trimmed suit. Nast, a native of Bavaria in Germany, remembered "Pelze Nichol" ("Nicholas with the Fur") of his childhood, who brought children presents. During the Civil War, the cartoonist cheered the Union soldiers and their families when he patriotically depicted the saint in a red, white, and blue outfit with his sleigh and reindeer, visiting the soldiers at their camp, and giving them holiday gifts.

Now, in this twentieth century, many persons wonder whether Santa Claus and the giving of presents haven't become too commercialized. Small children are bewildered when they see more than one St. Nicholas on the street or in stores. When we consider the traditions connected with him, we are amazed at some of the things that have happened to him.

What, for example, would the good old bishop think if he should read this advertisement which appeared in recent years in a great daily newspaper?

VISITS IN YOUR HOME

BY ST. NICK

Santa in person in your Home—Office—

School—Factory—Parties

Your child will thrill to a visit by Santa

Now—Dec. 4–25—Special Christmas Eve and

Christmas Day Visits

Approved by the Better Board of Santa Clauses

(Screen—Stage—Radio Actors)

This special group, known as Santa's Helpers, Inc., is well trained, and its members appear in good costumes and fine make-up. Before going to special assignments, they learn the names, ages, likes, dislikes, etc. of the young customers. When he reaches a home, Santa Claus opens a large order book, and conducts his interview with each child. The usual charge for such a visit is $15, from December 4 to 24; but on Christmas Eve, or on Christmas Day, the fee is $25. In some cities there are even schools that train the men in make-up, first aid, fire prevention, child psychology, and story-telling. At the end of the course some persons get degrees in "Santa-Clausing."

It is a bit surprising to read that also in conservative England some of the large stores have succumbed to the custom of hiring "Father Christmases," the equivalent of our American St. Nick or Santa Claus. And English children, like those here in the United States, happily visit toy departments and tell their gift bringer, "Father Christmas," what they want that year.

ALL ABOUT CHRISTMAS

Among the men who for several days each year, just before the holidays, play Santa to wondering youngsters are individuals from such different occupations as ministers, railroad conductors, engineers, and others.

According to an article in the *Saturday Evening Post* (December 22, 1951), the world's highest-paid Santa Claus is Bill Strother. He receives $1,000 per week for a month from a department store in Richmond, Virginia. During this time he also makes numerous visits to hospitals, orphanages, and the homes of shut-ins. Naturally, his outfit is of the best; and his "realistic beard, mustache, and eyebrows" alone cost $500, and must often be replaced.

One of the best loved St. Nicks in Southern California is genial Jimmy McGarrigle, a well-known singer of Long Beach. For about twenty years he has annually donned his red suit and white whiskers—ever since the day he first played Santa Claus on the old U.S.S. Lexington.

During a recent holiday season, he made more than forty appearances in this role before various clubs, orphanages, etc. Just before Christmas (1951) he met 186 airplanes at the International Airport in Los Angeles, and gave a gift to each incoming and outgoing passenger.

Jimmy McGarrigle, because of his love for children and all mankind, makes an ideal St. Nick. Once, when asked what Santa meant to him after all these years of impersonating the famous saint, he gave this sincere message: . . . "Santa Claus has even a greater meaning to me now. Santa Claus means watching the wonderment, surprise, and love that I see in the eyes of children as they look at me. It is the purest look that a human can behold." . . .

In recent years St. Nick has gone quite modern by arriving from his home at the North Pole in different manners. In many cases he seems to prefer to leave his eight reindeer and sleigh behind, and use a newer method of transportation. Cities, all over the country, vie with each other in finding novel ways to bring him to their communities. Not long ago Santa arrived in Chicago by parachute; he was luckier that year than a St. Nick who tried the same method in Florida, but got caught in some wires when making his descent.

Boston has received him all boxed up in a large crate, while youngsters in Maryland greeted him as he came riding in the cab of a locomotive. Not long ago, Salt Lake City imported some husky dogs from the North to pull Santa into town on a sled. At cities on the seacoast, he has arrived by boat; elsewhere, fire trucks, mule-drawn wagons, old-fashioned stagecoaches—all have been used for his transportation.

At one naval station St. Nick thrilled the youngsters as he stepped from a helicopter, carrying a big bag full of presents. When he arrived in a DC-6—escorted by fighter planes at Lockheed Air Terminal—a crowd of 25,000 people gave him a rousing welcome.

Several cities, including New York and Hollywood, have staged elaborate parades, featuring Santa Claus, that draw thousands of spectators. The film capital's "Parade of Stars" along Hollywood Boulevard, decorated with glittering trees, includes bands, horsemen on prancing steeds, and the good saint himself, dressed in a red velvet suit, and riding in a $25,000 sleigh.

In our country we have a town that glorifies St. Nicholas, the small community of Santa Claus, not far from Evansville, Indiana. In 1882, at their general store on Christmas Eve, it is said that some residents were discussing what to name their town, when Santa Claus walked in. At once someone called out, "Let's call it Santa Claus!" and so it got its unusual name.

Nowadays, at the Christmas holidays, this is one of the busiest places imaginable. Mail arrives here from every state and even from other countries to be stamped with the postmark, "Santa Claus." The small post office has been enlarged at several different times, for as many as three million pieces of mail pass through it at this season.

The local American Legion Post helps with this enormous job. Since 1935, one member, Mr. Jim Yellig, has played Santa Claus. For years letters addressed to St. Nick were destroyed by the Post Office Department. In 1938, the local American Legion Post offered to answer them, and to keep faith with as many children as possible. Sometimes posts in other localities assist in investigating worthy requests and fulfilling them when this can be done. Mr.

Yellig and his assistants send each child writer a letter signed "Santa Claus," stating he may not be able to answer all requests, but wishing everyone a "Merry Christmas."

Thousands of tourists, young and old, visit the town of Santa Claus annually, and enjoy the museum—the original postoffice of 1866—with its fine collection of toys from varying periods of time.

Also, there is the Santa Claus Park, with an "Enchanted Trail." Along it are dioramas of life-sized Mother Goose figures. On Kriss Kringle Street is a colored statue of St. Nick, twenty-three feet high, and weighing forty-two tons. On its pedestal are these words:

DEDICATED

TO THE CHILDREN OF THE WORLD

IN

MEMORY OF AN UNDYING LOVE

There's another village called "North Pole" or "Santa's Workshop" that was completed in 1949. It is located on the side of Whiteface Mountain at Wilmington, New York, near Lake Placid. This artistically planned project was designed by Arto Monaco, who formerly worked with Walt Disney. There are ten log houses, with steep roofs, a permanent home for Santa Claus, a post office, a blacksmith shop, and a small chapel with a charming nativity scene. Angels seem to be flying above the stable; and the entire scene is lighted by a beautiful star.

In some of the buildings Santa and his assistants are busy, making toys and other gifts. The money for buying the materials is given by crowds of tourists who visit the unusual place and throw coins into the wishing well. At Christmas, the presents are distributed to children in orphanages in several Eastern states.

On the grounds there's a real lollipop tree; also you can see the North Pole. Of course, the live animals, eight reindeer, burros, ponies, sheep, and goats get much attention from young visitors. "Santa's Workshop" is open from June 1 to November 1; and the spot has already attracted more than a quarter of a million people. And it is just one more evidence of the continued interest that Santa Claus holds, both for old and young.

Torrington, Connecticut, during the two weeks before Christmas, has a "Christmas Village" for its children. They can visit St. Nick in his workshop and see the elves working on toys of many kinds, while near-by shelves are loaded with gifts. Santa sits in a room, where presents hang from the walls and ceiling, chats with each youngster, who visits him; and gives him a little gift.

Santa's red sleigh is an added attraction for the boys and girls, who are thrilled by his eight real reindeer that include the popular holiday favorite, "Rudolph, the Red-nosed Reindeer." One of the most inspiring scenes, as at "North Pole," is the lovely representation of the nativity. The figures of Mary, Joseph, the Wise Men, and the shephards are almost life size; and the beloved Star of Bethlehem lights the straw-filled manger where the Baby Jesus is lying.

Not only in such places, but all over our land, the spirit of Santa Claus still lives. For weeks before Christmas, countless individuals work unselfishly preparing holiday cheer for underprivileged children and adults. So, no matter what the good old Saint is called— *Jule-nissen, Sankt Nikolaus, Sint Nicolaas, Santa Klaas, Father Christmas, Petit Jésus, Père Noël, Befana, Kriss Kringle,* or *Krist Kindlein*—his name is a synonym for unselfish giving.

In spite of his modernization, it is good that the memory of the generous bishop, St. Nicholas, is still alive today, for he is the personification of the true spirit of Yuletide and brings happiness to millions of children. We Americans are proud that St. Nicholas evolved here into his present character—a jolly, chubby Santa Claus —a *real* New World contribution to the world's store of happy holiday traditions.

4

"Bearing Gifts . . ."

"BEARING GIFTS, WE traverse afar" was the chant of the Magi or Three Kings, as they carried their precious offerings of gold, frankincense, and myrrh on that long journey from the East to the manger in the Bethlehem stable. There, joyful, because the star had guided them aright, the Wise Men bowed before the Holy Babe in adoration and presented Him their treasures.

Our age-old tradition of remembering relatives and friends with presents at the holidays is one of the most satisfying of our Christmas joys. This is especially true if such giving is done in an unselfish way without thought of like return, for it reveals the highest type of Yuletide spirit.

Because of the well-known incident of the coming of the Magi, many persons have the belief that the custom of giving gifts at our winter festival originated with their presentation to the Infant Jesus.

However, the idea was prevalent even before Christ's birth. The Romans, for instance, used to exchange gifts at this time. They went out to the forests and gathered vervain—boughs of laurel, olive, or myrtle, sacred to Strenia, goddess of health. People gave such branches, symbolic of health, happiness, and affection, to their rulers.

As years passed, the Roman emperors began to desire and demand more material rewards from the populace than mere greenery. Consequently, clothes and articles made of gold or silver, such as statues of the gods or goddesses, became the usual presents for royalty. Emperor Caligula even made a law compelling his subjects to present gifts to him; and he stationed himself on the porch of his palace and waited there to receive these offerings.

During their winter festival, the riotous Saturnalia, the Roman citizens used to give "good luck" presents, or *strenae,* to their friends. At first these consisted mainly of fruits, but later other things took their place. They gave "honeyed" gifts to make life sweeter; or lamps, to assure the recipients of light and a bright future; or gold, to provide for their wants in the coming year. Since the rich shared with the poor during the Saturnalia, the custom of less fortunate persons asking for alms is said to stem from this era.

In the fourth century, a Greek named Libanius wrote that the spirit of generosity seemed to take hold of individuals at this time of year, for then each one gave lavishly of what he had to make others happy. The writer asserted that this was indeed a good thing and served as an antidote against the individual hoarding of wealth.

In Egypt, at the winter solstice celebration, parents often placed presents, such as puppets, small chariots, and other playthings, on the tombs of dead children. These gifts were supposed to comfort the departed. In excavations of recent years, many toys have been found that were placed at the burial sites centuries ago by sorrowing parents.

In England, after the Norman Conquest by William the Conqueror, there was a revival of culture, along with the erection of great castles and abbeys. Then it became the custom for wealthy individuals to present costly presents to monasteries and schools. Such gifts usually were given on Church feast days, especially on Christmas Day. On December 25, 1067, just a year after William had come to England, he gave the Pope much of the loot taken when his men plundered Britain. This included the ensign of the Saxon ruler whom he had defeated.

Churchmen, too, during the Middle Ages in England were expected to share with their monarchs at Christmas. In 1252, for instance, Margaret, the daughter of Henry III, was married at Christmas to Alexander, king of the Scots, in the city of York. Henry attended with one thousand knights, while the Scottish king had sixty men in his retinue. Gay and long-continued festivities marked this event. The Archbishop of York presented the king with six hundred fat oxen for the feasting, besides giving a large sum of money to his sovereign to help pay the wedding expenses.

In 1268 this same monarch, Henry III, while putting on his annual holiday celebration, ordered all shopkeepers to close their places of business during the entire period of fifteen days. This was a severe blow to the merchants, so they appealed to him to be allowed to carry on their trade. Henry would not let them reopen until they had paid him the princely sum of two thousand pounds.

Often English monarchs took it as a matter of course that their people give them holiday presents. When the nobles and other subjects arrived at the royal festival, each was expected to bring a gift, in accordance with his rank and wealth. History tells that Queen Elizabeth used to acquire practically all of her extensive wardrobe by this Yuletide giving. At Christmas, 1561, a lady-in-waiting knitted Her Majesty a pair of silk stockings. Elizabeth was so pleased that ever afterward she refused to wear any other kind of hose.

When Charles II came to the throne, after the Cromwellian era, he permitted the custom of holiday giving to rulers to be revived. But he made some givers angry, as Pepys has reported in his famous diary. The latter said that the king had bestowed all these presents upon his favorite, beautiful Lady Castlemaine. This, Pepys wrote, was "an abominable thing."

After Henry VIII had broken away from the Catholic faith, St. Nicholas was not supposed to visit his country with presents for the children. About three centuries later, when Queen Victoria married the German Prince Albert, the latter brought back from Germany the St. Nicholas tradition to England. But the white-bearded old gentleman who is said to bring the Christmas gifts was called "Father Christmas," even though he is the counterpart of the earlier St. Nicholas and the modern Santa Claus. For many years now, English youngsters have hung up their stockings for Father Christmas to fill, and families exchange presents on Christmas Day.

Consideration for the poor has always been an important feature of holiday celebrations in England. December 26 is St. Stephen's

Day or "Boxing Day"; and it was almost as important as Christmas Day itself, for on it, in accordance with an old custom, the village priest would open the "poor box" at the church and distribute its contents to the needy.

Gradually it became customary on Boxing Day to give Christmas "boxes" to servants, and to those that performed public services, such as tradesmen, postmen, policemen, dustmen, parish clerks, beadles, crossing sweepers, milkmen, newsboys, and cabmen. These persons went around on Boxing Day with the hope of picking up some extra shillings.

Back in 1710, the noted writer Jonathan Swift complained that this had become a great burden (no doubt similar to modern tipping) and declared he would simply be "undone" by the expensive custom of Christmas "boxes." It seems that the attendants at the coffee houses—then popular meeting places—had raised their annual fees from half a crown to a whole one. Swift paid the money, not because he wanted to, but he didn't wish to be shamed before others, to appear too niggardly.

The source of holiday presents to children has been given different names in various places. However, St. Nicholas seems to be the most widely acclaimed source. Housewives in Northern Europe used to have their chimneys cleaned just before the Yuletide season, so their fires would burn better during the winter months. But they told the boys and girls that the chimney sweeps were doing the job so that St. Nicholas could get down them more easily to fill the shoes or stockings with gifts.

In Czechoslovakia, it is said, the youngsters believed the saint came down from heaven on a golden cord with a basket of presents for all good boys and girls.

In Northern European lands, such as Holland, Belgium, and Germany, children were told that St. Nicholas, dressed in his red bishop's robe with miter, crosier, and jeweled gloves, rode around on his white horse the night before his feast day—December 6—to bring their gifts. He was said to jump from roof to roof, then climb down each chimney. In shops in the cities at the holidays, there were always gingerbread replicas of the good bishop for sale.

ALL ABOUT CHRISTMAS

Often fathers, older brothers, or uncles on December 5 would dress like St. Nicholas and go to various homes to ask the children about their behavior in the preceding year. On this preliminary visit he had with him a servant, "Black Peter," who carried a heavy stick and a black bag.

At the time of his expected arrival, the children spread a sheet on the floor before the door, and sang songs to welcome him. Then, when the door opened, a shower of candies fell on the sheet, and after the scramble for the sugar plums, the boys and girls begged St. Nicholas and his servant to enter. Immediately the bishop asked about their actions, while Black Peter showed the bag in which he *might* carry them off. After the questions had all been answered, St. Nick promised to return that same night with gifts for those whose behavior had been satisfactory. Before they went to bed, the children put out some water; and in their wooden shoes placed carrots or hay for the good saint's horse. Sometimes their parents, too, would furnish a sheaf of grain for the steed. The youngsters' boxes or baskets stood waiting the hoped-for contributions. Next day—St. Nicholas's Feast Day—they were delighted to find he had left them ginger cakes, candies, toys, books, and various trinkets. Often the tables or chairs were tipped over to show that their patron had really been there. But naughty children found only switches, and the food they had put out for the white horse was left untouched.

In Austria St. Nicholas made his rounds with *Knecht Ruprecht;* there, boys and girls usually received practical gifts of warm mittens, other useful clothing, or food. When mists rose at this season in Belgium, parents said that the bishop was baking his Christmas cakes. As in other lands, doors suddenly opened on the eve of December 5, and candies fell inside the room. The saint's servant had different names in varied localities, including *Pelze Nichol* (or *Pelsnickol*), *Schmutzli,* and *Jan Haas.*

In Germany, after the Reformation under Luther, some sources assert that Protestants wanted to substitute the Christ Child (*Das Christlkindl*) for St. Nicholas as gift bringer. Therefore, in many homes, when the family had gathered happily around their glittering Christmas tree, the *Christkindl* would arrive. Sometimes a youth took the role; but often a young girl with long blond hair acted the part. She was dressed in a white robe, wore a golden crown, golden wings, and often carried a small Christmas tree in one hand. Even though these Protestants had changed their celebration from December 6 to Christ's birthday, many still continued to give or receive small gifts on St. Nicholas's Day, as before.

Germans have always been generous in their giving at Christmas. They buy numerous presents; and the women often spend months making fine pieces of needlework for their friends. Even the smallest children are encouraged to make simple gifts for their parents, brothers, and sisters.

When all the presents have been carefully arranged on a large table near the tree, along with plates of apples, nuts, and candies, and everyone is breathlessly waiting for the gifts to be distributed and opened, suddenly the door flies open. Then a large package is thrown into the room with a cry of *"Julklapp"!* Such presents usually have many wrappings; and when the receiver has finally taken off all the coverings, he finds a small but precious gift. At New Year's Day, Germans reward their servants and others who have been of service to them.

In some Swiss districts, the Christ Child is also acclaimed as the source of holiday generosity. Dressed as an angel, the Child rides around in a sleigh drawn by six reindeer. Candies, apples, oranges, cookies, Christmas trees, and other gifts are distributed. Everyone is happy; and that night all go to church to join in a midnight Christmas service.

In some Swiss communities St. Nicholas's Day is the time to begin the Yule celebration, while in others, it starts on December 13, St. Lucia's Day. On the latter, the women sit up late to finish their presents or to complete other holiday preparations. In Switzerland, too, sometimes a "jovial and red-faced 'Father Christmas'" (or St. Nicholas) dressed in a fur robe and accompanied by his wife goes around the neighborhood. He gives gifts to the boys, and she, to the girls.

During the weeks preceding Christmas, French children are much excited over the beautiful toys, dolls, etc. that are displayed so lavishly in the shops of their large cities. Also at the small booths along the boulevards, one can buy fascinating, but inexpensive presents. In France the youngsters receive gifts on Christmas after they have hung up their stockings or set out shoes for the Christ Child (*Petit Noël* or *Le Petit Jésus*) to fill for them.

New Year's Day is the time for French family reunions and gifts for adults. Boys and girls often give little homemade presents to their parents. On this same holiday it is customary for tradespeople to remember their patrons; also the servants and clerks are given bonuses for faithful work.

In Spain the church services and manger scene, or *nacimiento,* in the home are the chief Christmas features; and gifts have never played so important a role as in several other lands. However, as stated before, Spanish children set out their shoes on Epiphany Eve for Balthasar, one of the Three Kings, to fill on his way to the Holy Land.

It has been the custom for postmen, messengers, and others in Spain to give their patrons small leaflets containing holiday greetings; in return they are remembered with gifts. Landlords, doctors, ministers, and others often receive turkeys or other farm products, while the rich give food and clothing to the needy. This last is an old custom, originating in the superstition that bad luck might come if one failed to help the poor at this season of peace and good will.

When the candles are lighted on Christmas Eve in an Italian home, the "Urn of Fate" is brought out. This is filled with wrapped packages. The mother draws hers first, then the others follow. If anyone gets a package marked with his name, he keeps it; otherwise, he puts it back and tries again. That evening before the Feast of the Three Kings (Epiphany) Italian children set out shoes, or hang stockings, for *Befana,* the female Santa Claus, to fill. They go to bed, confident that she will ride through the air, come down their chimneys, and leave them presents.

(Years ago in Russia, children believed that a counterpart of *Befana, Babouschka,* was the bringer of good things at the Yuletide.

Now, in that country, January 1 is the day for family reunions; and the present Russian Santa Claus is known as "Grandfather Frost.")

There are several interesting beliefs and customs about Christmas gifts in Scandinavian Lands. In Denmark, for example, boys and girls believe that a small gnome, dressed in gray and wearing a pointed cap, is responsible. They call him *Jule-nissen,* and set out a large portion of rice pudding, their favorite holiday dessert, for him to enjoy.

In Sweden, little men with long gray beards, the *Tomtar* that live in dark corners or under boards, are said to leave surprise packages for children under cushions or in other hiding places. On Christmas Eve, after the boys and girls have put on their best clothes, the mother opens the door of the room where the tall, shining tree stands, with its star and other ornaments, and surrounded by a heap of packages. As the father distributes the gifts, they have fun reading aloud the original rhymes attached to the presents.

Gifts in Sweden are exchanged on December 13, the Feast Day of St. Lucia, a Sicilian maiden, who suffered martyrdom in the year 304. As she was noted for giving food and drink to the poor, it is customary on her day to perform such deeds as a memorial to her.

In Hungary on St. Lucia's day, boys go around singing chants that are supposed to make the hens and geese fertile. Then the mistress at each home gives the boys small tokens of some kind. Carolers in Albania carry gaily decorated sticks to which they fasten the gifts they receive in return for singing.

Christmas festivities begin in Mexico on December 6 and end a month later. Beforehand, many Mexicans are busy making toys and other articles in their homes. Just before Christmas, they carry their products in baskets to the market places in near-by towns. Tiny figures, for use in manger scenes, so popular in Catholic countries, are sold in large quantities. Mexican youngsters, like those in Spain and Italy, get their presents at Epiphany.

Since the spirit of generous giving fills the air at the Christmas holidays, in some lands, animals, too, are remembered. St. Francis of Assisi wanted "all creation" to share in Yuletide happiness, so he gave domestic animals an extra amount of food at this time. A Russian legend tells that at the night of Christ's birth barnyard animals and fowls helped spread the joyful tidings. Therefore, on Christmas Eve, they ate a special "Holy Supper." In the Scandinavian countries, sheaves of wheat or barley are placed on roofs or poles for the birds to enjoy; also bits of suet are fastened to trees for these feathered friends.

In modern times, the purchase of Christmas gifts has become "big business"; often all sales' records are broken at this season. (For instance, in 1950, fourteen billion dollars was spent in the Christmas trade.) Naturally, many luxury articles are given, but useful and practical ones are gladly received, too.

Many individuals are trying to counteract the commercial side of Christmas by making their own presents; or, when buying, they select things carefully, keeping in mind the tastes of friends for whom they are intended. Wise parents often teach their children to go without certain things in order to give to the less fortunate, or they show the boys and girls how to make simple presents for others.

In spite of the fact that there is some selfishness in our gift-giving, Christ's birthday seems to bring out the best qualities in countless individuals. Philanthropic citizens begin, many weeks in advance, to plan gifts for shut-ins, for inmates of hospitals and other institutions, and for servicemen, far from their homes.

This Yuletide consideration for others is a tribute to the Founder of Christmas Day, for the spirit that moves human beings to think of others, and to give liberally, even when it means sacrifices, is an attribute of the "Giver of Perfect Gifts."

5

"Deck the Halls . . ."

DURING THE SIXTEENTH century, the English poet, George Wither, wrote his delightful Christmas poem, containing these lines:

> So now is come our joyfulst feast;
> Let every man be jolly.
> Each room with ivy leaves is dressed
> And every post with holly.

Nowadays, in our busy modern world, we still enjoy this old holiday tradition of "decking the halls." And, in doing so, we are following an ancient custom that has many interesting beliefs and legends associated with it.

Centuries ago the Jews used boughs of trees to adorn the booths they set up each autumn for their "Feast of Tabernacles." We remember, too, that palm branches were strewn along the way as Jesus rode in triumph on that first Palm Sunday into the city of Jerusalem.

The Romans believed that good fortune would be theirs if they exchanged green branches with their friends. It was also an early belief that if someone touched another person with a green switch, it would bring good luck. Children used to go around hitting neighbors with fresh branches, while reciting "good-luck" verses.

For the celebration of their winter feast, the Saturnalia (beginning about the middle of December), the Romans lavishly decorated their homes, temples, and statues of the gods and goddesses with green boughs, garlands, or flowers. In their processions during this period, they carried such greenery as laurel; sometimes they bore small trees adorned with lighted candles. This was fitting, for they were celebrating the return of the sun, and looking forward to the coming of spring.

Well before the Christian era, evergreens were used as an emblem of eternal life. For, although the cold winter weather killed most plants, the evergreens remained, symbolic of summer and life. In the Celtic and Nordic lands, the people almost worshiped the greens "that do not die," and believed that such plants as the pine, spruce, fir, holly, box, bay, mistletoe, ivy, juniper, rosemary, etc. shielded them from evil spirits. These pagans used to go out to the dark forests with their Druid priests to watch them cut down the greens, especially the sacred mistletoe.

Even after the Teutonic tribes gave up old beliefs and embraced Christianity, many of them clung to the use of evergreens at winter festivals. It is said that in early Christian processions, apples and rosemary were carried, typifying man's fall and his later redemption. At Christmas greens were used, not only for decorations, but to emphasize the nativity idea. One writer asserted that trimming homes and churches with evergreens reminded man of Christ's deity, and that the Child born at Bethlehem was both God and Man, "who would spring up like a tender plant, should always be green and flourishing, and live for evermore." The Christmas wreath is said to have originated from Christ's crown of thorns. Although connected more closely with His death than His birth, the wreath has been accepted and used as a holiday tradition.

"Against the time of Christmas," as an early description of the British celebration tells us, "everyman's home, as also their parish churches, was decked with holm, ivy, bays, and whatsoever the season of the year afforded to be green." Some, it is true, refused to use ivy in church decorations, for this plant had always been closely associated with Bacchus, the Roman god of wine. As a result, ivy was a reminder of the excesses to which revelers went at the Saturnalia. The "holm" referred to is "an evergreen oak with holly-like leaves."

Bay (or laurel) was connected with victory; the Greeks used to present winners of contests with laurel wreaths. (Today we still speak of one's "winning his laurels.") In the Middle Ages, rosemary was spread on the floor during winter celebrations because it gave out a spicy, pungent fragrance when the merrymakers walked over its branches. Some believed this odor would preserve their youth.

The rosemary is said to have received its fragrance from the fact that Mary laid the Christ Child's garments on its bush. This green, used for many years in England, lost its popularity during the Victorian period; and one authority calls this "a distinct loss."

The Yuletide habit of using greenery was furthered by the many legends which had arisen that, at the time of the nativity, trees and flowers had bloomed out of their regular season. As early as the tenth century, an Arabian geographer, Georg Jacob, told of such happenings; and in the thirteenth, an old French epic described a miracle—candles burning on blossoming trees at Christmas.

Also, there is the famous story of the Glastonbury thorn tree, which relates that Joseph of Arimathea (in whose tomb Christ was laid) landed with the Holy Grail on the coast of England, not far from the town of Glastonbury. While resting there, Joseph stuck his staff into the ground; and to the amazement of all, it took root. Thereafter, it blossomed each Christmas, and people came from long distances to see this miracle. Finally—so the account goes—one Puritan, disgusted with such superstitious beliefs, decided to chop the thorn tree down. But in doing so, he cut his leg badly; a chip flew up, and destroyed the sight of his right eye.

The legend asserts that, even though the trunk had been separated from its roots, it continued to grow; then slips were planted elsewhere, and produced flowers that were sold for high prices abroad to certain merchants as relics.

Since the use of greenery in churches was of heathen origin, some Church officials objected to its use. However, as with several other traditions, which meant so much to the people, the leaders had to show tolerance and permit the custom to be continued.

In England, opinions differed as to the proper time the greens should be taken down in the churches. Some insisted that all should be removed on Twelfth Night (January 6), while others wanted them to remain up until Candlemas, February 2 (or forty days after Yule).

ALL ABOUT CHRISTMAS

In some districts, the evergreens were left to decay naturally; but in others, like Shropshire, the discarded holly, laurel, bay, etc. were burned in fireplaces, either on Twelfth Night, or on the evening before Candlemas.

Robert Herrick, like his fellow poet, George Wither, has given us enjoyable Christmas poems, describing old traditions in "Merrie England." His "Ceremony upon Candlemas Eve" reveals the belief that those who did not destroy all the evergreens would be haunted by evil spirits.

> Down with the Rosemary, and so
> Down with the Bays and Mistletoe.
> Down with the Holly, Ivie, all,
> Wherewith ye dressed the Christmas Hall.
> That so the superstitious find
>
> No one least Branch left there behind.
> For look how many leaves there be
> Neglected there (maids trust to me)
> So many *Goblins* shall ye see.

Down through the centuries, holly has been a popular winter decoration. The Romans gathered it for use during the Saturnalia, carried it in their processions, and decked images of their deities with its glistening leaves. Holly was so highly esteemed in England that one early writer declared:

> Whosoever against holly do cry
> In a rope shall be hung full high.
> Alleluia!

The custom of using holly at Christmas was brought to the United States by the English settlers.

While some have stated that "holly" is a corruption of "holy," and the plant often has been called the "holy tree," the name really comes from the Old English *holen* or *holegn,* and was applied to the genus of trees and shrubs with glossy leaves and bright red berries.

There are more than three hundred species of holly; and it is found in almost every country in the world, both in temperate and tropical regions. However, the most highly prized type is the *Ilex Aquifolium* which is native to the British Isles; it grows best where the humidity is high, and the summers, cool. This is especially favored for Christmas use because of its sharp, shining leaves and brilliant berries.

In our country, holly is native to the Eastern states, and is found from Massachusetts to Florida as well as westward to Missouri and Texas. One of the largest Eastern nurseries is located in Robbinsville, New York; other holly-growing orchards are found in Rhode Island, Connecticut, Pennsylvania, Maryland, Virginia, and Florida. In our northwestern states and in British Columbia, holly is grown commercially; and each winter large quantities are shipped to distant places for holiday use.

The plant has male and female varieties, the latter being the type that produces berries. It takes eight years for the trees to mature before the growers know which will have the coveted berries. So, the business of raising this Christmas green is a gamble, unless the plants are propagated by cutting or grafting.

Among the numerous beliefs connected with holly is the Druid idea that its eternally green leaves proved that the sun never completely deserted the earth; so they considered it as sacred. Also, they thought the spirit of the holly tree kept its beauty all year round so the world would still be attractive when their sacred oak trees were bare of leaves.

Primitive tribes believed that the woodland spirits had to leave their homes and wander around in the cold during the pagan winter solstice feast. Therefore, they thought if they gave these creatures shelter, the spirits, in turn, would bring them good luck the rest of the year. So to entice them inside, people hung evergreens, especially holly (since it was symbolic of joy and peace), over their doors at the Yuletide.

There was a belief that holly had mysterious powers. If one planted it near his home, it could ward off witches and protect occupants from severe weather, thunder, and lightning. During the period of the Druids, it was customary for a person to put a sprig of holly in his hair when he went out to watch the priests cut the sacred mistletoe. A syrup concocted from the plant was certain to cure a winter cough; also, if one placed a bit of holly on his bedpost, he would have only pleasant dreams.

After the adoption of the Christian faith, a churchgoer always tried to get a sprig of the plant—that had been used as a church decoration—to take home with him. If anyone wearing a piece of holly entered a church on Christmas Eve, he was given supernatural power, and would see a procession of all the parishioners destined to die the coming year. Another belief was that the holly tree had been the "burning bush," from which God had spoken to Moses, in regard to his taking over the leadership of his people.

The plant, according to another legend, was symbolic of the Virgin Mary, the pure maiden, who had been chosen to be Christ's mother. When Jesus walked on earth, holly is said to have sprung up in his footsteps. Following this miracle, animals revered the holly, and never harmed it; and stubborn beasts could easily be subdued by the use of a holly branch.

Another story was that, when Christ's enemies were searching for Him, the plant concealed His whereabouts. As a reward, holly was allowed to keep its leaves throughout the year, thus becoming the emblem of immortality, with the promise of life everlasting.

According to some sources, Christ's crown of thorns had been fashioned from holly leaves. At first its berries were white; but when the crown was pressed down on His brow, blood drops turned the berries a bright red. Because of this miracle, early missionaries used holly in their preaching to picture the Saviour's suffering: the sharp, prickly leaves, reminiscent of His wounds, and the berries, of His sacrificial blood. The Teutons used holly, along with other greens, to adorn their churches at the Yuletide, as did the English; but the plant was not permitted in such buildings in France, Italy, or Spain.

Poets often have praised the holly; and these lines are found in an old carol:

> There comes the holly that is so gent,
> To please all men in his intent.
> Allelujah!

In "The Holly and the Ivy," an old French song, the writer says:

> Of all the trees within the wood,
> The holly bears the crown.

And the famous Bard of Avon adds his tribute to this plant:

> Then, heigh ho, the holly!
> This life is most jolly.

It was considered unlucky in some parts of the British Isles to take holly boughs into a home before Christmas Day. (Some insisted that every bit of the plant must be removed by Twelfth Night.) Since there were two kinds, the prickly and smooth, formerly called "he" and "she," there were certain beliefs about them. If the prickly variety was first brought into the home at Christmas, the husband would rule the household during the coming year; but if the smooth variety, the wife would be the head.

It was long a British tradition to place a piece of holly in each beehive at the holidays, for there was a legend that when the Baby Jesus was born at Bethlehem the bees sang a song in his honor, a song that they have been humming ever since.

Whenever a manservant in England failed to bring in holly to "deck the halls" (after the maids had asked him to do so), he was punished in this way: the girls stole his trousers and nailed them to the gate of the courtyard. Also he was not allowed to kiss any of the maids that year under the mistletoe bough.

In some places, it was customary for those who had quarreled to end their conflict beneath branches of the holly tree. A poet, Charles Mackay, has immortalized this, saying:

> Be links no longer broken;
> Be sweet forgiveness spoken,
> Under the Holly Bough.

Another favorite Christmas green, the mistletoe, has for years been used both here and abroad. (It is the state emblem of Oklahoma.) Varied ideas exist as to the origin of the word "mistletoe." The dictionary states that it comes from the Anglo-Saxon "mistel" plus "tan," and means "different twig"—perhaps because the plant forms such a strong contrast to the tree on which it grows. Its yellow twigs and green leaves are easily visible as it clings to the bare limbs of trees in the winter. One writer says, "The yellow color of the withered mistletoe may partly explain why the plant is thought to disclose yellow gold in the earth and reveal buried treasure on Midsummer Eve."

The Druids insisted that mistletoe had been brought from heaven by the missel thrush. Apparently someone saw one of these birds with a white berry stuck to its toe, and created the word, "mistletoe." Since birds feed on these berries, they are largely responsible for the plant's wide distribution.

This popular evergreen has many legends and traditions connected with it, and is often referred to as the "Golden Bough." In Greek mythology, it was believed to be a charm against evil. The Latin poet, Vergil, in his classic, relates that Aeneas was directed in a dream to seek out his father Anchises in the underworld. He was also told to pluck a "golden bough" to carry with him as a gift to Proserpine. When the boatman, Charon, saw the mistletoe branch, he allowed Aeneas to cross with him. In the Elysian Fields, he conferred with Anchises, and through the magic power of the "golden bough" was able to reach the earth once more.

Mistletoe also played a role in Norse legends, for it was held sacred to their goddess, Frigga, wife of Odin. The Druids believed in the plant's healing powers, and it was an important feature of their winter religious rites.

This evergreen belongs to the laurel family, and has pale grayish-green leaves and waxlike white berries. It has sometimes been called the "tree thief" since it is a parasite and grows without touching the ground. (One source suggested that mistletoe is symbolic of the link between heaven and earth.) Its aerial roots penetrate the bark of the tree that serves as its host. Gradually the mistletoe weakens the tree; and if the latter becomes too heavily infested with bunches of the parasite, it may die.

Several different species are native to America; and it seems to grow almost everywhere here. It is especially abundant in Alabama. In the Eastern states, it is said that the mistletoe appears to seek out tall trees, often hard to reach, including those of the sycamore and black gum varieties. The parasite grows abundantly in California, and is usually found there on poplars, willows, and oaks. Most of the commercial mistletoe is shipped from this state. Other trees to which the plant sometimes attaches itself are the red maple, tupelo, cedar, black cherry, and mesquite.

Among the Romans, mistletoe was considered a symbol of hope and peace. Therefore, when enemies met under it, they laid aside their weapons, kissed each other, and declared a truce until the next day. Other early people also observed such a custom, believing that only happiness could exist under the mistletoe, where they sealed their pledges of peace and friendship with kisses. This may have been the origin of the kissing custom under this plant.

Mistletoe played an important part in the Norse legend of Balder, the sun god, deity of light and good. He was the son of Odin and Frigga. When Balder told his mother he had dreamed of his coming death, she determined to prevent it. So she obtained a promise from every living thing, from the powers of nature—earth, air, fire, and water—that they would not harm Balder.

Since Frigga did not consider the mistletoe of much importance, she didn't ask it to make the promise. Then the lame god, Loki, who was jealous of Balder, made a sharp arrow of mistletoe wood, and placed it in the hand of blind Hoder, god of winter, who shot and killed Balder.

At once, the light of the sun decreased; and there was great mourning for the young deity. All the gods tried to bring him back to life, and after three days, through the power of his mother's love, Balder returned from the dead. Then his light shone again at the winter solstice.

Frigga's tears turned into mistletoe berries, symbolic of love that is stronger than death. Overjoyed by her son's return to life, Frigga kissed each person who passed beneath the mistletoe; she decreed that ever afterward, all who walked under it should receive that same token of affection. Later, the mistletoe was dedicated to Frigga with the provision that it would never harm anyone again. So it became a parasite, destined always to live on other plants, above the ground.

The Druids, a pre-Christian group of Britain and ancient Gaul, believed, as sun worshipers, that mistletoe was a sacred spirit. When they went out to cut it at the winter solstice, their ceremonies included the sacrifice of white bulls, and even human beings.

On the sixth day of the moon nearest the new year, the priests, clad in long, flowing white robes, marched in a solemn procession into the depths of the forest, followed by men, women, children. Heralds sounded trumpets before them; and bards chanted as they approached the tree on which the mistletoe was growing. Druids cut the plant only from their sacred oak trees.

The Arch Druid wore a heavy gold chain around his neck; and wide bands of the same precious metal decorated his arms. He carried a short curved knife that was kept for this purpose alone. After climbing to the first branch, on which the parasite was growing, the priest severed the mystic sprigs.

These branches were caught by other Druids in the folds of their garments, or by maidens holding "a fair, white cloth." For the mistletoe was not allowed to touch earth and be defiled by it, or it would bring bad fortune to all. Then at the foot of the oak, the priest blessed small sprays, and gave them to their followers, praying that divine favor would be theirs. Those who received mistletoe were expected to give the priests something in return. Later, they wore the sprigs around their necks as charms or placed them over doorways to keep off evil spirits. Those who entered received kisses from the owners to seal their friendship.

These primitive folk believed that mistletoe would protect their cattle from disease, so they fastened a "golden bough" over stable entrances. The plant was also associated with happy marriages, for the Druids asserted it would promote fertility. Some persons used to brew a drink from this plant, believing it would produce a prophetic nature. Others made divining rods and knife handles from the mistletoe because of its mystic powers.

At a summer ceremony, the Druid priests cut the mistletoe, or "guidhel," for medicinal uses. They maintained that it could cure many ailments, including wounds, ulcers, poisoning, and the "falling sickness," epilepsy. One authority says that in Holland and England, down to the eighteenth century, some doctors were still prescribing mistletoe for epilepsy. Among Indian tribes in America it was customary to chew a bit of the plant to cure the toothache. (In 1952, a report by competent doctors told of a new drug, Protoveratrine, derived from mistletoe, that is being used to reduce blood pressure.)

Some early Christians associated the plant with evil, for they believed it had been the "forbidden fruit" of the Garden of Eden. Others asserted that Christ's cross had been made from the wood. One legend is that, originally, the mistletoe had been a noble forest tree like the mighty redwood. But after the Saviour's death, it was so ashamed of its part in His suffering that, overnight, it shrank in size.

Also, because of its connection with pagan Druid rites and the Druids' worship of the "golden bough," many Christians regarded mistletoe as "an emblem of unwholesome superstition." Consequently, even though used in homes at Christmas, it was not allowed as a church decoration.

However, there was one notable exception in England to this rule: at the stately York Minster, a large spray of mistletoe was laid on its altar each Yuletide. Some believe this was significant of the fact that man is dependent upon God for life, just as this plant is on the tree to which it clings; or the rite may refer to God's healing powers, because of mistletoe's medicinal quality. Still others think of its white berries as a symbol of Christ's pure life.

An unusual procedure took place in York while the mistletoe rested on the altar there. Men stood at the city gates and proclaimed pardon for the guilty, and freedom for those held in prisons. During the twelve joyous days of Yuletide festivity, prisoners were released, allowed to come and go as they pleased, and beggars were given food and shelter.

Mistletoe, like the holly, has often been spoken of in literature. Sir Walter Scott in *Marmion* tells us:

> The damsel donned her kirtle sheen,
> The hall was dressed with holly green.
> Forth to the wood did merry-men go
> To gather in the mistletoe.

Shakespeare, no doubt, remembered its connection with Christ's cross, for in *Titus Andronicus* the Queen of the Goths, Tamara, speaks of "the baleful mistletoe." An English ballad, "The Mistletoe Bough," tells of Christmas revelry that ended in a tragedy. A bride, as a joke, decided to hide from her groom and the guests. She hid in an old chest, and its lock spring closed over her; everyone searched for her with no success; and great mourning followed her unexplained disappearance.

During the happy holiday season in "Merrie England" at great manor houses, the mistletoe always hung high because of the ancient belief that the plant should never touch the ground.

> The mistletoe bough on the festive throng
> Looks down, amid echoes of mirthful song . . .
> And who is she that will not allow
> A kiss claimed under the mistletoe bough?

A girl, kissed under these circumstances, was considered lucky; those who weren't, were destined to remain husbandless for another year. With each kiss, the man was supposed to pluck a white berry from the bough and give it to the girl. When all were gone, the mistletoe was said to lose its mystic powers.

Another English poet, Oliver Herford, paid tribute to the old tradition in these words:

> It hath been writ that anye man
> May blameless kiss what mayde he can,
> Nor anyone shall say him "no"
> Beneath the holye mistletoe.

During the Victorian period, the British often hung up a "kissing ring" or "bough" as part of their holiday decorations. It was made of wires, covered with gay ribbons; sprays of mistletoe were fastened to it; and sometimes it was adorned with apples and lighted candles.

The "ring" was suspended from the ceiling, and many girls were kissed beneath it. Some people follow this same idea today or concoct a "mobile"—a bare branch, decorated with sprays of mistletoe and hung from a chandelier, where it sways gracefully whenever there is movement in the room.

In addition to our traditional Yuletide greenery, a colorful tropical plant, the gay poinsettia, now is recognized as one of our most highly cherished Christmas emblems. Everyone enjoys a gift of a potted poinsettia; and pictures of the brilliant plant adorn our greeting cards and gift wrappings. Contrary to general belief, the blossoms are *not* the red brachts or leaves, but the small yellow flowers in the center of the attractive clusters. The rich red and green coloring make this plant most appropriate for Christmas decorations.

A native of the American continent, it was discovered in 1828 in Mexico by Dr. Joel Roberts Poinsett (1779–1851) of Charleston, South Carolina, and given his name. Dr. Poinsett spent four years (1825–1829) as our first minister to that country. When he came upon the distinctive flower, called by the Mexicans and the people of Central America *Flor de la Noche Buena* (Flower of the Holy Night or of Christmas Eve) or "Flame Leaf," he was delighted with his discovery. The Mexicans have a story that when blood fell on the earth from the broken heart of a young girl, a poinsettia plant grew from each drop.

Dr. Poinsett sent some cuttings in 1828 to Philadelphia to a nurseryman, Robert Buist, who specialized in collecting new plants. The latter named it *Euphorbia poinsettia;* later it was given the botanical terms, *Poinsettia pulcherrima;* but most people called the unusual plant the poinsettia. Some were sent to the botanical gardens in Edinburgh, and the famous naturalist Dr. Henry Perrine also brought public attention to the new discovery. When Dr. Poinsett returned to the United States from Mexico, he visited his friend, John C. Frémont, in California, who may have helped start the plant in this region.

Poinsettias grow well outdoors in what is called California's Poinsettia Belt"; and from this region, the plants are shipped to every state in the Union. Ventura, north of Los Angeles, is called the "Poinsettia City"; and it is a real thrill to visit this community when the plants are at their best.

Credit for the original development of this flower goes to Albert Ecke, a Swiss farmer, who started to raise vegetables near Los Angeles during the 1890's; then he became interested in growing and improving the tropical plant. He made his first sales in 1906, and in recent years his son, Paul Ecke, has made Encinitas, about twenty miles north of San Diego, the poinsettia capital of the world.

Just before Christmas each year, you can see a picture you will never forget, near the great Marine Corps Reservation, Camp Pendleton. There, on three hundred acres leased by the Eckes, the unique Christmas flowers are in full color.

Since Albert Ecke's death, his son has carried on the business; he has developed stronger varieties that stand up better against the wind; others that keep their foliage longer; and types that can be grown at lower temperatures. One variety, the "Albert Ecke," honors his father, while a beautiful double poinsettia, the "Henrietta Ecke," bears his mother's name. Cuttings from such improved plants have been sent to Mexico, and also to Dr. Poinsett's home, Charleston, South Carolina.

As San Diego has become the center of production of this flower, a "Poinsettia Fiesta" is staged there, featuring a parade, a ball, and a football game in the Poinsettia Bowl. The climax of the week is a pageant, *Christmas in Many Lands.* In 1952 two queens were chosen to rule over the fiesta: one was a civilian; the other, a Wave, from the Naval Station at San Diego.

We are truly indebted to the cultured diplomat, Dr. Poinsett, who recognized the possibilities of this plant, and to the Eckes, who have developed it. For the lovely poinsettia adds grace and beauty to our homes and churches at the holidays; and it has rightfully won its place along with our older, traditional greenery as a cherished Christmas decoration.

There is a modern wreath that has become very popular in recent decades—the unusual Della Robbia wreath, "a live replica" of the relief carvings of fruits and leaves that surround the artist's charming Bambino medallions.

These wreaths are made by members of the Boys' Republic, at Chino, California. Mrs. Margaret Fowler (who gave some of the buildings for this unique institution) was so impressed after seeing the Bambinos in Italy that she suggested to the boys that they try to make some such holiday wreaths in their handicraft classes.

This project began in 1923, and has proved most successful. Almost all the year around the boys gather various leaves, seed pods, cones, etc., and later combine them with colorful fruits. Now their products are sold in every state and also abroad. Recently, in one season, they made and shipped out over fourteen thousand wreaths, many to noted personages. The money is used to help support this worth-while school, and for additional recreational facilities. The Della Robbia wreath adds an attractive and unusual touch to many homes during the Christmas holidays.

Decorating for this festive period is not only a happy event in individual homes, but has also become a worth-while community project. For example, in Birmingham, Michigan, near Detroit, the local branch of the Women's National Farm and Garden Association has for several years sponsored a "Christmas Open House and Flower Show," or a "Sharing of the Greens."

The object of this gala affair is to exchange ideas with others for home adornment. Young and old assist in decorating their Community House; many bring exhibits, using certain plant materials to carry out suggested themes. These often include shrubs with attractive berries, and other kinds of greenery, not so well known.

The children also take part, and give good suggestions. Young people from different schools contribute their Christmas music, and add to the spirit of holiday gaiety. After each annual show, many of the decorations are taken to homes for the aged, or to hospitals, to bring cheer to shut-ins—a real Yuletide "Sharing of the Greens."

Out in the West—a long way from Birmingham, Michigan— honor, too, is paid to our Christmas greenery at the Colorado College for Women. Here, each year, the students stage an impressive pageant, *The Hanging of the Greens*.

Young women, in evening dress, carrying garlands of greenery, enter the large dining hall, singing "Joy to the World," accompanied by their orchestra. The balcony and stairway are lined with girls holding a chain of feathery, pungent pine. Then the narrator begins, with these words:

> List the chimes are sweetly sounding
> Christmas happiness abounding.

After grace, all are seated and the Christmas dinner is served. Then the plum pudding is brought in, in gala fashion, by men faculty members in medieval dress. A quartet of men teachers, in high hats, adds to the festivities with their caroling. A series of tableaux follows, including the "Song of the Angels" and "Mary and the Holy Babe," with the worshiping shepherds.

Members of the choir, carrying lighted candles, take their places on the stairs; and the inspiring strains of "O Holy Night" bring to a close another presentation of the "Hanging of the Greens." This is a fitting tribute to a beloved tradition which has come down to us from olden times when halls were "embowered with Holly, Ivy, Cypress, Bays, Laurel, and Misselto."

6

"O Christmas Tree! O Christmas Tree!"

[In about two thirds of the homes in the United States—statistics tell us—we center our holiday gaiety around lighted Christmas trees. For this beloved holiday tradition, symbolic of the ever-living spirit of the Yuletide, brings a delightful forest aroma into our homes.] Nowadays, too, such trees are used in great numbers in churches, clubs, business houses, schools, and for street decorations. ["O Christmas Tree! O Christmas Tree!" ("O Tannenbaum! O Tannenbaum!"), a well-known German song, expresses their great love for this evergreen, whose year-round verdure is, to them, an emblem of immortality. Although the German people have often been given the credit for using the first lighted and decorated trees, the idea really started centuries earlier.

Primitive tribes revered nature, and believed that everything had life; therefore, by legends they tried to account for various natural phenomena. They revered trees, and used them, not so much with the idea of adorning their homes, but rather "for bringing the world of nature indoors." The Egyptians, for example, during their winter solstice rites, took the green date palms, significant of "life triumphant over death," indoors.]

During the Saturnalia, Romans trimmed trees with trinkets and small masks of Bacchus. Sometimes they placed twelve candles on a tree with an image of the sun god at the tip. The noted Latin poet,

Vergil, once wrote of the custom of decorating trees with swinging toys.

In Northern Europe, the Druids, at this same season, honor their chief god, Odin (or Woden), by tying to tree branches gilded apples, emblematic of his favor toward them in giving them different kinds of fruits. These offerings to Odin also included cakes, made in the shape of fish, birds, or other animals. The Druids, too, put lighted candles on boughs as a tribute to their sun god, Balder.

When these pagans accepted Christianity, they continued their winter rites, but changed them to honor Christ. And the evergreen tree came to denote His bringing new life to the world after the long dark days of winter.

In his story *The First Christmas Tree* Henry van Dyke tells of its reputed origin. In heathen times, the Druids offered sacrifices at the sacred oak to their god. Winfried, a missionary, went from England to the continent to preach Christianity to these people.

At the Thunder Oak, he and his companions arrived just in time to save a young prince from death. Then Winfried told the assembled crowd the story of Christ's coming to earth at Bethlehem. He begged them not to worship their heathen gods any longer, with bloody sacrifices, out in the dark forest. He pointed to a tiny fir tree, and asked them to take it into their homes, and with singing and rejoicing, celebrate the birthday of the Christ Child.

In Europe, before the use of trees became general, it had been the custom in some places to take into their homes, in the fall, branches of cherry or hawthorn. The people would put the boughs in water, keep them in a warm spot, and by Christmas, they were in beautiful blossom.

Sometimes decorated branches were suspended from the ceiling; but by the middle of the sixteenth century, standing trees were in vogue, in Alsace, for instance. In some countries, instead of using a living tree, a frame was made in the shape of a pyramid. This was covered with evergreens, and trimmed with candles and other decorations.

In Northern Europe, where many persons lived in forests and revered trees, it was quite natural for them to use trees at Christmas.

An outcome of old pagan rites, this custom spread to other countries from the Rhineland.

[The great reformer, Martin Luther (1483–1546), even when a boy, loved holiday celebrations. As a young man in Eisenach, he went out with his friends to sing carols. The story goes that, after he had married and had a family, one Christmas Eve he was walking home through the forest. Luther was deeply impressed that night by the myriads of stars in the winter sky, and by the beauty of the stately evergreens.

[When Luther reached home, he tried to explain the glory of the scene to his wife and children; but words failed him. So he went out, cut down a small fir, and placed lighted candles on it, to represent the starry sky above the stable the night that Christ was born. One of Luther's chief desires was to make ordinary people understand and appreciate Yuletide joys. Although he is said to have started the custom of lighted Christmas trees, the idea spread slowly, and was more popular in Protestant regions than in Catholic lands.]

In Strassburg—an old volume reveals—in 1605 some citizens set up Christmas trees in their parlors, firs which they adorned with "roses, cut out of many colored paper, apples, wafers, gold foil, sugar, etc." But there was no mention of candles on the trees.

During the Thirty Years' War (1618–1648), it is reported that an officer of the Swedish army, who had been badly wounded, was well cared for by kind-hearted Germans in Leipzig. At Christmas, to show his gratitude, he set up a lighted tree in one of their churches.

Some of the clergy, as late as the eighteenth century, objected to the use of holiday trees, one minister declaring that many persons spent more time on their Yule trees than they did on their Bible reading. He also suggested that it would be better if the children were dedicated to the "spiritual cedar tree, Jesus Christ."

After the custom had spread through Germany, it reached Finland, Denmark, Sweden, and Norway by the nineteenth century. Austria is said to have had its first tree, in 1816, when Princess Henriette set one up at Vienna. In 1840 Princess Helene of Mecklenberg introduced the idea in Paris. Various lands devised their own types of decorations; the Lithuanians, mostly farmers, fashioned windmills or birdcages from straw; Norwegians used fish nets, reminiscent of their national industry; while other Scandinavians made strings of small flags; and the Poles attached feathers, ribbons, or colored papers to their Christmas trees.

Germany long was known for her Yuletide celebration, which always has centered around the tree on Christmas Eve. This was only for family, relatives and intimate friends. The weeks before the holidays were filled with important preparations. In the marketplaces, there were trees of various sizes and prices so that every family, large or small, rich or poor, could have a *"Weihnachtsbaum."*

It was always a thrilling moment in the life of each German child when the door opened, revealing the tree in all its glory, decorated with a star, an angel, sweetmeats, tiny toys, tinsel, gilded nuts and wax tapers. Gifts were placed on a near-by table. After the exchange of presents, the father read the Bible story of Christ's birth. Later, everyone joined in singing such Christmas favorites as "Stille Nacht! Heilige Nacht!" "Vom Himmel Hoch," and "O Tannenbaum! O Tannenbaum!"

Another German carol, "The Christmas Tree" written by Peter Cornelius, has been translated by H. N. Bate, and begins with these lines:

> The holly's up, the house is all bright,
> The tree is ready, the candles alight;
> Rejoice and be glad, all children tonight.

In England, trees were not a holiday custom at a very early date, although one writer speaks of "three trees" that stood on the table during a Christmas feast, honoring Henry VIII. In 1829 a German, Princess Lieven, living in London, put on a holiday party for her children. On a table were decorated trees lighted by varicolored candles with the presents arranged near by. A few years later— 1836—a German woman at Queen Charlotte's court created a tree for the royal children by fastening an evergreen bough to a board.

Prince Albert of Saxe-Coburg, the consort of Queen Victoria, in

1841, the year their first son was born, set up a Christmas tree for the holidays at Windsor Castle to carry out the old beloved tradition of his native land. It was beautifully decorated; and an angel with outstretched arms was placed at the top. Everyone at court was delighted with this spectacle; others soon followed Albert's example; and the idea spread through England. The Queen spoke of the happiness of her children in their annual Christmas tree; also Prince Albert wrote his father of the pleasure the tree, with its bright ornaments and wax tapers, had given all the royal family.

During the evolution of the Yuletide tree, several legends became associated with it. One is that a French knight saw a tree with lighted candles; some of them stood erect, while others were upside down. At the top of the fir was a Child with a halo around his head. This vision was later explained in this way: the tree represented the world; the Child, the Saviour; and the candles, both good and evil human beings.

It is said that, in Alsace, good St. Florentin wanted to make the holidays happy for the little children. But, as he was very poor, he had no money to buy them gifts. However, in the woods, he had noticed a perfectly shaped little fir tree, glistening with snow and ice. Florentin chopped it down, took it into his house, trimmed it with nuts and apples, and lighted it with tiny beeswax candles. The children all were pleased with the unusual sight.

Another often-heard story is that, once on Christmas Eve, a cold, hungry child was welcomed at the modest home of a forester. After supper, the small son gave up his bed for the stranger to sleep in.

Next day, when the family awoke, they saw a dazzling light, and discovered that their guest was the Christ Child. In return for their kindness, He said He would give them a gift. Then He broke off a fir branch, planted it in the ground, and declared it would always be green and bear fruit, so they would have plenty to eat at this season. A similar legend says that, after the Holy Child had been given shelter by a poor farmer, He disappeared, but in His stead, the family discovered a blossoming tree.

There is an interesting explanation as to why we use tinsel as a decoration. One woman had trimmed her tree carefully; and that night spiders spread their webs all over it. When the Christ Child saw this, He knew she would be unhappy next day; therefore he turned all the webs into silver. The woman was overjoyed the following morning at the unusual and unexpected beauty of her Christmas tree.

A legend, found in a manuscript in an old monastery in Sicily, asserts that on the night of the Saviour's birth, all the living creatures on earth journeyed to the stable in Bethlehem to honor the new-born King, and to give him presents.

Even the trees of the forest went: the olive, to give its fruit; and the palm, its dates. But the little fir had no gifts; besides, it was so weary it could hardly stand. The larger trees pushed it into the background, and almost hid it completely. A near-by angel felt sorry for the tiny tree, looked up at the stars, and asked some of them to come down and rest on its boughs. The stars obeyed, and shone there like candles. When the Baby Jesus saw the lovely sight, He smiled, blessed the happy little tree, and declared that at Christmas fir trees should always be lighted to please little children.

How the fir was chosen as the Yuletide emblem is explained in another story: on that first Holy Night, God sent three messengers, Faith, Hope, and Charity, to light the Christmas tree. In searching for the right one, they selected the fir, because each bough resembles a cross, as the twigs are at right angles to the branches.

Some sources say that the fir was the original "Tree of Life" in the Garden of Eden, and at that time had fruit. But after Eve had plucked it, the tree no longer bore. Its leaves turned to tiny needles; and only on that first Christmas did it bloom once more.

Here, in the United States, the first decorated Christmas trees are said to have been the ones set up during the American Revolution by the homesick Hessian soldiers. They had been hired by King George III, and came over from Germany to fight the rebellious colonists. But the custom of having holiday trees did not come into general use here until years later.

Authorities seem to differ about who should have the honor of having set up the first Christmas tree in our country. Recent research has shown that Charles Follen, a German professor at

Harvard (who began to teach there shortly after his arrival in the United States in 1824), did have a tree each year for his son, Charles, at their home in Cambridge, Massachusetts. This fact was stated by his wife in the biography she wrote about her husband.

The Follen tree was first set up in 1832. That Christmas, a famous Englishwoman, Harriet Martineau, was a guest at their home. Later, in her book, *Retrospect of Western Travel,* she described her visit to the home, giving a delightful picture of the tree, with its decorations of dolls, glittering ornaments, and seven dozen wax tapers. Miss Martineau also made the prediction that the Christmas tree would, no doubt, become a regular New England holiday tradition.

For some time, credit for having the first tree here in the United States went to August Imgard of Wooster, Ohio, who, in 1847, decorated a small spruce for his young nieces and nephews. Neighbors and friends who came to see the unique sight soon took up the idea for their families.

At first, the Christmas tree decorations were quite simple: tufts of cotton, strings of popcorn and cranberries, gold, silver, or colored paper ornaments and chains, stars, candy canes, dolls, gilded nut shells, and angels. The small wax candles were in tin holders, clamped onto the branches.

According to Hertha Pauli, Pastor Henry Schwan in 1851 had the first Christmas tree in a church, in Cleveland, Ohio; however, some of his parishioners objected to this as a pagan practice. A few members of the congregation were threatened with harm, if they ever again should take part in such a ceremony. But the good minister did some research, and was able to prove that the use of Christmas trees was a Christian rite. Next year Pastor Schwan again had a tree in the church; fortunately, opposition soon stopped; and within a few years, Christmas trees were used in many homes and churches.

Lavishly trimmed trees were featured at annual Christmas Eve Sunday School entertainments. Such an event was the high point of the year for the youngsters—especially for those who did not have trees at their homes. For weeks beforehand, the boys and girls practiced their recitations, songs, and little plays. When the great evening came, they entered the church, and were enraptured by the lighted tree. Of course, the climax was the arrival of Santa Claus with loud jingling of sleigh bells. Then he and his helpers, the Sunday School teachers, distributed presents from the tree, and also delighted the children with the "treat"—boxes of hard candy, perhaps accompanied by an orange or a popcorn ball.

New England, which in early days had frowned upon the observance of Christmas, did not generally adopt the custom as early as some other regions. However, in 1860, a German did have a trimmed tree at his home in Westfield, Massachusetts; and he invited his neighbors to come on Christmas Eve to enjoy it with him.

During the fifties, while he was President, Franklin Pierce and his wife entertained the entire Sunday School of the New York Avenue Presbyterian Church, with a Christmas tree at the White House. In 1891 President Benjamin Harrison had a Christmas tree there, and played Santa Claus for his grandchildren. He referred to it as "an old-fashioned Christmas tree," and expressed the wish that all families would follow this example.

As such trees became more popular in our country, some individuals began a campaign opposing the use of evergreens for this purpose, declaring that if the cutting of Christmas trees was continued, our forests would soon be depleted. President Theodore Roosevelt —noted for his campaign for the conservation of our natural resources—promptly banned the use of such trees for White House festivities.

Shortly afterward, he was surprised and very angry when he discovered that two of his boys, Archie and Quentin, had smuggled a tree into the mansion and had set it up in Archie's room. At once, the boys appealed to their father's good friend, Gifford Pinchot, "America's first professional forester," and explained the situation. Pinchot talked to the President and convinced him that, if young evergreens were properly cut, it was helpful, rather than harmful, to our forests. So the Roosevelt boys were allowed to keep their tree that year; and ever since the White House has had an indoor tree.

The American Forests Products Company asserts that Christmas trees can be as readily replaced as our holiday turkeys, and are just as important for Yuletide gatherings. From a commercial standpoint, the sale of these trees has become a significant business. In one year, recently, in this country, more than twenty-one million Christmas trees were sold for about $50,000,000.

The states along the Canadian border furnish most of the trees we buy, although about nine million annually are shipped in from Canada. The majority are young evergreens from naturally wooded areas. Most of these would have been eliminated by nature herself in the struggle for forest space. So, by clearing them out, room is given to other trees to make better timber, and to mature to log size.

In addition, about one and a half million trees are grown on established plantations, especially for holiday sales. Franklin D. Roosevelt used to write "Farmer" after his name, when he voted. For at his Hyde Park estate he had planted thousands of young Norway spruce trees, which were sent to New York markets when they reached the proper size.

The fall months are busy ones for the Christmas tree industry. The trees must be selected; laborers, hired; and after the trees are cut, under efficient supervision, they are graded, tagged, tied in bunches, and delivered by trucks to freight cars for shipment to distant states.

Americans show varied tastes in selecting their trees. The most popular one is the balsam fir that grows in the northeastern part of our country. Second choice is the Douglas fir, a West Coast product. Other popular types include the black spruce, red cedar, white, red, Engelmann, and Norway spruces; cypress, hemlock, juniper, and Scotch and Southern pines.

Nowadays, the early, simple, homemade ornaments for Christmas trees are a thing of the past in most homes. Varicolored electric lights have taken the place of wax candles. Sometimes the boughs are overloaded with garish, factory-made ornaments; but luckily, many people select artistic decorations. The making of such ornaments has become an important industry in the United States in recent years.

Until World War II opened in 1939, we imported many Christmas tree decorations from Germany. They were made mostly in the Thuringian Mountains; in the town of Lausche, for instance, entire families often worked fifteen hours a day making them. Then, at the end of each week, their products were taken to Sonneberg, thirteen miles away.

Because of the scarcity of such ornaments here, during the war years, the Corning Glass Company began to make them. With their improved methods they could make them more quickly and more cheaply than the imported ones. Now the town of Wellsboro, in northern Pennsylvania, is the center of the industry in the United States.

Early in this century, various communities adopted the idea of setting up large Christmas trees in their public squares for everyone to enjoy. In 1909, the citizens of Pasadena, California, decorated a tall tree with glittering tinsel and many electric lights. This stood on Mount Wilson, which towers over the city, and it created quite a sensation.

A few years later—1912—a community tree, "The Tree of Light," a 60-foot balsam fir, was placed at Madison Square Park in New York. On Christmas Eve more than 20,000 happy people met around it for holiday ceremonies. Philadelphia followed in 1913 with a 75-foot Norway spruce, "The Children's Christmas Tree," in famous Independence Square. Gradually the idea spread through the United States; and soon it became a regular custom to have programs and caroling under community trees on Christmas Eve.

Recently, in different American cities, outstanding trees have attracted national attention. The one said to be the world's largest living Christmas tree is the magnificent live oak (300 years old) that stands above the banks of the Northeast Cape Fear in Hilton Park at Wilmington, North Carolina. It rises to a height of 90 feet; its trunk has a circumference of 14 feet, while the limbs have the tremendous spread of more than 110 feet.

This oak is festooned with six tons of Spanish moss, and is

adorned with countless colorful ornaments. Seven thousand vari-colored electric lights burn brightly on its branches each night during holiday week. Under the spreading boughs, school children sing traditional carols and present a Biblical play. Near by is a beautifully arranged nativity scene, with the Baby Jesus and His parents.

Some communities seem to be vying with each other as to which one can set up the tallest or most unusual tree. For example, Los Angeles in 1948 celebrated at Pershing Square, around a 96-foot white spruce; while in Bellingham, Washington, that same year, stood a 134-foot Douglas fir, followed the next season by another of the same species, that towered to the height of 153 feet. So far, the tallest Christmas tree on record is a Douglas fir, used in 1950, at Northport, a shopping center not far from Seattle. This giant of the forest was 212 feet tall, and weighed 25 tons.

At Troy, Montana, citizens gather at a 100-foot ponderosa pine that grows right in their town; Minneapolis has a unique tree, fashioned from water pipes, attached like spokes of a wheel to a telephone pole. Their tree, in 1947, was 65 feet tall; and 135 individual Christmas trees were inserted in the pipes to serve as limbs.

Trees are featured at Bethlehem, Pennsylvania, during their nationally known festival, on the Hill-to-Hill bridge, connecting the northern, eastern, and southern sections of the city. On the middle arch stands a beautiful 60-foot tree, made up of more than 150 spruces, and lighted by 1,200 electric lights.

The tree that has, no doubt, been seen by more persons than any other is the one at Rockefeller Center in New York City. It is estimated that about 2,500,000 see it each year in all its beauty. Ever since the completion of the 70-story Radio City Building in 1933, formal trees have been set up and decorated there.

They have varied from 50-foot pines to 90-foot Norway spruces. Many unusual and interesting types of ornaments and lighting effects, including flood lights, have made the displays unforgettable. Decorations have been of tinsel, colored cellophane balls, great silver stars, sparkling snowflakes, brightly hued ornaments, and gold plastic balls.

ALL ABOUT CHRISTMAS

Other decorative effects are arranged near by to add to the distinctive setting, such as hundreds of lighted candles in the windows of adjacent buildings. There have been golden replicas of organ pipes; and here people enjoy recitals of Christmas carols.

One year, Mr. and Mrs. Santa Claus were featured guests at this Radio City tree; during another holiday season, live reindeer from the Bronx Zoo delighted visitors. Several outstanding skating pageants, such as *Hans Brinker and the Silver Skates, Stars on Ice,* and *Christmas Carnival* have been staged by professional ice skaters.

In a recent year, a 90-foot Norway pine, the highest one ever set up at the Center, caused a sensation, with its myriads of gold and silver electric light bulbs. The following season, a different idea was used, when a tall, silvered tree was put in place, and adorned with hundreds of plastic globes in five brilliant colors. Seven miles of electric wiring were used for the 7,500 lights.

At first, carols were sung at the glittering trees by church groups, Girl Scouts, or other organizations. But in 1939, a group known as the Radio Center Choristers was organized. It is made up of individuals of all kinds and professions, who are employed at the Center. Their traditional candlelight concerts are a "must" for thousands at the Yule season.

Far across the American continent in Altadena (a suburb of Pasadena) is the famous mile-long avenue, known to the world as "Christmas Tree Lane," and bordered by gigantic but graceful deodar cedars with branches that spread out to a distance of forty or fifty feet. (The word "deodar" means "tree of God," and has been extolled in poetry and legends.)

This unique roadway owes its origin to a pioneer resident, Captain Frederick J. Woodbury. When he was visiting in India, he was enthralled by the beauty of the deodars that he saw growing on the slopes of the mighty Himalayas. When the captain returned to California, he carried deodar seeds with him, and planted them on his ranch at the foot of the Sierra Madre Mountains.

Some years later (1885) his sons transplanted the seedlings, with the result that now two hundred large cedars border the road that once formed the main approach to the Woodbury ranch of nine hundred acres. Today it is a public thoroughfare, Santa Rosa Avenue, and stretches from Foothill Boulevard to Woodbury Road.

Each year, since the first lighting of these trees began in 1920 (sponsored by local Kiwanis Clubs), millions of persons, including visitors from many parts of the world, have seen and admired this unusual and inspiring Christmas spectacle. The Pasadena Municipal Light and Power Company uses more than ten thousand multi-colored bulbs in lighting these beautiful deodars.

In 1952 the noted lane was lighted each evening from Christmas Eve (from five to eleven P.M.) until New Year's, when the lights stayed on all night for the first time. On Christmas Eve, children from near-by churches meet at four P.M. at Woodbury Road and Lake Avenue to hear a talk about the significance of the trees. Then the "Queen" of the Altadena event turns on the lights, and the children join in singing "Silent Night! Holy Night!"

Just as darkness falls over the near-by mountains, the lights go on, all along the lane; then thousands of cars move slowly down the slope, with lights dimmed and motors off. The traffic is directed by Boy Scouts, under the supervision of Altadena and Pasadena Police and Highway Patrolmen.

As visitors make their way through this fairyland, they enjoy a thrilling Christmas experience, one they will always remember. One poet, Virginia Brasier, has described the memorable sight in stanzas that contain these lines:

> Against the jagged mountain background flames
> The Christmas lighting of the deodars.

As a nation, we celebrate at a tree in Washington, D.C., lighted each year by the President with suitable ceremonies. This Christmas Eve service was first observed in 1923, when a fir tree from Vermont was placed on the Capitol steps. The next year, a living Norway spruce was planted near the White House in Sherman Square; and later it was dedicated as a "National Living Christmas Tree."

The program in 1934 took place around a living Norway Spruce across the street from the White House in Lafayette Square. Since

1941, the "National Community Christmas Tree" has been one of the two Oriental spruces (now thirty-five feet tall) on the south lawn of the Executive Mansion. The tree is gaily decorated with large colored glass balls, one for each state, and is ablaze with glittering lights.

On Christmas Eve, December 24, 1952, the tree-lighting ceremonies were opened with a concert of Christmas music by the famous Marine Band. Then the Washington Community Chorus sang carols, after which a Boy Scout and a Girl Scout presented greetings from the city of Washington to the President and his family. The Chief Executive pressed a button that turned on the tree lights. His Yuletide message, broadcast to the entire nation, ended with this wish: "Now, my fellow countrymen, I wish for all of you a Christmas filled with the joy of the Holy Spirit, and many years of future happiness, with the peace of God reigning upon this earth."

In contrast to this observance in the East, there is a unique ceremony each Christmas on the Pacific Coast, when individuals of different faiths make an annual pilgrimage to King's Canyon National Park in central California. At an elevation of 6,500 feet, a Christmas program takes place under a giant redwood, the General Grant, dedicated in 1926 as the "Nation's Christmas Tree."

It is a *Sequoia gigantea,* usually called a Sierra redwood, and stands 267 feet high. Its first limb is 130 feet above the ground; and the base has a diameter of 40 feet. Its mighty trunk has a circumference of 107 feet. It has been estimated that the General Grant contains more than half a million board feet of lumber.

This tree, more than 3,500 years old, is considered the oldest living thing on earth. Its top is scarred, as it was struck by lightning; but it still stands proudly erect, although many centuries have gone by since it started as a tiny seedling. The General Grant is worthy of being called our "Nation's Christmas Tree," for it was growing on the mountain slope when Christ was born in Bethlehem.

This sequoia was discovered in 1862 by Joseph H. Thomas; and in August, 1867, Mrs. Lucretia P. Parker named it to honor our Civil War hero. The General Grant Park area was set aside in

1890, mainly for the purpose of protecting this tree. When Congress passed a bill in 1940 creating King's Canyon National Park, this section—now named the General Grant Grove—became part of the larger area.

Sanger, California, fifty-four miles distant from the tree and the entrance to King's Canyon National Park, is the nearest large community to the General Grant. In 1925 some of the townspeople conceived the idea of establishing a national Christmas tree. That year a group journeyed over the snow-filled roads, and at high noon on Christmas Day, held a service under the General Grant. The following spring, on April 28, 1926, the tree was officially dedicated as the "Nation's Christmas Tree."

Each holiday season since then, except when deep snows have cut off access to the giant sequoia, a Christmas program has been presented at its base. Park officials annually lay a wreath under the great redwood to honor it.

Sanger has adopted this forest tree, and calls its yearly holiday celebration "The Nation's Christmas Tree Festival." They put up gay, colorful street decorations; merchants hold open house; carols sound through the business section; and special Yuletide programs are put on. The whole community joins together to make this an outstanding event.

In 1952, a cavalade of cars started as usual from Sanger; and Bishop Donald H. Tippett conducted services at the General Grant. Choirs from Fresno and Sanger joined in singing carols. Some years the program has been broadcast across our country; and Sanger sends holiday greetings to everyone in the nation.

This tree is becoming more noted each year as a national institution, and is visited annually by thousands of summer travelers. It is to be hoped that the serenity which the General Grant, our "Nation's Christmas Tree," displays may become a reality throughout the whole world. For the age-old custom of celebrating Christ's coming around a Christmas tree is a cherished tradition; and the evergreen branches, symbolic of immortality, inspire us each time the Yule season returns.

7

"Kindle the Christmas
Brand . . . "

ONE OF "MERRIE ENGLAND'S" most enjoyable holiday customs was bringing in the massive Yule log, and seeing it burn in the great fireplace at the Christmas feast. During the days of George II, some-one wrote of watching "a bouncing Christmas log in the chimney, glowing like the cheeks of a country milkmaid." And Charles Lamb once declared that "a large, heaped-up attractive fire" is one of our choicest winter pleasures. Also to us moderns, a blazing Christmas fire is the emblem of warmth, light, and happiness, even though it is an ancient custom that started far back in primitive times.

For many centuries, fire has been the symbol of home and safety. According to Norse mythology, their goddess, Hertha, was the deity of the home and domesticity. It was their belief that she descended to them in the smoke of their fireplaces, and that her coming would bring good fortune to the household. All enjoyed the bright glow as they warmed themselves by the hearth; and firelight often was the only means many early people had of lighting their homes after the sun went down.

As the Celts and Teutons held their winter festivals to commemorate the rebirth or return of the sun, the source of light, heat, and life, fire naturally played a vital role in the celebration. High on the hills, they built immense bonfires to honor their great god, Odin; and as the flames leaped up, young men engaged in such sports as jumping over the bonfire.

"Kindling" the Yule log originated in Northern Europe, where the Druids carefully selected a large log, preferably from a fruit-bearing tree, such as the apple, or oak. Then at a solemn gathering, they blessed the log, and prayed that it would burn forever.

This custom is said to have been associated with the Scandinavian worship of their mystic tree, Yggdrasil, or the "Tree of the Universe." No one had ever seen it; but tradition declared it was so mighty that no human being could even conceive of its size. One root was said to be in heaven; another, in hell; and the third, on earth. The entire universe, they believed, would be destroyed when the serpents that were continually gnawing at its roots made their way completely through the mighty tree, Yggdrasil.

When the northern tribes accepted Christianity, their old winter celebration was replaced by Christmas, the feast honoring Christ's birth. Since the Christian leaders wanted to do away with the pagan belief about Yggdrasil, they finally persuaded their followers to burn the log, which represented the ancient tree. This rite was to signify that the heathen ideas were no more; and it also became symbolic of Christ as "The Light of the World."

It is generally conceded that the Yule log custom came to English-speaking people from their Scandinavian forebears and their pagan ceremonies. In England, many persons selected their logs from oak, pine, or ash trees, while the Scottish people preferred those from birches. In some cases, the ash was most highly regarded because of the legend that Mary washed and dressed the Baby Jesus for the first time by the light of an ashwood fire.

The Yule log was chosen months before the Christmas holidays in order that it would be thoroughly dry, burn more easily, and send out a brighter light. The brand was always as large as the fireplace would accommodate; and often the log had its gnarled roots still attached to it.

There was a firm belief that all who helped bring in the Christmas brand would be insured against harm from witchcraft in the coming year. Therefore, it was customary for the whole family and all their retainers to go out to the forest to drag the trunk into their home. On such occasions, the log was often draped with garlands of Yuletide greenery. Oxen or horses sometimes assisted in pulling the trunk; but usually members of the household and the servants did the work, using ropes or chains. There was always much fun and noise on these yearly excursions; jokes were played; and someone might even try to drop the log on another's toes.

As the procession moved along, cheerful songs were sung; on some large estates, the owners hired minstrels to honor the Yule log by greeting it with such special songs as "The Old Oak Bough," "Welcome Yule," or Herrick's rollicking song that began with these lines:

> Come, bring with a noise,
> My merrie, merrie boyes,
> The Christmas log to the firing.

Often when travelers met a Yule log parade, they would doff their hats to the holiday brand. As the gay celebrants neared the manor house, the loud noise of horns and shouting announced their arrival. Then, with the aid of everyone, from the oldest to the youngest, the log was triumphantly dragged into the great hall. Sometimes, a young man would ride in on the brand, with all the girls of the household pulling on the ropes.

Next, each person sat on the log, sang a song to it, and kissed the trunk. In some places the oldest member of the family poured wine, three times, on the log, as he prayed that health, wealth, and happiness would come to all; that the spirit of good fellowship would prevail as long as the Christmas brand was aflame; and that all the inmates of the household would be kept in safety until the next Yuletide. Sometimes everyone drank a cup of spiced ale together, before the log was put in place.

When the great brand had been settled in the fireplace, the remains of last year's holiday log were brought out to kindle the new one, for it was an important part of the ceremony to save part of the old brand until the following season as Robert Herrick has related in his poem:

> Kindle the Christmas Brand and then
> Till sunset let it burn,
> Which, quenched, then lay it up again,
> Till Christmas next return.

Part must be kept wherewith to tend
The Christmas log next year;
And where it is safely kept, the fiend
Can do no mischief here.

While the fire burned briskly and sent out its cheery gleam, children danced in the firelight under the boughs of mistletoe and other holiday greens. Everyone was happy, for he believed that the Yule log had power to protect his home from evil spirits, and to destroy old hatreds and misunderstandings. Around the hearth at Yuletide, estranged members of the family often were brought together; and many old friendships were renewed as toast after toast was drunk to the blazing Christmas brand. Of course, the tables were spread with many kinds of holiday foods; and all ate their fill.

As the flames leaped higher and higher, the household joined in playing games. They dived for apples in a tub of cold water or took part in sack races. Sometimes, with their hands tied behind their backs, they tried to catch and eat Yule cakes that hung from the rafters.

One of the favorite and most popular pastimes at Christmas festivities was the game of snapdragon. Somebody placed raisins in a bowl, poured liquor over them, and set it afire. The object of the game was to snatch the burning raisins quickly, and stick them in one's mouth. There were always barrels of ale on hand for holiday revels, and another game consisted of placing a lighted candle in a can of ale or cider, and drinking the contents.

When they had tired themselves out with all the romping, singing, dancing, and playing vigorous games, the revelers sat around the fire, while the Yule log continued to glow and send out its welcome heat and light. Then they told, or listened to, weird legends and tales of great deeds done by heroes of bygone times, until bells announced the midnight hour, and it was time to go to rest.

France, like England, had its Yule log tradition. Often the entire family, dressed in their best clothes, went out to the woods together. There the father and oldest son cut down the log and dragged it home. The mother and the rest of the children followed, carrying freshly cut greenery to decorate the house. On some French farms, most of the laborers left early the day before Christmas to go to their own homes; but the unmarried ones remained, and helped bring in the Yule log, sometimes using a yoke of oxen.

The brand was carried in with much ceremony through the doorway, the youngest member of the household being at one end, and the oldest at the other. Three times they circled the room with the log before placing it in the fireplace. Sometimes, the father poured a glass of wine over it, while the others joined in a chant, expressing their joy at this happy Yuletime event.

After the head of the house had lighted the log, its fire was used to cook the Christmas supper which the family would enjoy on their return from attending midnight Mass at the village church. In some places it was customary for the father to sprinkle the brand with holy water before lighting the fire at midnight; and they waited to do this until they had heard the church bells joyously pealing out the glad tidings of Christ's birth.

In Provence, as the Yule log was brought in, a child poured wine on it in the name of the Holy Trinity. After the brand was completely burned, the charcoal was carefully gathered and saved as a remedy for such ailments as chilblains. They believed it to be a cure for certain diseases of animals, including the "staggers."

Before the Yule log was put in place in some regions of France, the prettiest girl of the family was seated on it, while all drank a toast to her. Sometimes, they lighted the brand, and let it burn for just a short time. After taking it from the fireplace, they covered it with a cloth. Then the children had fun; and all beat the log with sticks to drive away the evil spirits in it. Soon their parents sent them outside, telling them to pray for forgiveness for their wrongdoing. When the boys and girls were allowed to come back into the house, they peeped under the cloth covering the log, and found gifts waiting for them.

Since large cities like Paris do not have so many fireplaces now, where Yule logs can be placed, the custom is no longer observed in towns. However, city dwellers are still reminded of the old tradition, when, in their bakeries, they see special cakes—baked for the season—Christmas cakes, shaped like logs, and covered with chocolate icing to resemble the bark of a tree.

Some homes in Germany used to burn Yule logs during a three-day Christmas celebration; but it was not a general practice in that country, noted for its devotion to the Christmas tree. In Norway, the father went out alone to bring in the brand. When it had been lighted and was burning well, he told his family that the light of the flames would banish all hatred from their home.

In various districts of Italy, there were long, special rituals observed in connection with the Christmas Yule logs. At times, when the entire family was gathered around it, the boys and girls struck it hard with sticks. Then the father, in the name of the Blessed Trinity, placed the brand on the fire, put some juniper branches under it, and poured wine on it three times.

Often the log was gaily trimmed with paper flowers and bright ribbons. When the youngest child poured wine on it, he expressed the wish that the hungry would be fed; the tired, find rest; and that all would at last attain the peace of heaven. For twenty-four hours Italian families maintained a strict fast; and it was not until after midnight that they sat down before the glowing Yule log to eat their Christmas meal.

Most people in Yugoslavia preferred the oak for their Yule brand. They placed it on the hearth, threw corn and wine on it, while all prayed that the New Year would bring abundant harvests. In Bulgaria, when the father bore the log inside, members of the family stood in two rows, each holding a lighted candle. As he passed along between them, it was customary to throw corn and wine at him.

The Serbian habit was for the young men of each home to go out to cut an oak tree on which they scattered wheat, while they chanted a greeting to the Christmas log. In felling it, they planned that the trunk should fall toward the east, just at the exact time the morning sun rose above the horizon. It was considered bad luck if the tree fell in the opposite direction. Then the trunk was cut into two or three pieces, and taken home; but they did not carry it into the house until after the sun had set on the day before Christmas. Candles were lighted on each side of the door as it entered; the mother threw grains of wheat on it; and the children sang their Yule log carols. As soon as the brand was burning well, a young pig was placed before it to roast for their Christmas feast.

As centuries passed, it was natural that different superstitions grew up in connection with the Yule log in various countries. For example, there was the belief that when a barefooted, or "squint-eyed" person entered a room where the Christmas brand was burning, bad luck would follow. If the maidservants did not wash their hands before touching the log, it would burn dimly. It was a bad sign, too, when the fire failed to last through the entire night. As the brand was considered a protection to the home from the ravages of fire, lightning, thunder, and hailstones, people used to carry small fragments of the log to bed with them to guard against such catastrophes.

Ashes from the brand were certain—many thought—to make the earth more fertile; consequently, they buried them at the roots of fruit trees to make them produce abundantly, or they scattered ashes on the branches. The remains of the Christmas log had power to rid cats of vermin, to cure the toothache, and to keep well water pure and safe for drinking. In some Slavic lands, the embers were left undisturbed, for they feared their ancestors might fall into hell.

The flame of the Yule log was considered symbolic of the light that came from heaven when Christ was born. In numerous localities Christmas festivities lasted as long as this light kept glowing. However, a most important belief was that the partially burned brand must be stored away and kept to light the Yule log when the next holiday season came around.

Today, in some places, the century-old Christmas brand tradition has been revived. For instance, at the Ahwahnee Hotel in Yosemite National Park, the trunk is dragged in with colorful rites of earlier times. Each year at this hotel, lovers of a "White Christmas" and of the old customs of "Merrie England" gather for a gay and festive holiday celebration.

The Yule log is given the place of honor, too, each year at the hospitable Empress Hotel in Victoria, British Columbia. Many Britishers, who came directly from England, live in this delightful city. Just before the Christmas feast is served at the Empress, choristers, in costumes of the days of "Good Queen Bess," herald the entrance of the Christmas brand, always an immense log. After it is brought in, and anointed with wine and oil by certain dignitaries, the Yule log is lighted by a "Very Important Person," who uses a piece of wood saved from the brand of the preceding year.

In our country there is a community, Palmer Lake, Colorado, that has attracted much attention because of its annual Yule Log Hunt —the only public one in the United States. (This event was well described by Katherine Best and Katherine Hillyer, in the December, 1951, *Good Housekeeping* Magazine.) Palmer Lake, a small town of about three hundred people, through this Christmas project, draws large crowds of participants and interested spectators each season.

In 1934, Miss Evalena Macy, pastor of the Little Log Church at Palmer Lake, heard through a visitor, Miss Lucretia Vaile, of the invitational log hunt at Lake Placid, New York. The latter suggested that Palmer Lake would furnish an ideal setting for such a Christmas ceremony, so the small community decided to carry out the idea.

Naturally, this involved a great deal of special planning and many days of hard work, in order to arrange the countless details for such an undertaking, which is offered free to the public. First, permission had to be obtained from the United States Forestry Service to cut down a tree; also, it was necessary to build a large fireplace in their Town Hall, raise funds for the "wassail" (spiced cider), bake many cookies for their numerous guests, and contrive costumes for the performers.

This successful community celebration takes place the Sunday before Christmas; visitors come from distant states, and even from abroad, to take part. Christmas carols are heard in the streets; and when a trumpet sounds, the hunters follow their leader past the Little Log Church, through Vaile Gulch, and up Sundance Peak.

The log is always cut down and hidden weeks beforehand; when

83

the hunters get near it, a signal is given, and all start searching for the trunk, which has a rope fastened to it. The one who finds it is hailed as the winner, and is allowed to ride back to town on the log while his fellow hunters do the pulling.

Outside the Town Hall is a blazing bonfire, and inside, the victor is given the first drink of the steaming "wassail." The carolers sing "Kindle the Christmas Brand" and other fitting songs, while the log is carried in and thrown on the flames. The fun continues; everyone is filled with the spirit of Christmas; and this unique ceremony brings much joy to all who are fortunate enough to visit the community of Palmer Lake on this festive day.

In many homes all over our country, where people are lucky to have real fireplaces, they enjoy gathering around holiday fire. Our own New England poet, John Greenleaf Whittier, in his "Snow-bound," has given us an unforgettable picture of the family of a century ago as they enjoyed the comfort of their hearth.

> Shut in from all the world without,
> We sat the clean-winged hearth about,
> Content to let the north-wind roar
> In baffled rage at pane and door,
> While the red logs before us beat
> The frost-line back with tropic heat;
> And ever, when a louder blast
> Shook beam and rafter as it passed,
> The merrier up its roaring draught,
> The great throat of the chimney laughed.

Such lines as these serve to remind us vividly of the rollicking custom of bygone days, when the Yuletide festivities were ushered in by our forefathers, who enjoyed carrying out their annual tradition of "Kindling the Christmas Brand."

8

"Away in a Manger . . ."

"AWAY IN A Manger"—the old carol attributed to Martin Luther —is still a favorite with modern children. And many boys and girls get a vivid impression of the circumstances under which Christ was born from miniature, or larger, Nativity scenes. These show the Baby Jesus in the manger, watched over by Mary and Joseph, while near by, in the attitude of worship, are the shepherds and the Wise Men from the East.

This Christmas custom, which has become very popular in recent years here in the United States, is said to have originated in the church, perhaps as early as the eighth century. Its Latin name was the *praesepio,* which in Italian was *presepe,* meaning "stable." However, it was St. Francis of Assisi who popularized the re-enactment of the birth of the Christ Child as part of the Christmas observance, when he set up a simple manger scene at the little town of Greccio, Italy, in 1224.

During the Middle Ages there were only a few books; even if there had been more, most of the people could not have read them. Naturally, the church ceremonies were conducted in Latin, so such holidays as Christmas and Easter held, perhaps, little meaning for many church attendants. This worried St. Francis, known as "The Little Brother of Mankind," for he wanted to humanize the teachings of the Scriptures, and to show his followers that Christ also came from humble beginnings.

The good saint was filled with an overwhelming desire to help his hearers understand sacred truths, so they might have a deeper religious experience. It is said that just three years before his death St. Francis saw some shepherds sleeping in the fields near Greccio;

and this gave him the inspiration for depicting the coming of the Saviour in a way all could understand. In his life of St. Francis, St. Bonaventure says, ". . . he was minded to celebrate the memory of the Birth of the Child Jesus, with all the added solemnity that he might, for the kindling of devotion."

Before making his plans, St. Francis went to Rome to discuss with Pope Honorius III the idea of setting up a nativity scene. After the pope had given his consent, the saint asked a wealthy nobleman ("a certain Knight, valorous and true, Messer John of Greccio, who for the love of Christ had left the secular army, and was bound by closest friendship unto the man of God") to help prepare the representation. St. Francis said, "For I would fain make memorial of that Child who was born in Bethlehem, and in some sort behold with bodily eyes His Infant hardships; how he lay in the manger on the hay with the ox and ass standing by."

Before Christmas came, the news spread rapidly through the town and countryside; therefore, crowds of worshipers, many with torches and carrying presents for the Holy Babe, thronged to see this unusual way of teaching the sacred story. Tradition tells us this took place in a cave on the hill above Greccio, not far from Assisi.

Here Messer John (or Giovanni) had assembled the necessary properties, including the manger, straw, and a live ox and an ass. Real persons took the parts of Mary, Joseph, and the shepherds. St. Francis himself arranged the scene, and placed a life-sized wax figure of the Christ Child in the manger.

There were shouts of joy from the peasants when they saw the nativity group and ". . . that august night was made radiant and solemn with many bright lights, and with tuneful and sonorous praises." For the first time, it is asserted, many understood the true meaning of that event in the stable at Bethlehem.

As St. Bonaventure related the story in 1263:

> The man of God, filled with tender love, stood before the manger, bathed in tears, and overflowing with joy. Solemn Masses were celebrated over the manger, Francis, the Levite of Christ, chanting the Holy Gospel. Then he preached unto

the folk standing around the Birth of the King in poverty, call-
ing Him, when he wished to name Him, the Child of Bethlehem, by reason of his tender love for Him.

St. Francis begged his listeners to put all hatred from their
hearts, and to think only of peace at this Christmas season. So,
more than seven centuries ago, "Of Greccio there was made, as it
were, a new Bethlehem." As the saint stood before the manger, he
led his people in songs that, no doubt, were among the first Christmas carols ever sung. He encouraged the children to sing around
the manger to the Baby Jesus, and from this custom have come
several noted lullabies to the Christ Child.

St. Bonaventure states that Messer John afterward declared, when
St. Francis lifted the Child in his arms, that the Holy Babe seemed
to waken from His sleep. This, the saint avers, was confirmed
later by reports of miracles that took place. That night at Greccio,
peasants carried the straw home with them. Soon stories were current that this straw had cured sick animals, and had also served as
"a prophylactic against divers other plagues."

The worshipers at this first nativity replica at Greccio were so
impressed by the novel Christmas ceremony that they repeated the
rites, year after year. Soon the idea was adopted by other Italian
towns; then the custom gradually spread to Spain, Portugal, France,
England, etc., and to other distant parts of the world.

Since domestic animals were used in these Yuletide representations, a legend arose that on Christmas Eve all the beasts knelt in
their stalls, in adoration of the Holy Infant. There was a widespread
belief, too, that on this holy night the animals had the power of
speech; and that it was a sin to try to "listen in" on them.

At first the *presepi* or Christmas cribs in churches were quite
simple; but as years went by, they became very elaborate, and
numerous figures were added, besides the Biblical ones. This holiday custom reached its height during the seventeenth and eighteenth
centuries in Italy. The figures—many life size—were artistically
carved from wood, or carefully modeled from wax or clay, then
painted or gilded by skilled artisans.

The "Bambino" or Christ Child often had many changes of

apparel that included richly embroidered robes of fine materials. For example, in the Church of Ara Coeli at Rome is one of the most noted Bambinos. It is said that a monk carved it of wood from the Mount of Olives in the Holy Land. The Christ child is dressed in rich clothing, and wears many jewels given Him by wealthy visitors. Various miracles have been ascribed to this Bambino. At Christmastime, Roman children come here and recite a "piece," or sermon, to the Holy Babe; each year the image is taken up a long flight of steps to bless the city of Rome.

In the lavish Christmas Crib scenes, the Virgin Mary is sometimes dressed in robes presented to her by royalty. Blue satin is often used for her costumes. However, Joseph is usually shown in ordinary garb, while the Magi wear jeweled turbans and robes of rich, colorful materials with long trains, carried by their retainers.

In addition to the rich costuming, the Italian Christmas Cribs had elaborate backgrounds; sometimes hundreds of figures, arranged in special settings, depict scenes that seem somewhat out of keeping with the religious idea of the nativity. However, since the correctly dressed replicas give authentic pictures of life in their land, as it really was during the period when the Crib was assembled, they afford us an excellent idea of the era. For instance, in the crowd of people, supposedly on their way to worship the newly found Saviour of the world, we see representatives from different ranks of society and occupations.

In many cases, the making of the Christmas Crib figures and their arrangement have been important contributions to art. And, happily, members of the Holy Family—Mary, Joseph, and the Christ Child—with the shepherds and the Magi have been kept as the central and most important point of interest.

One of the most costly and complicated nativity scenes in Italy, the Madonna della Grazie, was built by Capuchin monks. The grotto, made of Sardinian cork, rose to a height of eighteen feet. The Three Kings, finely carved figures, and the shepherds were made to move down a mountain slope to the manger, where the parents were watching over the Holy Infant.

The famous German poet, Goethe, while visiting in Italy in 1787, described a Christmas Crib he had seen in Naples. It was an outdoor spectacle, constructed on a roof. This scene, with Vesuvius forming its background, made a strong impression on the poet.

In many great museums throughout the world are excellent examples of nativity scenes of former centuries. The Metropolitan Museum in New York City contains the noted Rossellino group, used before 1478. In the Tyrolean Alps the Christmas Crib has long been popular; and the people produce beautifully carved figures. The National Museum in Munich contains many such masterpieces, also delicate plaster figurines, set against interesting backgrounds.

The well-known Lang family of Oberammergau (many of whose members have taken part in the Passion Play) has produced a notable collection of figures and manger scenes. Alois Lang, who has played the part of Christ, is an expert at carving. During World War II, at the request of a young American officer, he carved a cross for a church in Los Angeles. When the man's mother wrote, praising him for his excellent work, Alois Lang sent her a delicately carved manger scene, including the stable, the Holy Family, and some angels.

Today, if you visit Rome, you can view what authorities declare is "The most famous Christmas Crib in the world" in the Basilica of Saints Cosmas and Damian, near the Coliseum. This famous *presepe,* "truly a work of art and the only one of its kind in the world," was created in Naples more than two centuries ago. A man and his wife, named Cataldo-Perricelli, who had inherited it from their ancestors, presented the scene to the Third Order Regular of St. Francis.

This unusual Christmas display is forty-five feet long, twenty-one feet wide, and twenty-seven feet high, and contains hundreds of wooden, hand-carved figurines. They are the work of several noted artists of the seventeenth century, and portray various phases of Neapolitan life of that period.

The blue sky contains stars, the moon, a comet; and there are several angels on their way to the grotto where Mary, Joseph, and the Babe are seen. One angel is waking a shepherd who has fallen asleep near his flock. In the background are several hills, valleys, the River Jordan, and lighted villages. On the balcony of his palace in Jerusalem, you can see Herod, pointing out to the Magi the way to the manger in Bethlehem.

There are farmlands with fruit trees and domestic animals. Numerous small buildings in the Crib have been made by cementing together thousands of tiny pieces of stone or tile. Figures of many different kinds of workers are engaged in their usual tasks. At an ancient castle, servants are working away busily; one maid is baking bread in an outdoor oven; another is roasting chestnuts; while, under rather primitive conditions, some women are washing their clothes.

There is a typical tavern of the day in the nativity scene, where food is being cooked; also, some diners seem to be enjoying their meal at a long table. To entertain them, a girl is doing an Italian country dance, the tarantella. Not far away is a fishmonger in charge of his small shop. These interesting scenes give us a good picture of how people lived and worked in Naples more than two centuries ago.

Naturally, the central and most important part of this Christmas Crib is the Holy Family. The Magi are dressed in colorful Oriental garments, decorated with gold and glittering stones. They are kneeling before the Infant Jesus, as they offer Him the rich gifts they have brought from their distant countries. This inspiring display reveals the spirit of the holiday season and shows the great love which the Italians have always had for their cherished *presepi*.

With the growth in popularity of the nativity scenes in their churches, many families began to set up simple mangers in their own homes. This was especially the case in Southern Europe, where the Christmas feast centered around the replica of the stable at Bethlehem, just as it did around the Christmas tree in northern lands.

In Southern France, notably in Provence, such a scene was called a *crèche;* in Spain, the *nacimiento;* and in the southern part of Germany, the *Krippe.* The Moravians, keeping the Holy Family as the center of interest, added various farm scenes to their *Putz;* while the Bohemians, in their "Bethlehem," used other religious figures besides the characters directly concerned with the Christmas story.

In the homes of well-to-do families the figures used were often carved or created by noted artists. These costly statues are highly cherished and handed down from one generation to another. In such representations the Holy Family is often seen resting in a building with high columns, over which angels are hovering while the shepherds and the Wise Men are kneeling before the manger. (Such a building is, of course, a bit incongruous when we remember the stable at Bethlehem.)

In Italy, even the poorest families enjoy their Christmas supper near the beloved *presepe*. The children place the inexpensive figures against a roughly painted background. The images, fashioned from cardboard, papier mâché, or plaster, can be bought very cheaply on the streets at open-air stalls. In Rome people throng to the Piazza Navona before Christmas to choose pieces for their *presepi*.

At twilight, on Christmas Eve, in an Italian home, all the members of the family gather around the scene. The manger is empty; but next morning the mother, in a special ceremony, places the Bambino in His bed. During the holiday week, the Italians enjoy going around to view the scenes their friends have set up; they kneel in prayer, and sing carols before each *presepe*.

For many French children, the *crèche* is the chief feature of their Yuletide observance. Often they add varied secular figures—all types of characters—called *santons*. In Marseilles a fair is held on the streets before the holiday season, and patrons hunt for novelties to add interest to their scenes.

A day or two before Christmas, French children like to go to the woods to gather holly, laurel, lichens, stones, and moss to use in arranging the *crèche*. Often it stands on a table in the corner of the room; there is a hill with a cave in its side where the Child is seen in the manger. By means of flour, they create the effect of snow, while shepherds are huddled around a tiny fire made with tinfoil. On the mantel above, three candles of differing colors—emblematic of the Holy Trinity—shed a flickering light on the scene; and the star of Bethlehem adds its glow.

ALL ABOUT CHRISTMAS

Each evening until Epiphany (Twelfth Night) French boys and girls celebrate around the *crèche*. Sometimes they make small manger scenes in cardboard boxes which they carry around to show to their neighbors. When they sing carols, they are often rewarded with little gifts.

The Spanish children rejoice around the *nacimiento;* and sing or dance to the accompaniment of tambourines. In Spain, the making of figurines for Christmas nativity scenes is quite an art. In the "Spanish Village" (at Barcelona), which contains replicas of buildings from all the provinces of Spain, visitors are delighted by the displays of all sizes and types of statues created for the *nacimiento.*

In Germany, especially in the southern part, during the Middle Ages, boys and girls gathered around the Christmas *Krippe,* with a figure of the Baby Jesus. In their excitement, during the singing and dancing, they often rocked the Crib too vigorously. This was called "cradle-rocking," and was opposed by some of the clergy. But from this custom, certain carols and lullabies to the Holy Infant have come down to us.

The idea of setting up nativity scenes spread to England from the Catholic countries; but it was never so popular there as on the Continent. Although banned by the Reformation, some remains of it still exist in certain rural districts, according to Michael Harrison. Mention has already been made of the English "kissing ring" ("bough" or "bunch") in connection with mistletoe; sometimes three dolls, representing Mary, Joseph, and the Child, were placed in this Christmas decoration.

Here in the United States, nativity scenes are becoming more popular each year. During the eighteenth century, because of religious persecution, many colonists came to this country from Moravia and Bohemia, settling at such places as Bethlehem, Pennsylvania, and Salem, North Carolina. With them they brought the Christmas *Putz,* which has now become a tradition in many American homes.

The descendants of these Moravians still set up their Yuletide displays in homes and churches. In the Brothers' House, built in 1769 in Salem, a large *Putz* gives not only a vivid picture of the first Christmas, but also has scenes from Moravian history, including pioneer settlement incidents.

In Bethlehem, many nativity displays are on a very large scale; and usually all the furniture is removed from the room. Besides the central manger scene with the Holy Family, there are miniature snow-covered mountains, farms with barnyards and animals, villages with roads, bridges, mills, and other buildings. The figures, often family heirlooms, are as highly cherished as their silver and linens. Originally the *Putz* was lighted by tiny wax candles, but now electricity is used. A star shines over the *Putz,* and by its light the mother reads to her children the ever-new Christmas story.

These Moravian people still go *"Putz*-visiting," beginning after the Christmas Eve vigil at the church, and continue the custom each evening of the holiday week. Often the women dress in the costumes of their ancestors to receive guests; and they proudly display new or old arrangements of the thrilling nativity scenes. Everyone keeps open house; strangers are welcome to enter and see the *Putz;* and there are always abundant supplies of delicious Christmas cookies made from age-old recipes for their numerous visitors.

Bethlehem, Pennsylvania, also has an outstanding Community *Putz,* which is displayed daily from December 16 to January 2, in the first Moravian Church. This elaborate scene rests on nearly fifty bushels of moss, and has a stream of water running through it. Here the Christmas story is shown in seven scenes, which have in them more than two hundred buildings. Herod's Temple is an accurate reproduction of the original; the Bible figures are carved by hand from mahogany; and the entire project represents much meticulous research and labor.

In a leaflet "America's Christmas City," issued by the Bethlehem Chamber of Commerce (reprinted from *Think,* December, 1941), Dr. A. D. Thaeler wrote:

> The Putz is a form of poetry, for though it is not written with ink on paper, nor painted with pigments on canvas, it is worked out with carved wood and moss and tinsel into a picture which stirs something back of the bare reason: the faculty of the imagination.

ALL ABOUT CHRISTMAS

The charm of visiting the various homes at this season is to see the special features of the Putz which speak particularly to the builder. It is not unusual to find little carved figures which have appeared year after year for three-quarters of a century. . . . It would be a distinct disappointment not to find them on the Putz under the old roof-tree. Naturally, certain parts come to be standardized, as the figures of the Holy Family, which can be purchased in stores. But the chief interest, needless to say, attaches to those portions of the Putz, perhaps even the weatherbeaten old stumps that represent rocks, which may have been in a family for many, many years. In other words, you cannot buy a Putz. You might spend a hundred dollars upon one, but it would not be worth a dime in real value. . . . It is one of the things that make up the real Christmas, for it keeps us linked with the one radiant truth, that through the Nativity of Christ there came to us all the light and life that the world knows.

Many individuals, today, all over the United States, are making a hobby of collecting Putz figures and arranging Christmas nativity replicas so that friends and strangers, too, can enjoy them. Mrs. Dorothy Green Miller of Springfield, Ohio, has a notable collection of such figures. Also, her library of hundreds of books on holiday customs and traditions shows the great interest she has always taken in Christmas lore.

Some years ago, Mrs. Miller decided to have a celebration that would bring happiness to many, and spread Yuletide joys over a longer period. So she began collecting materials for a Putz; and in 1931 set up her first simple scene under the Christmas tree. Now she has accumulated more than twelve hundred figures, many of which have been sent to her from distant parts of the world.

It is a tremendous task to unpack them each year and to place the varied and numerous scenes on simulated snow. Her Putz is now displayed in two rooms; and in addition to the sacred incidents, she arranges groups depicting favorite Christmas stories, Mother Goose tales, and fairy stories.

When everything is ready on Christmas Eve, the Millers hold open house; and both children and adults are thrilled as Mrs.

Miller explains the different groups, and reads the incomparable Christmas story as told by St. Luke. Her display is shown until Twelfth Night; and each year hundreds of visitors, including many strangers, enjoy the Putz. So it's not surprising that she has become known as the "Christmas Lady." Once, when asked what she would like for the holidays, she said:

> If I were to be granted one wish this season, I would wish for nothing more than that everyone might be permeated with the sort of Christmas spirit that makes one thrill when he sees a lighted Christmas tree; a glistening ornament; a solitary candle sending out its shaft of light in silent appeal; the darkening silhouette of the landscape against a covering of snow; a child's merry face; a spirit so radiant that even the red and green of the traffic lights will make one feel like shouting "Merry Christmas!"

In many communities, families, churches, and other groups are helping today to make the holidays more significant by arranging outdoor nativity scenes for passers-by to enjoy. These wayside mangers help bring the Christmas story to people's attention. From New York to Florida, from Seattle to San Diego, in almost every part of our land, there are outstanding representations of this kind during the holidays.

In the South, for example, some scenes are decorated with palm leaves, while "up North," real snow often adds the right decorative touch to an outdoor replica. At the University of Missouri in Columbia, students create a Crib which thousands of persons come miles to see and enjoy.

In and around Baltimore, Maryland, families arrange what they call "Christmas Gardens," miniature landscapes, under their trees. Details differ; sometimes incidents in local history are shown; but most "gardens" still have the Holy Infant as the center. This custom, which goes back at least sixty years here, is said to have been started by persons who had visited the Moravian towns of near-by Pennsylvania, and brought back the *Putz* idea.

A Baltimore paper, a few years ago, reported that one "Christmas

Garden" enthusiast, Mr. Vernon Engleman, had spent more than a decade on his project, which contains accurate replicas of different buildings, including a music hall, from which carols sound, and his "prize structure," a diminutive Catholic cathedral. It has real chimes and an organ that plays a tune. Other persons in Baltimore have unusual "gardens" with indirect lighting, mountain scenes, waterfalls, and hand-carved figures and buildings.

In 1939, a German, Christian Mayer, who had been in the United States only ten years, was inspired by a picture on a Christmas card to set up a nativity scene. In a stable made of rough slabs and filled with real straw were life-sized figures (made from wall board, and painted by Mr. Mayer) of the Holy Family and the worshiping shepherds. Since his family was in Germany, he had decided to make "a Christmas present for everyone to enjoy"; and hundreds of passers-by were inspired by his scene.

It is wonderful, too, the way the Yuletide spirit prevails among business houses. Their outstanding window displays attract enthusiastic spectators. During World War II, for instance, one Western department store had inspiring scenes in their eighteen large windows, with backgrounds in rich colors, and figures of simulated marble, telling the Christmas story. As someone said, this was "window-trimming at its highest plane." These replicas were prepared by the owners "to help bring a ray of hope into the wartime Christmas."

Recently another firm in the Midwest had an unusually attractive manger scene with live animals—cows, donkeys, sheep, and camels; on Epiphany, the arrival of the Three Kings, in their colorful dress, climaxed this outstanding display.

If good St. Francis of Assisi could return to earth, he, no doubt, would be amazed to note what has developed from the simple Crib he set up several centuries ago. But these modern representations of the Christmas story *do* inspire many to feel more deeply the significance of the birth of the Christ Child. And each nativity scene, large or small, reminds us of that night when the shepherd saw a Babe, "Away in a Manger" in far-off Bethlehem.

9

"The Boar's Head
in Hand Bring I"

> At Christmas be merrie,
> And thankful withal;
> And feast with thy neighbors,
> The great with the small.

DOWN THROUGH THE centuries, "Eat, drink, and be merry" seems to have been a Christmas tradition. No matter how well fed people have been the rest of the year, at this time, they enjoy serving their families and friends an abundance of choice foods. This custom comes down to us from the ancient winter feasts when everyone was happily looking forward to the coming of a new year.

Eating certainly was emphasized at Christmas in the "good old days" of "Merrie England," when weeks of preparation preceded the most important feast of the year. The English rulers set their people the example by staging great banquets. At first only nobles and clergy were present; but gradually the middle class and the poor were included. The latter were made happy by gifts of food, and in some cases were fed at the great castles or manor houses.

The first important Christmas feast occurred in 878 during the reign of King Alfred, who had decreed that Yuletide be observed for a period of twelve days. It is said that at this celebration foods were served on gold and silver platters.

In 1171, Henry II entertained at his holiday banquets the Irish kings and princes, who were amazed at the foods served them. Henry III celebrated with his nobles for a week in 1248 at Winchester; and also ordered, this same Christmas, that the poor be well fed at Westminster Hall. Four years later, when his daughter, Princess Margaret, was married on Christmas, the Archbishop of York supplied six hundred beeves to feed the assembled guests.

On one occasion, Edward I invited a hundred lords and ladies to share his holiday banquet; and they ate at a great round table, reminiscent of the days of King Arthur. Richard II, who ascended the throne in 1377, at a notable celebration at Litchfield engaged two thousand cooks to prepare the food, for history states that ten thousand people were fed at this affair. This same monarch also entertained lavishly when the King of Armenia visited him.

At Christmas, 1400, Henry IV held a splendid feast to honor the Emperor of Byzantium, while his successor, Henry V, noted his marriage to Queen Catherine by giving a holiday banquet in the great hall at Westminster. Many notables were present, including the king of the Scots and the Archbishop of Canterbury. The menu featured brawn (boar's meat), several kinds of fish, and "jelly covered with flowers." During the reign of this same monarch there was "a glutton mass celebration" in 1415 that lasted five days. It was long remembered for the vast amounts of food and drink consumed "with the most furious zeal and rapidity."

During the years Henry VI was king (1422–1471), such dishes as roast heron, capon, venison, mutton, beef, boar, and "custard royal with a leopard of gold sitting therein" were served, according to Michael Harrison, who tells us that spices and herbs at that period were added to nearly all foods. This was done, perhaps, to cover up odors, or to vary the monotony; and, since spices were expensive, the wealthy liked to show their ability to buy them.

Henry VII (1485–1509) also kept up the lavish holiday customs, usually at Westminster. Besides the many meat and fish dishes, he served "frumenty," a popular dish made by boiling hulled wheat in milk, then adding sugar and spices. One of his most sumptuous banquets was given at Christmas, 1492 (when Columbus spent the day in the New World), to honor the Lord Mayor and aldermen of London. The king, queen, and members of the court were served a total of 120 different dishes, with the peacock as the outstanding one. However, the mayor and his associates had to be satisfied with "24 dishes and an abundance of wine."

By this time, cooks had developed some very fancy and unusual desserts known as "subtleties." They were elaborate concoctions, made from sugar, or molded of blanc mange or jellies in the shapes of animals, ships, castles, persons, or scenes showing historic events. At Christmas, they were usually made in the form of the Wise Men, the Virgin Mary, a cradle, a manger with the Holy Infant. These "subtleties" were carried in with much pomp, served as table decorations, and then eaten as dessert.

Lavish holiday feasts continued during the reign of Henry VIII. One Christmas at Greenwich, there "was such an abundance of viands served to all comers of anie honest behaviour as hath been few times seen." Once this king used a gold tablecloth that had cost more than $3,000. His daughter, Elizabeth, continued to serve Christmas dinners with many courses.

Such feasts, given by rulers or nobility, often began at noon, and lasted eight or nine hours. Sometimes the banquets had twelve courses, symbolic of the twelve disciples.

The host, surrounded by his family and friends, sat on a dais in his great hall. The tables were loaded with fruits, plum puddings, mince pies, and "subtleties." There were loud trumpet blasts to announce the entrance of the servants with huge platters of roast beef, haunches of venison, roasted hares, turkeys, swans, herons, capons, pigs, geese, and, of course, the two most heralded foods—the boar's head and the peacock. Vegetables, including turnips, carrots, beets, and parsnips, were served on these occasions.

To entertain the guests during the long-continued meal, there was the "Lord of Misrule," in charge of the mummers and jesters. But, in many cases, diners paid little attention to the antics around them, for they were too busy consuming food. Dogs hovered near by and enjoyed bones and foods thrown their way.

Wild boars were plentiful in England in Druid days; and such animals were offered in sacrifice by priests to the goddess Frigga. The boar was revered by these people because, since it dug its tusks into the earth, it was said to have suggested to men the idea of ploughing the ground. Sometimes a roasted wild boar was served at the winter feasts; and after the acceptance of Christianity, the people continued to eat the flesh of this animal.

The serving of the boar's head, with great fanfare, at the Christmas feast is said to have originated in this way: one of the students of Queen's College, Oxford, was walking in Shotover Forest, deeply engrossed in reading Aristotle. Suddenly, without any warning, a wild boar rushed out and attacked him. The surprised scholar had no time to draw his sword, so he quickly jammed his book down the animal's open jaws, and choked him to death.

Then the ingenious Oxonian cut off the boar's head and, in triumph, carried it back to his college. It was roasted and borne into the hall, in an impressive ceremony, and served to the students. Ever since, Queen's College has observed this custom; now, however, a false head, with a piece of brawn under it, is carried in the procession.

A single voice sings the "Boar's Head Carol"; and as the platter advances, everyone joins in the chorus. The head is placed before the provost, who carves slices of the brawn and serves those at his table. Then the dish is sent to the other diners.

This college custom was soon taken up by early English rulers and members of the nobility. It became a tradition and a favorite Christmas rite. As years passed, the ceremonies attending it grew more elaborate. Its coming was announced by music, played and sung by hired minstrels. Everyone stood up when the Master of the Revels entered and ushered in the Chief Cook. Usually, the latter was given the high honor of bringing in the boar's head.

Sometimes, two tall men, chosen from the most important servants, carried in the huge gold or silver platter on which the head, decorated with holiday greenery, lay, with an apple or a lemon in its mouth. The bearer, at times, was preceded by a man, holding a dripping sword; this was supposed to be the weapon with which the animal had been slain.

Singers joined in the traditional carol, always sung during this colorful part of the Yuletide feast:

> *Caput apri defero*
> *Reddens laudes Domino.*

The boar's head in hand bring I,
With garlands gay and rosemary;
I pray you all sing merrily,
Qui estis in convivio.

For many years the old custom continued, but naturally it was banned by Cromwell. With the Restoration, the rite was brought back, although it never again regained its old popularity. Several times the ancient tradition was carried out during the reign of Victoria. Sir Walter Scott in his vivid description of holiday festivities in "Marmion" describes the boar's head ceremony:

Then was brought in the lusty brawn
By old blue-coated, serving man.
Then the boar's head frowned on high,
Crested with bays and rosemary.
Well can the green-garbed ranger tell
How, when, and where the monster fell;
What dogs before his death he tore,
And all the baiting of the boar.

Another elegant and royal meat dish, served in medieval days at Christmas, was the roast peacock. This dish was termed "food for lovers and meat for lords." The cooks carefully removed the skin with all its brilliant plumage. After the fowl had been baked and partly cooled (it was stuffed and seasoned with various spices), the feathers were replaced and the tail spread out gracefully.

The handsome bird rested on a large platter, with its crested head proudly erect. Sometimes, a sponge, soaked in spirits, was placed in the gilded beak, and lighted just before the bearer entered the hall. The peacock was sometimes made into a pie, and served with its head sticking out of one side of the pan, and the tail on the other. As the meat was rather dry, plenty of gravy was used with it.

This is referred to by Massinger, in *The City Madam,* and shows the extravagant way in which this fowl and other meats were prepared for the great Christmas feasts of long ago:

Men may talk of country Christmases,
Their thirty pound butter'd eggs, their pies of carps' tongues;
Their pheasants drench'd with ambergris; the carcasses

Of three fat wethers bruised for gravy to make sauce
for a single peacock.

The peacock was never borne in by a servant, for this honor was given to the most charming, or distinguished, lady present. As she carried in the platter, the court ladies, or those of the nobility, followed in her train. Musicians, playing on ancient instruments, such as the viol, cithern, or lute, furnished appropriate music.

When the bearer reached the dais, she mounted the steps, and carefully placed the colorful dish before the host or most highly honored guest. Before the fowl was served, each knight came up, placed his hand on it, and swore a solemn oath to perform some worthy deed.

It is said that one of the last times the peacock tradition was carried out was while George IV (who reigned from 1820 to 1830) was still Duke of Clarence; and he was amazed when this ancient dish was served by his host.

Our Christmas dessert, mince pie (also known in early days as "shred" pie or "Christmas" pie), has been popular for more than five centuries. During the Middle Ages, it was named "mutton pie." The earliest known recipe called for chopped or minced partridges, pheasants, hares, instead of the beef later used in its making. Gradually, other ingredients were added; one recipe called for chopped meat, suet, sugar, apples, molasses, cider, raisins, currants, citron, cloves, and nutmeg. Some early pies contained as many as six pounds of meat alone.

Some sources state that, at first, mince pies were made in oblong shape to represent the manger at Bethlehem; and the latticed tops of some of these pies were symbolic of the hayrack in the stable. The apples were significant of the growth and fertility to come with the new season; the Oriental spices, reminiscent of the gifts of the Wise Men.

As one poet has sung, the "Christmas pie" was an emblem of holiday joy:

Without the door let sorrow lie,
And if for cold it hap to die,
We'll bury it in a Christmas pie,
And everyone be merry!

In medieval days, after the mince pies were baked in England, their owners took special precautions to prevent their being stolen. In these lines, Robert Herrick warned his contemporaries:

> Come guard this night the Christmas-Pie,
> That the Thief, though ne'er so sly,
> With his Flesh-hooks, don't come nigh
>
> > To catch it.

> From him, who all alone sits there,
> Having his eyes still in his ear,
> And a deal of mighty fear
>
> > To watch it.

Mince pies sometimes were called "wayfarers' pies" since they were given to all holiday visitors. There was a common belief that eating this dessert brought good luck, especially if one ate twelve such pies between Christmas Day and Twelfth Night. In addition, one would have a happy and fortunate day for each pie eaten, on condition one consumed them at twelve different places. Any person who refused to eat this pastry would lose a good friend during the coming year. Remains of the "Christmas pies" were always distributed to the poor at the end of the Yuletide season.

Perhaps the most famous holiday pie ever baked was the one made in England in 1770 for Sir Henry Grey. It was prepared by his housekeeper, Mrs. Dorothy Patterson at Horwick, and sent to his London home. The pie was about nine feet in diameter, weighed 165 pounds, and was served from a four-wheeled cart. In it was the minced meat of several partridges, pigeons, blackbirds, geese, rabbits, turkeys, and ducks—not to mention twenty pounds of butter, and a couple of bushels of flour.

(In December, 1949, a large *modern* mince pie was made at Salt Lake City, Utah, and hailed as the "World's Largest Pie." It measured 3½ feet across, and weighed 140 pounds. This "Christmas Pie" was presented to the children of St. Anne's Orphanage in that city.)

There's a legend to the effect that once an English king, when hunting, had to remain in the forest over Christmas Eve. So his cook put into a pot all the food he happened to have with him—some chopped meat, flour, apples, dried plums, eggs, ale, sugar, and brandy. He stirred the concoction together, put the sticky mass in a bag, and boiled the first English plum pudding.

This may or may not be true; and some historians believe that "plum pottage" or "plum pudding" is in reality the successor to frumenty, sometimes called "frumante" or "furmety." At first the dish was made by boiling grains of wheat until they burst. The mixture was strained, and broth, or eggs and milk, stirred into it. Later, other ingredients, such as sugar, lemons, raisins, currants, nutmeg, suet, ginger, mace, and cloves were added to improve the taste.

The original "plum pottage" was always served with the best meats at the first course of a Christmas feast. Gradually, the dish seems to have evolved into a sweet, stiff pudding, and was used as dessert. A Mrs. Fraser, "sole teacher of the art of cookery in Edinburgh," wrote a cookbook in 1791 in which the dish was named "plumb pudding" for the first time. (It has been said that, since "plum" meant to "rise" or "swell," the dish got its name because of the swelling of the raisins.)

Cakes, of several kinds, were a popular holiday food in England. When poor persons came around singing carols or carrying figures of the Madonna and the Child, people gave them presents of Christmas cakes.

Since the Puritans frowned upon any observance of Christ's birthday, they denounced the baking and eating of holiday foods. A poet of the day expressed himself in this fashion about the Roundheads:

> The high shoe lords of Cromwell's making
> Were not for dainties—roasting, baking;
> The chiefest food they found most good in
> Was rusty bacon and bag pudding.
> Plum broth was popish, and mince pie—
> O that was flat idolatry!

Wassail, usually a mixture of hot ale, sweetened, and spiced with nutmeg, or ginger, was drunk, chiefly on Christmas and at Twelfth Night. Well-to-do hosts used wine instead of ale, and added cream, eggs, almonds, cloves, and cinnamon. Roasted apples, bobbing on the surface of the wassail, were known as "lambs' wool" because of their smoothness and softness. Wassail at first in England was served in a great wooden bowl; later, finer utensils were used; and often a canopy of Christmas greenery was placed over the container.

The custom of serving wassail originated, so tradition tells, when the beautiful Saxon maiden, Rowena, presented Prince Vortigen a bowl of wine, and greeted him with "Wæs hæil!" This meant the same as our modern "Here's to you!"

Gradually, the ceremonies associated with wassail drinking became more elaborate. With much pomp, a steward brought in the great bowl; and he was followed by the gentlemen and castle servants. As he called out "Wassail! Wassail!" all joined in a carol praising the drink, and crowded around for a taste of the steaming mixture.

Our American writer, Oliver Wendell Holmes, in "On Lending a Punchbowl," eulogized this custom:

> This ancient silver bowl of mine, it tells of good old times,
> Of joyous days and jolly nights, and Merry Christmas chimes.

Several superstitions in England were connected with holiday foods: a loaf of bread was left lying on the table after the Christmas Eve supper, so that there would be plenty of bread in the home during the coming months. Also, in order to enjoy good health the next year, it was customary to eat apples at midnight on Christmas Eve.

In Polton, and near-by places in Bedfordshire, there was a special holiday dessert—"Apple Florentine"—no doubt similar to our modern deep-dish apple pie. It was made in a huge pan, "filled with good baking apples, sugar and lemons to the very brim, with a covering of rich pastry." When the dish was baked, the crust was lifted off, cut into triangles (to be replaced later), and hot, well-spiced ale poured over the apples.

During the time of Cromwell, even though Yule feasts were forbidden, many people continued to enjoy the old holiday dishes in their homes. From several English writers we gain a good idea of what different individuals ate for Christmas dinner. Pepys, for instance, tells us in his diary that he enjoyed "a mess of plum pudding and a roasted pullet" on the Christmas of 1662, adding that he sent out for a mince pie, as his wife had been sick, and hadn't been able to bake any. He dined in 1666 on "good ribs of beef roasted and mince pies."

Addison writes that Sir Roger de Coverley kept open house for his friends at Yuletide; and that he had killed eight fat pigs, and given portions of meat to his neighbors. Also Sir Roger had ale on tap, and "cold beef and mince py" on the table to treat any of his tenants who came by.

In his stories, Charles Dickens has immortalized Christmas dinners; and no one can forget his incomparable description of the meal at the Cratchit home on that memorable Christmas. And what an inviting picture of holiday cheer he gives us in this description: "They sat down by the huge fireplace of burning logs and a mighty bowl of wassail. Something smaller than an ordinary wash-house copper, in which the hot apples were hissing and bubbling with a rich look and a jolly sound that were perfectly irresistible."

Our own American author, Washington Irving, in his essay "The Christmas Dinner" in *Sketch Book,* gives us an inimitable picture, along with all the fascinating details, of the holiday feast he enjoyed during his travels in England. His host, the squire, kept up, in the nineteenth century, the old Christmas traditions.

When everything was ready, the cook struck his rolling pin on the dresser, as a signal to the servants to carry in the platters of food, just as Sir John Suckling described the old custom:

> Just in the nick the cook knocked thrice,
> And all the waiters in a trice
> His summons did obey.
> Each serving man, with dish in hand,
> Marched boldly up like our train-band,
> Presented and away.

Then the butler, with a servant on each side of him, holding high a lighted candle, carried in the pig's head, adorned with rosemary, and placed the famous dish before the squire. As the harpist struck a chord, all sang "The Boar's Head" carol.

The table was loaded with good things to eat; "Ancient Sirloin" occupied a place of honor; and a pie was decorated with peacock feathers. (However, the host admitted it was made from the meat of pheasants.) Finally, Squire Bracebridge stirred the contents of the great silver wassail bowl, drank from it, as he wished everyone a "Merry Christmas," and then sent the vessel around, so all could enjoy its contents.

On the continent of Europe, foods served at the holidays have changed somewhat during the years; but many older ones are still featured. In Central Europe, a suckling pig with an apple in its mouth often is served; while in Hungary, Germany, Belgium, Holland, and Yugoslavia, geese are stuffed with prunes or apples, or served with apple fritters. The Bulgarians sometimes cook geese on beds of sauerkraut to take away the strong flavor.

Roast turkey is the chief dish in some French homes, but, in Provence, for example, their Christmas supper included snails, mullet, olives, celery, ending with apples, raisins, almond nougat, and other dainties.

Since the fish was an important symbol among early Christians, stewed eels were often eaten at the Christmas supper in Italian homes. Chestnuts have long been popular there, and are used in several ways in holiday cookery. Also a special bread, *panettone* (made with spices and filled with currants), is given to friends and relatives at this season.

In Norway, Sweden, and Denmark, fish forms the chief item on the Yuletide menu. The largest, finest ones are saved for this important occasion, and are blessed by priests. *Lutefisk,* a Christmas delicacy, is made from dried cod. It is soaked for some hours in lye water; then the flaky bits are cooked and served with melted butter and lingonberry sauce. Carp, with a gingersnap sauce, is a favorite in Poland and Germany. Salt cod, with a special sauce, is often eaten in Spain at the holidays. In Finland, boiled cod, seasoned with allspice and accompanied by creamed potatoes, is enjoyed by some families, while others serve suckling pig or fresh ham. The Finns also bake a special Christmas bread.

Children in Ireland like to help their mothers prepare nuts and fruits for holiday puddings. Delicious bread, containing eggs and raisins, is served with afternoon coffee in Scandinavian lands and in Switzerland. Austrians sometimes bake two large loaves of bread, representing the Old and New Testaments. A favorite dessert in Denmark, Norway, and Sweden is rich rice pudding with raisins, cinnamon, and one almond; the finder of this nut is sure to have good luck.

In many lands special cakes are planned for the holidays; the French have one in the shape of a Yule log; the Hungarians use poppy seeds in theirs; and some cakes are decorated with embossed figures of the Holy Infant. In Rumania, a cake is made with folds symbolic of the swaddling clothes. The Serbians hide a coin in their cake, guaranteeing someone a fortunate new year.

Cookies are popular in many countries; and some say they came from the confections given Roman senators during the Saturnalia. German *Pfefferkuchen,* hard, round, spicy cookies, are always associated there with Christmas. The Moravians are famous for varied types of tempting cookies they prepare for their *"Putz-*visiting"; and the Scandinavian housewives, too, spend days baking tasty, characteristic Christmas cookies for afternoon coffee parties.

At the holidays, sharing food with the poor and giving extra to animals are customary in several places. Just before the Yuletide, cartloads of sheaves of grain are brought to town in the Scandinavian lands. Even the poor save small coins to buy a bunch of grain to place on the fence, roof, or pole for the birds' Christmas. Also, in Northern Europe, boys and girls put out food for St. Nicholas's white horse, while in Spain, they supply hay for the camels of the Three Kings.

In the Tyrol, before going to Midnight Mass, some set out a pan of milk for the Christ Child and His Mother. Children of Ukrainia often carry gifts of foods to relatives or friends so they can partake of the same Christmas meal. Tyrolean housewives bake cakes with the sign of the cross on them; and they give one to each maid to take home to share with her family. In Greek churches, sometimes a plate of figs and nuts is placed before the statue of the Virgin. In Polish homes, one seat at the table is left vacant as an invitation to the Christ Child to eat with them.

If a stranger comes to the door while a Hungarian family is eating its holiday meal, it is customary to ask him to share their food. At some Christmas Eve services in France, farmers place gifts of their products before the *crèche* at church. Later, this food is presented to the poor. In Provence, a special bread called the Christmas loaf is baked. Members of the household do not eat any of this until one-quarter of it has been given to the first needy person who comes to the door.

Since many American settlers came from Britain, they brought with them English menus for the Christmas festivities. But in Puritan New England, most newcomers frowned upon the celebration with its mince pies and plum puddings. As a result, it was not until late in the last century that Christmas dinners became a general custom in that region.

But in the South, especially in Virginia, it was a different story. There, well-cooked and beautifully served holiday meals were important events on great plantations and in town. The steaming bowl of wassail was carried in at the end of the feast; one recipe, brought from England and used in the South, called for wine, sugar, nutmeg, cinnamon, and the whites of twelve eggs. After the hot wine had been poured over the beaten egg whites, baked apples were added.

Olive Bailey, in her *Christmas with the Washingtons,* has given a vivid picture of those holiday dinners. There were baked fowls, capon stuffed with oysters, roast veal with herbs, baked ham, oyster pies, yams, several kinds of jams, preserves, pickles, cornbread, pies, and cakes. Martha Washington's recipe for her "Great Cake" is still extant, and calls for such items as forty eggs, four pounds of butter, and other ingredients in almost unbelievable amounts.

During the hard winter at Valley Forge (1777), the general and his officers had meat, fowls, and a few vegetables for Christmas dinner; but no bread, tea, or coffee were to be had. Three years later (1780), Martha Washington joined her husband, and managed to prepare for him and his staff a meal that included beef, mutton, turkey, pies, pudding, apples, and nuts.

The Moravians of Pennsylvania and Salem, North Carolina, have added to our American list of Christmas foods their "mintcakes, pepper nuts, *Kümmelbrod,* sugar cakes, mince pies," and numerous kinds of holiday cookies, made from recipes brought from their former homes in Europe. Such cookies are often cut in the shapes of fish, turtles, bears, lions, horses, birds. Many are gaily decorated, and are used to ornament the tree and *Putz,* as well as to eat.

The Scandinavians in our Middle West still serve such holiday favorites as their noted rice pudding. Because of the many nationalities that have settled here, our list of holiday foods is a long and unusual one.

Nowadays, we have become accustomed to a rather uniform Christmas dinner, one that includes as its main feature a delicately browned turkey—a truly American holiday tradition—served with all the "trimmings."

When the Spanish entered Mexico, early in the sixteenth century, they found turkeys had been domesticated by the Aztecs. By 1519, these birds were taken to Spain, then to Italy, and by 1541 were being raised in England. From there they were brought back to what is now the United States, although some also came overland from Mexico. French peasants, it is said, began to tame wild turkeys during the seventeenth century; and one authority says that France is the only European land where roast turkey is the chief item on the Christmas dinner menu.

Our cranberries, now the regular accompaniment to turkey, were first used by the Indians, who told the Pilgrims at Plymouth they were good to eat. Today, cranberries still come chiefly from Massachusetts, where they are grown on more than fifteen thousand acres.

In the *Ladies' Home Journal* (December, 1897) this menu was suggested for Christmas dinner:

Oysters on the half shell
Clear soup
Custard and spinach blocks
Deviled spaghetti
Roast Turkey—Chestnut Stuffing
Sweet-Potato Croquettes
Peas in Turnip Cups

"The Boar's Head in Hand Bring I"

Ginger Sherbet
Lettuce Salad Cheese Balls
Toasted Crackers
Plum Pudding—Hard Sauce
Coffee Bonbons

In the twentieth century, we still serve some of the same dishes, including turkey as the main course. But, as has been the custom for centuries, housewives plan weeks ahead, to serve their choicest foods to families or friends at Christmas dinner.

It's rather strange that in this hectic, modern age some individuals like to revert to the Yuletide feasts of medieval times, and to re-enact old traditions. At several colleges and hotels in America, ancient holiday dinners are now being staged annually. One of the most colorful events of this type occurs at the Ahwahnee Hotel, in Yosemite National Park, where heavy snows often add the right touch to the scene.

Here, for the "Bracebridge Dinner," settings and costumes of thirteenth-century England are revived with great "pomp and circumstance" for the visitors who are privileged to attend. The large dining room, hung with holly wreaths, other Yuletide greenery, and ancient banners, is transformed into a medieval baronial hall. On a wide sideboard is a generous supply of game and fruit to delight the eye.

The great window, that usually affords a view of Yosemite Falls, is covered to make a replica of a stained-glass window. This forms a good background for the raised dais, where the squire and his lady, in period costumes, take their places. The eager guests are summoned to the feast with a fanfare of trumpets, blown by properly costumed pages.

Each of the four courses or "presentations" is brought in, with fitting ceremony, by lackeys in correct dress. Each dish is presented to the squire for his approval before the guests are served. Sometimes he adds a bit of spice or dubs the roast beef, "Sir Loin." When the boar's head comes in, choristers sing the carol written about it. Of course, there is also a peacock pie; and the meal is topped off with delicious plum pudding and the age-old wassail.

ALL ABOUT CHRISTMAS

A harpist plays while the meal is in progress; the "Lord of Misrule," in cap and bells, goes around to amuse the guests. Waits sing traditional carols; and the carefully carried out details make this Christmas feast a long-remembered experience. At last, the squire and his family rise; and as they leave, they give each visitor a personal holiday greeting.

A ceremony, similar to the one at Yosemite, takes place at the Empress Hotel at Victoria, British Columbia. Their dinner, too, is featured by the boar's head procession. So, at these places, and in other localities, the clock is turned back at Christmas; and we get a glimpse of the times when kings and nobles held great banquets, and large amounts of food were consumed amid gay revelry; then the carol "The Boar's Head in Hand Bring I" was heard echoing through many an old castle.

These dinners remind us of the important role food has always played in holiday festivities. As long as we continue to "keep" Christmas, families will "break bread" together at the holiday season. During this joyous period, let us remember the advice that Poor Robin gave in his *Almanack for* 1700:

> Now that the time has come wherein
> Our Saviour Christ was born,
> The larder's full of beef and pork,
> The granary's full of corn.
> As God hath plenty to thee sent,
> Take comfort of thy labors,
> And let it never thee repent
> To feast thy needy neighbors.

10

"No Candle Was There . . ."

"No CANDLE WAS there . . ." so a Christmas song tells us, in the stable at Bethlehem. But from ancient times candles have been used at winter feasts. At the Saturnalia, Romans fastened them to trees to denote the sun's return to earth; the Jews celebrated their "Feast of Lights" with candles for eight days to commemorate a victory for religious freedom. Christians lighted them in the Catacombs; and today candles are universally used as Yuletide decorations.

The Christian use of candles, symbolic of Christ, the "Light of the World," is said to be a combination of Roman and Hebrew customs. At first, tallow candles were chiefly used, because of the high cost of wax tapers, for church services. When the later became cheaper, they were preferred, as an emblem of Mary's purity, for wax is the product of virgin bees. Many persons believed that bees had come directly from heaven; and usually religious institutions kept swarms of them. An early writer, Durandus, said the wax represented Christ's body; the wick, His soul; and the flame, His divine nature.

About A.D. 492 Pope Gelasius established Candlemas Day as the time for blessing candles in the churches. This feast commemorates the "Purification of the Virgin" and the presentation of Jesus by His parents in the Temple, when Simeon greeted Him as "A Light to lighten the Gentiles."

During the time Christ's birthday was celebrated on January 6, Candlemas—forty days later—came on February 14. But with the change of Christmas to December 25, Candlemas fell on February 2. This marked the end of Yuletide festivities (in some places) when all greenery had to be taken down and burned. Herrick wrote of this date:

> End now the White-loaf, and the Pie,
> And let all sports with Christmas die.

Some sources believe that Candlemas may be a Christianized form of the Cerealia, when Romans carried candles through the streets in honor of Ceres, who had thus searched for her daughter, Proserpine. The Romans also burned candles to the goddess, Februa, mother of Mars; therefore, Christian Church officials, not able to persuade their adherents to give up old customs, perhaps turned this one to honor the Virgin Mary. Tapers were widely used in homes—so St. Jerome states—as an expression of Christmas joy.

Candlemas ceremonies at churches were elaborate; and people carefully kept at their homes fragments of the candles blessed on this feast day, believing they would keep all harm away. In Brittany such candles were burned whenever anyone was ill, or during thunderstorms.

In medieval Europe, it was customary to light a candle "of monstrous size, called the Christmas candle," so that it could shed its glow on the festivities. This burned each evening until Twelfth Night. At St. John's College, Oxford, there is an old stone candlestick, used for holding the Christmas candle, that always stood on the "high table."

Martin Luther, as mentioned before, is credited with starting the practice of placing tapers on Christmas trees; and soon others followed his example.

Bayberry candles with their delicate odor are popular at Christmas, and are said to bring good luck to a home. Also there is a belief that if sweethearts (who are separated at Christmas) light bayberry candles, the scent will be wafted from one to the other, even across the world, if they are truly in love.

In certain lands, it was the habit to place candles in windows to guide the Christ Child, or weary travelers, to shelter; many thought He would knock, in the guise of a stranger, to test their hospitality. Therefore, no one was turned away; and several stories have been based on this idea.

The Irish would place a candle in the window, and then leave the door open to attract the Holy Family, searching for lodgings on their way to Bethlehem. So strangers were always given food and shelter for the night. Also, in Ireland, only girls named Mary had the right to put out the candles in the churches on Christmas Eve. Sometimes the Irish set up a sieve with twelve candles for the Apostles, and a large candle in the center, representing Christ.

In the Scandinavian countries, the mother always lights the candles on Christmas Eve, while the boys and girls sing carols around the tree. Norwegians believed that Yule candles bestowed blessings; therefore, they used to spread out food and clothing, and set out their silver and pewter that the light might shine in benediction on them.

In Denmark two candles on the table represented the man and his wife. These Yule candles were made tall and thick; the family watched them through the night, believing that if one went out, it foretold a death in their family. No watcher was allowed to touch the candles with his hands.

The remains of these Christmas candles were considered to have magic power: farmers fed them to their fowls, or smeared their plowshares with the candle ends to assure abundant crops. Sometimes people used the fragments to mark crosses on cattle to protect them from harm.

Swedish people have always featured candles at the Yuletide; they placed them at their windows, burned small tapers on their trees, and at their Christmas gift exchange, used them to melt the wax with which packages had been sealed.

Here in the United States, in some Swedish communities, a colorful ceremony is still observed at the Christmas morning service. The meeting is announced in these words: *"Valkonna alla Svensker till Julottan!"* which means, "Welcome all Swedish people to early Christmas matins!" When the members arrive at dawn, and open the church doors, they are thrilled to see a lighted candle at each seat.

The Swedish Christmas celebration begins December 13, the feast day of St. Lucia—mentioned before as a gift bringer. Many girls in Sweden used to believe that St. Lucia could reveal the

115

future to them on her day, so they prayed to her to let them know the names of their husbands-to-be.

(St. Lucia—so we read—lived at Syracuse, in Sicily, during the days of the Roman Empire. She gave her dowry to some Christians who had been persecuted for their faith. Then her angry fiancé told authorities that she, too, was a Christian; and Lucia died a martyr's death.)

The Swedish people admired her courage and generosity, and celebrated her feast day. It was long a custom for the eldest daughter to dress in white with a red sash to represent St. Lucia. On her head she wore a crown with several lighted candles. As soon as the first cock crowed, she went around the house, carrying coffee to each member of the family, and sang a special carol for this day.

(Although many sources connect the "Lucia Bride" with the Christian St. Lucia, one writer—Michael Harrison—says that the girl really signifies "light" as a natural phenomenon, and that her name came from this.)

The Swedes and Swedish-Americans annually choose a beautiful "Lucia Bride." In 1949, for instance, a girl from Chicago with four companions flew to Sweden to take part in their "Feast of Lights." The "Brides," in white robes and wearing crowns of lighted candles, compete for the honor of being the national "Lucia Bride."

In Spain each family places a burning taper above its door, while in Italy the candles stand at the windows to light the Holy Child on His way. On Christmas Eve, in Italian homes, small wax tapers surround the nativity scene; and a large one lights the supper table where the family gather after their twenty-four hours' fast.

In some parts of Italy, it was customary for the father and his shepherd boy on Christmas Eve to light the animals to their stalls. First, the man and boy, each carrying a lighted candle, went into the stable, and held the candles for a minute in each corner. Then the two stood at the door with their candles high, as they lighted the animals in for the night's food and rest.

In Serbia, it was an old custom to place a candle in a box of wheat and hang it in the kitchen. On Christmas Eve, the head of the house lighted the candle and prayed that their crops would be abundant in the new year; and that all the family would have health and happiness. Then the members of the household exchanged greetings. Also, when the Yule log was carried into the kitchen, a large candle burned at each side of the door.

Bulgarian peasants went to their stables with lighted tapers, and greeted the domestic animals with "The Child is born, and blesses you tonight." As the Yule log burned merrily in French homes, children placed small candles around their *crèches,* usually three, to symbolize the Trinity. In Southern France, when these were burning, it was considered a bad omen if the wick bent toward any particular person.

When the Austrians placed lighted candles at their windows on Christmas Eve, they sang a hymn. First, the father, then each member of the family held a candle before they sat down to eat and to give thanks for the birth of the Saviour.

Candles were popular in England, too, at the Yuletide; and Irving tells us that, in front of the cups and beakers on the sideboard at Bracebridge Hall, "stood the Yule candles, beaming like stars of the first magnitude."

On the first Sunday in Advent, in many English homes, an Advent wreath with four tapers (two red, two white) was placed in the window. Just before the evening meal, the first candle was set aflame. On the second Advent Sunday, two were lighted, and so on, until the four were burning. Years ago, in Lancashire, the boys and girls used to take candles to school to give to their teachers on the day before Christmas. Grocers and chandlers also presented them to their customers.

In a mining district in Shropshire, down into the nineteenth century, miners would carry around boards to which several small lighted candles were fastened. And, in Wales, on Christmas morning, at about four A.M., young men carrying torches walked to church with their minister. There, colored candles lighted the room where the communion was observed, or carols sung.

On Christmas Eve, on the Isle of Man, at their caroling parties, one person would hold a burning taper, while he sang a carol alone. If the light went out, he had to stop his song. When the holiday

117

festivities ended in the British Isles on Twelfth Night, often a game—jumping over a lighted candle—was played. If one could do this twelve times without putting out the flame, one was going to be very fortunate during the next twelve months.

In the United States, candlelight Church services, especially carols by candlelight, have become very popular. One of the most impressive meetings of this kind happens each year at the Central Moravian Church at Bethlehem, Pennsylvania.

This Christmas Eve vigil was started in 1741 when the leader of the Moravian religious group, Count Nicholas von Zinzendorf, with a lighted candle in his hand, led his people into a near-by stable. There, all joined in singing the old carol:

> Not stately Jerusalem,
> Rather humble Bethlehem
> Giveth that which maketh life rich . . .

So they named their settlement Bethlehem, to honor the Christ Child.

Each Christmas Eve, the Moravian Church is decorated with evergreens, and is aglow with the light of candles. A simple but impressive service is held that includes organ and orchestral music, the reading of the Christmas story from the Bible, prayer, and the singing of familiar carols. Ushers, or *Diener,* pass through the congregation with trays of slender beeswax tapers, each in its own small holder. These are made in the apothecary shop of Simon and Rau, the oldest drugstore in our country.

Each attendant lifts a candle from the tray, and holds it during the caroling. The climax comes at midnight when a child soloist (whose name is not revealed until that moment) leads the antiphonal singing. Everyone who is privileged to attend this vigil, in the church scented with evergreens, where tiny candles send out their flickering lights, remembers the scene as one of life's unforgettable experiences.

In American homes, even though wax tapers are now banned on Christmas trees, candles still play an important role in our holiday decorations. Tall ones stand at the windows; lower, thicker ones on the mantel, while others in a mass of greenery or red-berried holly branches form an attractive centerpiece for the Christmas table. Slender white candles before a statue of the Madonna make an effective picture; and tall ones, at each side of the fireplace or the front door, add festive touches.

Almost every town and city in our land now puts on special lighting effects for the holiday season. Boston is said to have started the custom of placing lighted candles in windows on Christmas Eve. In recent years, such simple lighting has given way to elaborate electrical effects that draw thousands of spectators. For example, Denver uses more than thirty-three thousand lights in the magnificent display at her Civic Center. In contrast, at Richmond, Virginia, is the soft glow that illuminates an outdoor nativity pageant which has been a Yuletide community project since 1928.

An old Spanish custom is still observed in some places in the Southwest. *Luminarios* (candles placed in paper bags, partly filled with sand) are set on walls, or the edges of roofs, and shed their gentle glow on Christmas Eve. At this time, bands of carolers with candles go around singing.

At the San Francisco fire stations, the firemen create unusual and colorful lighting effects each year. The vicinity of Chicago's old water tower is radiantly lighted by the glow of countless bulbs from a tall Christmas tree. Kansas City also features a lavish display in its Country Club Plaza district, which is ablaze with lights for five weeks. This project uses twenty thousand colored lights and sixty miles of wiring.

All over the United States our celebration has truly become "A Feast of Lights." Even though electricity now plays the major part, we shall always enjoy the soft glow of candles at this season. In a recent year (1950) Americans spent $13,000,000 in buying more than 250,000,000 candles. Many are used in churches where they have a deep religious significance for innumerable worshipers. It is to be hoped that these ancient lights will, during many more Christmas holidays, continue to remind us of the birth of Christ, "The Light of the World."

11

"There's a Star in the Sky"

MEN, FOR CENTURIES, have revered the stars as God's work, ". . . the moon and the stars, which thou hast ordained"; and the Christmas star or "Star of Bethlehem" is a favorite Yuletide symbol. Christ's coming was foretold in Numbers 24:17, "There shall come a Star out of Jacob"; and in Revelation 22:16, He is called "the bright and morning star."

The star, too, is always associated with the story of the Wise Men. In Matthew 2:9 and 10, we read, ". . . lo, the star, which they saw in the east, went before them, till it came and stood over where the young child was. When they saw the star, they rejoiced with exceeding great joy."

In our stately carol, "We Three Kings of Orient Are," the poet hails it as:

> Star of wonder, star of night,
> Star with royal beauty bright,
> Westward leading, still proceeding,
> Guide us to thy perfect light.

Others have also praised it in such songs as "Star in the East," "Have You Ever Seen the Star?" "O Star of Bethlehem," "The Star of Midnight," "How Brightly Beams the Morning Star," "The Wise Men Saw a Light Afar," and "O Lovely Star That Shone So Bright."

A lighted star is a popular Yuletide decoration in many churches. When one sits in a darkened sanctuary, and suddenly a brilliant star flashes on, we are vividly reminded of that first Christmas night.

120

At the holidays in our homes, places of honor are given to stars, at the top of the Christmas tree, in windows, or on porches. Candles glow in star-shaped holders; cookies are baked in this shape; and stars add beauty and meaning to Christmas wrappings and greeting cards.

In Winston-Salem, North Carolina, at Moravian homes, their characteristic Moravian stars gleam in the doorways. They are fashioned of white paper cones, fastened together with an electric light in the middle. To the descendants of early settlers, these stars are a continual reminder of the "Light that shineth in darkness." One of their favorite songs begins:

> Morning Star, O cheering sight!
> 'Ere Thou camst how dark earth's night!

In some lands, including Spain, Italy, and Russia, the people would wait until the first star appeared in the sky on Christmas Eve before beginning their Yuletide celebration. Sometimes, at this season, European girls went out to the fields to pray to the stars to bring them husbands.

At the feast day of the Three Kings (January 6), "Star-Singing" (mentioned in connection with the Magi) is still carried on. Tyrolean boys dress as the Wise Men, shepherds, and Herod with his retinue. The procession is led by a man bearing a star-shaped lantern on a tall pole. This lamp, lighted by candles, revolves as it is carried along. When the "star-singers" stop at a home, they stamp on the ground to insure good crops, sing their carols, and receive coins, cakes or drinks.

Swedish boys and girls, wearing tall white hats trimmed with silver stars, are headed by a child with a large star, which has bells on each of its five points. Also, singers from the Passion Play, in Oberammergau, go out to "follow the star" with a large star-shaped lantern; they stop to sing carols at the church, postoffice, and various homes. Rumanian children carry the *steaua* with a small candle burning in it.

Members of the Greek Church in Alaska continue this old European tradition. The first night the singers go around bearing the star, they are invited into homes to sing, and are given refreshments. But next evening, the character of the affair changes; the carolers are pursued by boys in fantastic dress who represent Herod's soldiers out to destroy the children of Bethlehem. The boys try to catch the man with the star, and to get rid of it. This causes much fun; and each year the young people look forward to this event.

After supper has been eaten on Christmas Eve in Poland, the "Star Man" appears, usually the village priest, who examines the boys and girls to find out whether they have studied their catechism. Later, three children, dressed as the Wise Men, knock and leave gifts. Polish children used to be told that the good "Star," a beautiful veiled lady, brought their presents to them from heaven.

All over the United States, cities feature stars in their special Christmas lighting. Some, several feet across, shine at the tops of community Christmas trees, shedding their light around for a long distance.

In 1934, the people of Palmer Lake, Colorado (famous for their Yule log hunt), placed a star that is five hundred feet across on the side of Sundance Peak. This brilliant "Star of Bethlehem" is visible for twenty miles. People in cars slow down to see it; and those on trains are thrilled as they pass by. The Mayor of Palmer Lake says that it is "our little village's symbol of hope for peace on earth."

Each year, Van Nuys, California, renames its main street, "Bethlehem Star Lane"; and it is decorated with illuminated stars. In their annual parade, the citizens carry out the true holiday spirit, for this procession contains no commercial floats. Various churches prepare religious floats, depicting such scenes as the Wise Men following the star, the annunciation to the shepherds, and the adoration at the stable. In the procession men dressed as the Three Kings ride camels down "Bethlehem Star Lane."

Across the continent, at Bethlehem, Pennsylvania, citizens of the "Christmas City" have erected a huge electric star, symbolic of peace and good will. This great display, built on a steel structure ninety-one feet high, stands on South Mountain, dominating the landscape. People can see the star, like the one in Colorado, miles away.

It is ablaze each evening from December 4 to January 2, attracting thousands of visitors. The first night it is lighted, there is a public service in Zinzendorf Square, near the site of the founding of Bethlehem more than two hundred years ago.

The official seal of this city is an appropriate one—the Star of Bethlehem with its five points representing the major interest of the community: religion, music, industry, recreation, and education.

Each Christmas, planetariums, including the Hayden in New York and the Griffith in Los Angeles, present displays of the "Christmas Sky." It is a thrilling arrangement of the heavens with the stars, moon, and planets in the same positions they held at the time of Christ's birth. As you watch this inspiring spectacle, you you can almost imagine you are with the shepherds on the hills of Judea.

Through the centuries, there have been many discussions and opinions as to what the "Christmas Star," mentioned by Matthew, really was. Some have declared it was just a legend—"a pious myth, beautiful to be sure, but of no historical value." Others maintain that it may have been a supernatural occurrence, Halley's Comet, a temporary new star, or the conjunction of two planets.

Dr. R. S. Richardson, astronomer, at Mt. Wilson Observatory, in discussing the theory, in 1949, that it may have been Halley's Comet (which will be seen again between 1985 and 1987), stated that, since the actual date of Christ's birth is not known, He may have been born several years earlier than has been believed. According to old manuscripts, in 11 B.C. "a spectacular celestial object" was seen. Records prove that, at this date, Halley's Comet was slightly north of Castor and Pollux, which in their daily journey passed through the zenith at Bethlehem. Therefore, as the Comet was very close to these stars, it, too, would have been directly over this location.

According to some sources, the star may have been a nova, a star "that suddenly increases its brilliance hundreds and even millions of times." Therefore, the unusual brightness of the Star of Bethlehem might be accounted for in this way.

123

ALL ABOUT CHRISTMAS

Robert C. Coles, Associate Curator of the Hayden Planetarium, stated in 1949, that perhaps the light was caused by the conjunction of Mars and Saturn, which occurs each two years, when they appear as a single star. About every eight hundred years they are joined by Jupiter.

This phenomenon was first noted by the astronomer Kepler in 1864. After making his calculations, he discovered that the three planets had been in conjunction about the time of Christ's birth. Records show that in 7 and 8 B.C. Jupiter, Saturn, and Mars were near each other.

In 1952 Dr. Alter of Griffith Planetarium said, "So far as astronomy is concerned, the story of the Wise Men's seeing the Star may be true in every word." However, some scientists believe none of the above theories is correct; and they assert that the story of the star of Bethlehem is a mystery that may never be solved.

But no matter what the astronomers say about the origin of the star that guided the Wise Men, whenever Christmas comes, we are thrilled again by the story told in the Gospel of St. Matthew, and by the glory of that ancient light, which the poet Josiah G. Holland described so well:

> And the star rains its fire
> While the beautiful sing,
> For the manger of Bethlehem
> Cradles a King.

12

"I Heard the Bells on Christmas Day"

ROUND THE WORLD today bells peal out the glad tidings of the Saviour's birth. In cities, chimes sound joyously from cathedral towers, while in the belfry of a small church a single bell spreads through the countryside the same message, "Christ is born!"

Long before His coming, bells, especially handbells, had been used during religious services. They were rung in Egypt at the Feast of Osiris; Jewish high priests wore gold bells on the borders of their robes, and used handbells in their ceremonies. The priests of Cybele at Athens did likewise; and at Rome, Emperor Augustus had a bell hung before the Temple of Jupiter.

It is believed that bells were first used by Christians on churches by Paulinus, Bishop of Nola, in Campania, Italy, about A.D. 400. These bells called the worshipers to Mass; before this, a man had gone around ringing a handbell.

Bells were introduced into France about A.D. 550; and in 680, Benedict, Abbot of Wearmouth, took a bell from Italy to England, the first one placed there on a church. Soon missionaries carried them to other parts of Britain. A Saxon king, Egbert, is reported to have decreed that all church services be announced by ringing bells.

Because of the early association with churches, bells soon acquired a sacred character. Usually religious inscriptions were engraved on them, "Glory to God" being a popular one. On a tenor bell, dedicated to St. Nicholas at a church of the same name in Brighton, England, was this inscription:

125

ALL ABOUT CHRISTMAS

Pray for our children,
Pray for our sailors.
Pray for this town.
I to the church the living call
And to the grave do summon all.

Bells were considered almost human in early times; they were given names of saints, sprinkled, anointed, and baptized at elaborate ceremonies with prominent individuals acting as sponsors. In the presence of many worshipers in 1878, the chimes of St. Paul's in London were blessed.

Before Christ's birth, bells had been used to announce both happy and sad events. But by medieval days, the pealing of bells had become closely associated with Yuletide rejoicing. At this season, poor persons went around with handbells to attract attention, and collect alms. Tradition tells that St. Nicholas, too, carried a handbell on his visits; and Befana, the Italian gift bringer, rang her bell as she went down the chimneys.

In Italian homes, when the church bells pealed out on Christmas Eve, the family lighted candles around the manger scene and began their festivities. The sound of the chimes in Scandinavia was the signal to stop all work, to close the shops, and to attend the church services. In Sweden, sometimes a masked couple with the man ringing a handbell, went to different homes. The person who answered the door received a gift from the woman's basket.

Jacob Riis tells of his childhood in Denmark in *The Old Town,* and describes the custom of "Blowing in the Yule." The village band climbed the church tower, and played four hymns, one in each direction, so no one would be forgotten. "When the last strains died away, came the big bells with their deep voices that sang far out over field and heath, and our Yule was fairly under way."

In Spain, church and cathedral chimes ring out at midnight; the streets are filled with people hurrying to the "Cock Crow Mass," where the priests perform the sacred rites. Also in South America, when the bells call everyone to church, the worshipers kneel there in prayer. Then as the chiming ceases, they rise and greet each other with a "Noche Buena."

"Down Under" in Australia, the church bells ring, too; but as it is warm weather there in December, the houses are filled with beautiful flowers. One blossom that is at its best at this season is the "Christmas Bell," a red bell-shaped flower fringed in yellow with bright green leaves.

Because of her many church bells, Britain has been called the "Isle of Bells." In some parts of the country, long before Christmas, the chimes announce its approach. During the Puritan era, this was forbidden; instead, a crier with a harsh-sounding handbell went around to remind citizens that no celebration would be allowed.

After Charles II's accession, church bells again honored Christmas on each Sunday in Advent (in some places three mornings before Christmas); and the air usually was filled with their melody on Christmas Eve when the Yule log was brought in. In Wolverhampton, the bells of St. Peter's ring for a quarter of an hour at this time. In 1640, Sir Roger Berkeley left a bell to the church of St. Martin's at Worcester, on condition that it be rung each night for several weeks before Christmas; also that it be named "Berkeley's Bell." But it gained the nickname of the "pudding bell."

A bell tolling for a dying person was called the "soul bell" or "passing bell." The Venerable Bede mentioned this as early as A.D. 680 when the bell at Whitby rang for the death of Abbess Hilda. It was thought that evil spirits waited to afflict the soul as it left the body; therefore, the sound of the tolling bell called people to prayer for the departing soul. Later, bells were heard after the death, as a mark of respect, and often struck the number of years the person had lived.

In some parts of England, where there was the belief that Christ had been born exactly at midnight, bells rang solemnly from eleven to twelve on Christmas Eve. This was "tolling the Devil's Knell" or the "Old Lad's Passing" to warn the powers of darkness of Christ's approaching birth. The instant that twelve midnight arrived, the tolling ceased, and joyful ringing announced the sacred event.

Years ago in Dewsbury, Yorkshire, the murderer of a young boy gave the parish church, as penance, a tenor bell. "Ringing the

Devil's Knell" there on Christmas Eve was done in this way: just after midnight, the tenor bell sounded for an hour; then, four times, four strokes were heard, the "Devil's Knell," followed by the same number of strokes as the years that had passed since the birth of the Saviour. The custom has been revived—so one source states—in recent years.

Fiends and goblins were said to hate church bells, as they summoned worshipers to prayer. Various superstitions arose, for many believed bells had the power to put out fires, ward off enemies and evil spirits, "purify the air" at times of pestilence, and drive away thunderstorms. It was also asserted that church bells rang at times when untouched by human hands; a bell at Saragossa, Spain, for example, sounded just before the death of a sovereign.

One old belief, especially in Germany, was that church or monastery bells that had been buried in the ground for safe keeping during wars would chime again on Christmas Eve, and could be heard by all who listened in the right attitude. A story, in Valencia, Spain, goes that an old woman kept insisting to the priests that she heard bells under the floor of a church there. When the authorities did some excavating, they discovered a large bell and a statue of the Virgin.

The idea was current years ago that if church bells were not properly baptized, harm would come to them. In the Dutch village of Lochen, two bells not christened with the usual ceremonies were stolen by the devil and cast into near-by ponds, where they could be heard only at Christmas, according to a local legend.

Another town in Holland, Been, considered a very wicked community, was celebrating with much debauchery one Christmas Eve. Christ, in the form of a beggar, wandered through the streets, but no one would give him food or shelter. Therefore, he caused great waves to cover the entire town; but on each Christmas Eve the sound of church bells could be heard coming from the waters that washed over the spot where the village once stood.

Bells at Yuletide have inspired poets in various countries; Longfellow's poem, with its message of peace, is still a Christmas favorite:

"I Heard the Bells on Christmas Day"

I heard the bells on Christmas day
Their old familiar carols play,
   And wild and sweet
   The words repeat,
Of "Peace on earth, good will to men!"

Charles Wesley is said to have written his immortal "Hark! the Herald Angels Sing," after hearing chimes on Christmas morning. Other tributes to such bells include the hymns "O Hark to the Bells' Glad Song," "Ring Out, O Bells, Your Joyful Sound," "Glad Christmas Bells," "Angels Singing, Church Bells Ringing," and "Glorious Yuletide, Glad Bells Proclaim It," "Ring on, Ye Joyous Christmas Bells," and "On Christmas Eve the Bells Were Rung."

On hearing the bells of Waltham Abbey in Essex on Christmas Eve, Alfred Tennyson immortalized this Yuletide symbol in these beautiful lines from "In Memoriam":

The time draws near the birth of Christ.
   The moon is hid, the night is still;
   The Christmas bells from hill to hill
Answer each other in the mist.

In the United States we are constantly reminded of the close association of bells and Christmas, for many communities use them for festive street decorations. In our shopping districts, we hear the sound of handbells, asking us to help "keep the pots boiling" so that the needy may have good Christmas dinners.

Attractive greeting cards, with bells of different sizes and colors, catch our eyes in shop windows. Real bells or replicas hang on outdoor wreaths, or on pine sprays in windows, or from chandeliers. Bell-shaped ornaments, in gay hues, or gold and silver, deck our Christmas trees, while delicious cookies in the shape of bells give a festive touch to holiday refreshments. Tiny bells on gaily wrapped boxes add their merry tinkle to the joy of opening Christmas gifts. And, of course, Santa Claus wouldn't be complete without his merry sleighbells. It is said that Clement Moore, author of "A Visit from St. Nicholas," had Santa's bells suggested to him as he drove home in his sleigh one snowy night.

ALL ABOUT CHRISTMAS

One of the joys of last-minute shopping is to hear Yuletide carols coming from towers of downtown churches. As Eleanor Hunter has so well expressed it:

> From every spire on Christmas Eve
> The Christmas bells ring out
> Their messages of goodwill and cheer.

Another special holiday treat is hearing bells of great American churches or of European cathedrals through the miracle of radio.

For many decades bells were an important part of the equipment of each church. But, for some time, the custom gradually died out. However, according to a recent article by George W. Cornell, there is a decided revival in their use; and numerous churches are buying carillons.

Within the past ten years, one company alone has installed bell equipment in more than three thousand churches here. Now in many places, bells are once more ringing out their invitations to attend church services. The head of one Chicago firm states that "more churches every year come to regard bells as a means of communicating their message." Ministers have said that "bells bring a distinct overtone to the life of the community . . . they help to heal life's discords," and "are a source of inspiration."

This revival of interest will not only add a religious tone to communities, but will help tell the world our real reason for celebrating at Christmas. It is to be hoped that many churches, now silent, will add bells. Then, as one poet has said, at Christmas we can hear

> A thousand bells ring out and throw
> Their joyous peals abroad.

And, when these holiday messengers chime out, we can appreciate more fully the good news they bring to mankind.

> Wake me tonight, my mother dear,
> That I may hear
> The Christmas bells, so soft and clear,
> To high and low, glad tidings tell
> How God, the Father, loved us well.—John Keble

13

"Joy to the World"

EACH YEAR, HUNDREDS of extra postmen are added here in our country, to help deliver at least one and a half billion Christmas cards (according to post office figures), an average of about sixty per family. Most of us take this custom for granted; but sending Yuletide greetings is really one of our youngest Christmas traditions. Starting in England, it has spread throughout the world during the last hundred years; and designing and manufacturing Christmas cards is an important industry.

The holidays would seem strange without such greetings, for they do bring much "joy to the world," a world that surely needs to be cheered by these friendly messengers. Many of us neglect our correspondence; but when the holiday spirit begins to fill the air, our thoughts travel across the miles. We wonder what has happened to certain friends and relatives since we read their last Christmas cards. And it's pleasant, too, to hear, unexpectedly from old classmates or former neighbors. Fortunately these Yuletide missives help preserve friendships that might otherwise be completely broken.

So, it's blessings on him who first invented Christmas cards! Although their exact origin is in doubt, some sources assert that the idea started with the fancy, handwritten holiday pieces that schoolboys, away from home, used to concoct to inform parents of their progress in their studies, and to insure themselves plenty of Christmas gifts. The boys wrote letters, in their best penmanship, on sheets printed especially for this purpose. (They sold for sixpence, but cheaper in quantities to schools.) Such papers often had fancy engraved, or printed, borders and headings, adorned with scrolls, flourishes, Biblical scenes or characters, drawings of birds, flowers, etc., some of which were hand-colored.

The question as to who actually created and sent out the first Christmas greetings, and when this happened, is still unsettled at this date, even among the best authorities in England. For there are at least four claimants to the honor. Charles Dickens wrote his immortal *Christmas Carol* in 1842; and this and his other holiday stories revived interest in holiday celebrations. It was during the decade of the 1840's that the earliest cards were produced.

A vicar of Newcastle, the Reverend Edward Bradley (also a novelist) is said to have sent, in 1844, to his friends, holiday greetings that he had had lithographed. Some sources assert that an artist of the Royal Academy in London, W. A. Dobson, while head of an art school in Birmingham, sent out hand-colored cards in 1844; also, that next year, this same artist created a second card and had copies lithographed for his relatives and friends.

Another claimant is William Egley (1826–1916), son of a miniature painter. The boy lived in a garret during the early years of Victoria's reign; he showed artistic talent when quite young, and became an apprentice to an engraver. It is said that the youthful artist was imbued with the warmer attitude toward the holiday season in England, and wanted to share his feelings with others.

His first Christmas card (given to the British Museum in 1931) was produced in 1842 or 1849—according to the way one reads the last figure in the date on the greeting, as Michael Harrison states in *The Story of Christmas.*

Egley's design was produced when he was only sixteen, if 1842 is the correct time. This shows several current holiday activities, a Christmas dinner, a dance, carolers or waits, skaters, a Punch and Judy show, and the giving of soup to the poor. The card carries the familiar message, "A Merry Christmas and a Happy New Year"; and it is reported that William Egley had one hundred copies made of his design to send to friends. (Harrison reports that James Haver, an authority on women's dress, says the costumes on the Egley card are more like the styles of 1842 than those of 1849.)

The *London Times* in 1884 tried to settle the dispute, and after investigation stated that credit for the first Christmas card belongs rightly to John Calcott Horsley, R.A. Sir Henry Cole, a close friend of Prince Albert (who set up a Christmas tree for the royal children), asked Horsley to design a Yule greeting to send his friends, instead of writing letters.

The result was a three-paneled affair, showing a grapevine twined around a trellis, with side panels depicting the usual holiday acts of "feeding the hungry" and "clothing the naked." The center panel pictured three generations of a family celebrating Christmas by drinking wine together. This caused many protests from temperance adherents in England who declared this card promoted drunkenness. They especially objected to the fact that a child was sipping a glass of wine.

About a thousand of these greetings were produced by a lithographer, Jobbins of Warwick Court, Holborn, colored by a man named Mason, printed by Joseph Cundall, and sold by a gift book company in Old Bond Street, where they each brought about a shilling apiece.

In his *Story of the Christmas Card,* George Buday says that the Cole-Horsley greeting appeared in 1843. Harrison states that Horsley tells in his advanced years of making the design in 1845 or 1846; however, Harrison believes that the artist's memory may have failed him, for the date, 1843, seems to be quite plain on one of the extant cards.

Even though authorities do not yet agree as to who originated Christmas cards (and the matter may never be definitely settled), we do know that, by the end of the fifties, such greetings were on sale. Since they were rather costly, they did not come into general use until much later, when a new process of color printing brought down the prices.

The first publishers of holiday greetings were men of high ideals; and in England they employed artists who were members of the Royal Academy. The royal family asked noted painters to submit paintings; and several of the best entries were reproduced.

In the 1860's, the firm of Goodall and Son created some rather simple, but beautiful cards, that helped make the custom of sending

Christmas messages popular. Their designs carried the usual printed greeting, with sprays of holly or mistletoe, embossed figures of Cupid, and winter landscapes with robins in the snow. In 1868, they created a popular card, featuring Little Red Ridinghood. One greeting of this decade showed "Father Christmas" in a red coat and blue trousers; he carried a Christmas tree, and was followed by a group of happy children.

The well-known London firm of Raphael Tuck and Sons also played an important part in keeping up standards of the cards made in the second half of the nineteenth century. In 1882 one British company paid $35,000 for original paintings for their greetings. Two years later, there was a $10,000 prize contest; and it was during this period that holiday cards reached their highest point in artistic value.

Naturally, some purchasers enjoyed buying "novelties"; so different types were created to suit varying tastes, including cards made in panels, in the shapes of palettes, ovals, or stars. Others were "frosted," adorned with "jewels" or iridescent materials; some were hand-painted on plush, satin, or porcelain, with sprays of flowers or landscapes. Often the greetings took the form of booklets, containing Christmas poems or other fitting sentiments. "Trick" cards, also, were fashioned; for example, one showed two faces, which were entirely different if the card was turned upside down.

The Marcus Card Company is credited with introducing Christmas greetings into the United States. Because of their immediate popularity here, Louis Prang started such a business at Roxbury, Massachusetts, in 1874. Prang, a German emigrant, had reached America almost penniless. During his first six years of hard work, he saved $600; and with it, opened a small lithograph shop. An excellent craftsman, Prang perfected the process of making colored pictures; and he soon became known for floral prints, especially those of his favorite Killarney roses.

When he produced his first Christmas cards, with simple flower designs and the words, "Merry Christmas," Prang wondered about public reaction to them. But his product soon became so popular that by 1881 he was turning out five million per year; and this became the major branch of his business.

That same year, Louis Prang offered prizes amounting to $3,000 for acceptable designs; and more than six hundred sketches were submitted. The following season, he repeated the offer. The high quality and beauty of Prang cards made them popular, not only here but abroad, for he produced them in as many as twenty colors.

Because of the increasing demand in this country for cards, other firms began to make large numbers of cheap, inartistic ones, in sharp contrast to the former beautifully designed and colored greetings. Many foreign cards, too, in violent colors and of poor design, flooded local markets; and for several years our Christmas cards suffered from a lack of artistry.

Fortunately, early in this century, there was a revival of interest shown in messages of better creation and workmanship. For many persons felt the true Christmas spirit had not been expressed by the majority of the recent offerings. Artists and manufacturers cooperated in producing cards of higher quality; so today our holiday messengers of joy are a real delight, both to send and to receive.

American ingenuity has developed such products at reasonable prices—cards that we are proud to send to our friends. Now thousands are employed in this outstanding industry; hundreds of versemakers contribute the sentiments; some of our best artists create designs for the greetings.

In recent years one company has promoted an annual international contest, open both to amateurs and professionals, for paintings for Christmas cards, with awards totaling several thousands of dollars. More than ten thousand artists have entered each contest; and this gives them the opportunity to express their varied ideas. Exhibits of a hundred of the best paintings, fifty foreign and fifty from our country, have been held in several American cities. This affords many art lovers a chance to see recent works of artists both here and abroad.

Each year, the American Artists' group presents a fine assortment of designs to the makers for their approval. In recent times, Christmas greetings have been adorned with the work of such celebrities

135

as Norman Rockwell, the inimitable Grandma Moses, and several talented movie stars. Winston Churchill, England's prime minister, has also contributed paintings for cards.

Our output plays its role well in improving public taste; and the cards are of sufficient variety to suit varied kinds of buyers. The serious type appeals to some individuals, while others enjoy those of a humorous turn. There are plain, but beautifully engraved ones, and others with more detail and ornamentation.

Often reproductions of old paintings are used; and the cards that are universally enjoyed include typical winter scenes, with stage coaches and sleighs bringing home Christmas trees along snowy roads or through old-fashioned covered bridges. Our many Christmas symbols—holly, mistletoe, candles, bells, Yule logs, Christmas trees, colorful tree ornaments, sprays of pine cones, stars, poinsettias, and the jolly face and figure of Good St. Nick—always retain their popularity.

Religious subjects, the Madonna and Child, the Magi, manger scenes, with the kneeling shepherds, lighted churches, organs, carolers, are often used; and such designs show that many like greetings that convey the real significance of why we celebrate Christmas.

From time to time, there have been certain fads in our Christmas cards; these include pictures of Dutch children, fawns, Scottie dogs, frisky lambs, modernized angels, and humorous figures. Unusual materials are sometimes used, such as parchment, transparent plastics, and thin sheets of silver or copper-colored metal.

In spite of the fact that we have many beautiful and unusual cards, some people prefer making their own personal greetings by using linoleum block patterns, painting little scenes, or by taking clever snapshots of the family, especially of the children. Such messages are doubly appreciated, for the receivers realize the thought and work that have gone into their making.

In selecting "boughten" cards, the makers urge us to use the "personal touch," and choose special greetings for the family, relatives, and certain friends. There is a wide selection of individualized messages—cards just for doctors, teachers, ministers, servicemen, for baby's first Christmas, and for many others. It's a nice touch to choose a greeting while keeping in mind the particular person for whom it is intended. And it certainly shows that the sender *does* put some thought and effort into his selections.

Since we receive so many artistic cards, we've developed the delightful custom of displaying them effectively during the holidays in several interesting ways. Some people attach them to draperies, or hang them on ribbons, fastened to curtain rods, and extending to the floor. Others cover door panels, stand cards on the mantelpiece; or hang them on the popular "Friendship Tree." But any method that gives us a chance to enjoy their beauty increases our pleasure in receiving these reminders of love and friendship.

It's a good thing, each year, to revise one's Christmas card list, and give a bit of cheer and happiness to some persons to whom we usually don't send cards. Perhaps you can congratulate somebody on a special achievement; recall a courtesy, or an enjoyable social event of the year. Cards, naturally, are doubly welcomed by shut-ins and those who live alone.

We'll probably never fully realize what Christmas cards have meant to the men who were far from home during the recent World Wars. These messages brought them the feeling that the "folks at home" hadn't forgotten they were away serving their country. One soldier declared that his pack of holiday greetings actually saved his life. Pfc. Ernest R. Bennett wrote his grandparents in Fresno, California, that while in Korea, he had stumbled over an American flare trap, and some shrapnel struck him in the chest. But luckily a large bundle of Christmas cards in his pocket absorbed most of the shock.

If we choose our Yuletide messages thoughtfully, and send them in the true holiday spirit, they'll continue to bring much "joy to the world." For this custom—one of our youngest Christmas traditions—can be an excellent means of showing "good will toward men."

14

"Christmas Voices"

EACH DECEMBER, IN more than forty countries, millions of persons buy Christmas seals to use on holiday mail. These stickers, real "Christmas voices," carry a message of hope to those suffering from tuberculosis; and they have helped thousands to recover.

This holiday tradition is one of the world's most altruistic customs. Everywhere volunteer workers unselfishly give their time and energy to sell the stamps, for the seals are symbolic of consideration for those afflicted with the dread disease. The money is used, not only to bring victims back to health, but to educate the public about this illness.

The idea of Christmas seals originated with a postal clerk, Einar Holboell, born in Denmark in 1865. While stamping letters and Christmas cards, in 1903, in the post office at Copenhagen, he remembered many needy children in his country were suffering from tuberculosis. He realized that they needed hospital treatment, but he knew there were not nearly enough institutions to take care of them.

Suddenly, a wonderful plan occurred to Einar Holboell. Why not have a special Christmas stamp printed to sell for just one penny? It could be placed on mail, in addition to the regular postage, and the funds from the sale used to build a hospital for the children of Copenhagen. At once he began to talk of the plan to the post office head and to his friends. Soon King Christian and several prominent citizens became interested in the project, for Holboell's great faith helped him put the idea across.

In 1904, the first Christmas seals were printed and sold at the regular post offices in Denmark. They had a portrait of Queen Louise, encircled by a wreath of roses. At the bottom was the date, 1904, and at the top, *Julen,* the Danish word for Christmas. That season more than four million stamps were sold, bringing in about $18,000 in American money. Even business letters carried the new decoration. The same year Sweden adopted the plan, and Norway, two years later. For these countries realized how much good could be done if all co-operated in buying the seals.

Jacob Riis, the noted Danish immigrant to the United States, a great philanthropist, was an editor and social worker, much interested in the general welfare. When he received a letter from his mother in Denmark, bearing several Christmas seals, he inquired about them. Riis was delighted to discover that they were intended to save children with tuberculosis. This news struck home, for six of Jacob Riis's brothers and several other relatives had succumbed to it.

At once he resolved to get the movement started here, in his adopted country. Riis wrote an article, "The Christmas Stamp," which was published in the *Outlook,* July 6, 1907. He explained what Denmark was trying to do, and the need for such seals in the United States, too. Riis told of the ravages of the disease here; and stated that each year 100,000 died from it, many of whom might have been saved with proper care and treatment. He urged all Americans to follow the Danish example, and get behind the stamp project. Although many were deeply moved by his forceful appeal, others felt the task was almost hopeless. For how could they fight this insidious enemy with such a small weapon—a penny Christmas stamp?

Among those inspired to work for the cause, through Jacob Riis' article, was Miss Emily Bissell, of Wilmington, Delaware, State Secretary of the Red Cross. She was especially interested because the local tuberculosis institution—Brandywine Sanitarium—needed the mere sum of $300 to keep functioning. She had been trying, but hadn't succeeded in raising this amount. Now Miss Bissell wondered whether the new idea might not be the means of saving their local hospital.

She kept thinking of the plan and decided to start it in Wilmington. Emily Bissell tried to interest others, but gained little attention at first. She herself made the simple design for the original American Christmas seal. It had a half wreath of holly and a cross, with "Merry Christmas" in the center and "Happy New Year" at the bottom.

After she had persuaded a kind-hearted printer to do the work, Miss Bissell talked at women's clubs, schools, lodges, and other groups to explain the undertaking. The result was that she holds the honor of introducing the use of Christmas seals in the United States.

The first stamps were put on sale December 7, 1907, at the Wilmington, Delaware post office. The first customer—so a story goes —was a ragged newsboy, who put down a penny, and said, "Gimme one, my sister's got it."

But the seals sold slowly; apparently the public was not convinced that the project would amount to anything. In spite of this, Emily Bissell refused to be daunted. She went to near-by Philadelphia to see the editor of the Philadelphia *North American*. At first he was not too interested, but when she talked to Leigh Mitchell Hodges (who wrote a column, "The Optimist," for this paper), she convinced him that she *did* have a worth-while idea. Hodges promised Miss Bissell to promote the movement; and the editor also championed her cause.

The result of this co-operation was that soon civic and national figures, including President Theodore Roosevelt and the Chief Justice of the Supreme Court, gave their endorsement. That year, 1907, Emily Bissell and her helpers, much to their surprise, made more than enough to keep the sanitarium open.

Even with this success, such an indefatigable person as Miss Bissell wasn't satisfied with a local victory. She wanted others to share in it. So she persuaded the Red Cross to support the sale of holiday seals. This was quite successful in 1908, with total sales amounting to $135,000. Until 1910, the Red Cross conducted the project alone. Meantime (1907–1910) the National Tuberculosis Association had also been soliciting funds to fight the plague. From

1910 to 1920, the two groups worked together to sell the Christmas stamps, with a red cross on them.

In 1919 the double-barred Cross of Lorraine was selected as the permanent emblem. This had been used by Geoffrey of Lorraine, a leader of the First Crusade, when he was chosen ruler of the Holy City of Jerusalem. This symbol, so familiar to early Crusaders, is a fitting one for modern individuals in their unending struggle against tuberculosis.

The Red Cross, in 1920, decided to devote its efforts for obtaining funds entirely to its annual roll call. Then the National Tuberculosis Association began to carry on the Christmas seal sale alone, as it has done ever since.

Each year, the organization selects a new design for the stamp, featuring the Cross of Lorraine. Collectors value these seals highly; and early issues bring good prices. However, it is not the first stamp that costs most, but the 1911 edition, made for vending machines. A group of people, named the "Christmas Seal and Charity Stamp Society," collects the various editions.

In recent years the seal designs have been of varied kinds, created by high-ranking artists, including Rockwell Kent, Thomas M. Cleland, and Steven Dohanos. The 1948 stamp was the work of an internationally known painter, Barry Bart, some of whose works hang in the Louvre and Avignon galleries. His design showed a small boy in red pajamas, sitting by a fireplace, from which stockings hung. Bart made this design, after seeing his little nephew slip downstairs, one Christmas Eve, to watch for Santa Claus's coming.

The 1949 seal showed a dove in flight, symbolic of hope for world peace and health. It was designed by Herbert Mayers, a young German-born artist, who saw service in World War II with the Eighth Air Force. Especially attractive was the 1950 stamp with three charming little modern angels, two playing instruments, while the other is singing a Christmas carol. In 1952 the seal depicted a candle, in an old-fashioned holder, emblematic of the light of knowledge. This design was the work of Tom Darling of Amityville, New York.

141

ALL ABOUT CHRISTMAS

Now, more than three thousand organizations are affiliated with the National Tuberculosis Association. Since the first sale of Christmas seals in 1907, the disease has dropped from first to seventh as a cause of death in this country. However, it still claims fifty thousand victims each year. In some communities the money from the sale of seals helps combat heart trouble and rheumatic fever.

The work of the association is preventive, and its funds are used to educate the public to protect themselves, for research, chest X-ray programs, child welfare work, and free clinics. Six per cent of the money raised goes to the National Association, while the rest is used in the state where the funds are given.

In regard to this worthy project, one chairman (Percy C. Scott of Long Beach, California) said, "We must continue to fight it with every means at our disposal. We make use of a powerful weapon against tuberculosis every time we purchase Christmas seals."

Leigh Mitchell Hodges (the newspaperman who aided Emily Bissell in her campaign) is the last survivor of the four founders of the Christmas seal sales. In 1950, at the opening of the annual drive, he declared:

> Remember you are not selling seals; you are selling happiness, health, homes unbroken by illness, the most valuable things in the world at the bargain price of a penny each. . . . When Miss Bissell showed me the seal, I could visualize it as a flaming banner to be carried at the heads of hosts of people, proclaiming that the white plague was preventable and curable. Since that time, deaths from tuberculosis in the United States have declined from 180.6 per hundred thousand population to 26. . . . Lick the foe by licking the seals.

An incident occurred in 1949 showing our gratitude to Denmark for starting this program. A six-year-old boy, Douglas Pfuetz, gave Mrs. Eugenie Anderson, our ambassador to Denmark, a package of American Christmas seals to present to Danish King Frederick.

When Einar Holboell died on February 23, 1927, he had been decorated by several monarchs for his work for world betterment; he had been knighted; and his name was known far and wide. If the seal idea had not occurred to him while stamping mail, perhaps

Holboell would have died unknown. The end came twenty-three years after he had started the movement; but during that period he had already seen good results.

For the penny stamps had built several hospitals and paid for the care of countless patients. Einar Holboell had the satisfaction of knowing that his project had not only saved lives, but had brought nations closer together (forty-five countries now sell such seals) in his unselfish efforts to make the world a happier and more healthful place.

When he died in 1927, Denmark used his portrait that year on their Christmas stamp. On his gravestone are the words: "The Father of the Christmas Stamp." We should be grateful to him and Denmark for inaugurating this Yuletide custom, and each time December comes around, we should buy seals for our letters and packages. In this way we can express the Christmas spirit, and help these "Christmas Voices" carry their message of better health to the world.

15

"Shout the Glad Tidings"

EVER SINCE THE angels sang that "glorious song of old,"

> Glory to God in the highest,
> And on earth peace, good will toward men,

Christians have continued to "shout the glad tidings" of the Saviour's birth. One of our finest holiday customs is singing Christmas carols: and many, who never sing at any other time, are tempted to join in. No matter whether the carols are old traditional ones, whose authors are unknown, or later hymns by great composers—we thoroughly enjoy singing all of them.

The origin of the word "carol" is obscure; some say it is related to the "circle" or "ring" dance from *carolare* (meaning to sing), and originally denoting "a dance accompanied by singing." In early religious rites, worshipers joined hands and danced in a circle, as they sang together. Certain sources believe that "carol" may be derived from the Greek word for "flute player," referring to the musician who accompanied the singing of the dancing group.

After the pagan winter feast had merged with the Christian, the Latin and Teutonic peoples still danced around nativity scenes to songs set to dance tunes called *Wiegenlieder* in Germany; *Noëls* in France; and *carols* in England. The people loved the custom, for in it they could express their joy at the Christmas season.

Today, the word "carol" also denotes happiness to us, and is a joyous narrative, treated in familiar style. In the *Oxford Book of Carols,* they are defined as "songs with a religious impulse that are simple, hilarious, popular, and modern." In contrast, the hymn is a more dignified song, often theological in nature.

At Christmas A.D. 129 Bishop Telesphorus of Rome urged his people to gather in the churches and sing the "Gloria in Excelsis Deo," or the "Angels' Song." St. Jerome also mentions the use of carols in the fifth century. Several Latin hymns celebrated the holy birth, including one of the eighth century, "Christ Is Born! Tell Forth His Name!"

Early carols have characteristics of true folk poetry—simplicity and joy. Some are a curious combination of the sacred and the profane, while others are rather naïve, or even absurd. In "I Saw Three Ships a-Sailing," Bethlehem is represented as a seaport, with Mary and her Son nearing it in a ship. Certain carols reveal mythical aspects of Christmas; and others express the emotions and reactions of ordinary people to their times; and, for this reason, these songs have survived. Since various carols were handed down, by word of mouth, from one generation to the other, we often find several versions.

St. Francis of Assisi is usually credited with being the "Father of the Christmas Carol." For at his nativity scene in Greccio in 1224, he led his followers in songs of praises to the Christ Child; and from "his jovial singing" came a new idea about the holiday season.

By the fourteenth century carols had more melody, and were being used between the acts of the mystery plays, by which Bible incidents and other religious conceptions were taught to the people. In time, many of the carols proved to be more popular than the dramatic episodes themselves.

According to Professor Saintsbury, our carols really date from the fifteenth century, for then the minds of men were beginning to be freed from the old period when the Church had "suppressed the dance, and the drama, denounced communal singing, and warred against the tendency of the people to disport themselves in church on the festivals."

At this period, there was a distinct growth in the "democratic spirit of music and drama"; and some began to express their own feelings in regard to Church music, preferring to sing in their own tongues, instead of the Latin. As a result, carols developed in the vernacular, sometimes with Latin refrains.

ALL ABOUT CHRISTMAS

There was a gradual "substitution of folk songs and dance tunes" for the solemn church music. The worshipers "wanted something less severe . . . more vivacious." The growth of ballads, too, had a strong influence; and such songs as "The Coventry Carol" (a lullaby sung in a mystery play by the women of Bethlehem before the coming of Herod's soldiers) and "The Cherry Tree Carol" became popular. The latter, an ancient story, was first found in a play performed in the church; later the words were set to a melody, originating a quaint early carol.

In this song, a miracle happens when Joseph and Mary are walking through a cherry orchard. The latter tells him of the Angel Gabriel's assertion that she would bear the Christ Child; and doubt enters Joseph's mind. When he refuses to pluck some cherries for her, a tree at once bends down its topmost branch; and she says:

> Thus you may see, Joseph,
> These cherries are for me.

In contrition, he falls on his knees and begs her pardon. Sometimes the last stanzas of this long carol are used as a separate song, called "As Joseph Was a-Walking."

Other carols showing reverence for the Virgin Mary include "A Babe Is Born All of a Maid," "A Virgin Most Pure," "When Christ Was Born of Mary Free," and "Lo How a Rose E'er Blooming." The last also refers to the old conception that at the Yuletide plants frequently bloomed out of season.

Various early carols deal with the angel's annunciation to Mary, the Virgin birth, announcement to the shepherds, their journey to the stable, visit of the Magi, the Holy Family's flight to Egypt, and the massacre of the children by Herod's soldiers.

The shepherds are the subject of the old Bohemian song "Come All Ye Shepherds"; the Welsh carol "Abiding in the Fields"; the Austrian "As Lately We Watched"; and "The First Nowell." Several songs were inspired by seeing the Holy Babe in His manger or cradled in His mother's arms, and include "Gentle Mary Laid Her Child," "What Child Is This?" "Immortal Babe," "A Child Is Born in Bethlehem," and an Alsatian carol, "O Sleep on, Sleep

146

on, Thou Fair Child Jesus." The last is one of the many lullabies to the Holy Infant.

The coming of the Wise Men or the Three Kings has been celebrated in the old English carol "The Golden Carol of Melchior, Balthasar, and Kaspar; in the Portuguese "From the Orient They Came a-Riding"; "Eastern Monarchs, Sages Three"; "The Kings of the East Are Riding"; "Three Kings in Great Glory of Horses and Men"; "The March of the Three Kings"; and "There Came Three Kings from Eastern Land."

As many early people worshiped nature, it was natural that some carols were concerned with its aspects. One of these, "The Holly and the Ivy," is believed to have originated in France. The words were known in the eighteenth century; but it is thought to be of a much earlier time. Cecil Sharpe, an authority on folk songs, collected the tune. "The Holly and the Ivy" is a struggle for supremacy between the "male" holly and "female" ivy; and the song may have come from the pagan dances between groups of boys and girls. In this carol, which is a blending of nature worship and Christianity, the production of the berries is likened to Mary's bearing the "Sweet Jesus."

> The holly bears a berry,
> As red as any blood.
> And Mary bore sweet Jesus Christ
> For to redeem us all.

One of the most popular English carols, "God Rest You Merry, Gentlemen," tells "in a naïve but touching manner" of the coming of the Saviour. (The title means "God Keep You Merry, Gentlemen." Often the comma after "Merry" has been misplaced.) The origin of the carol is still a mystery; some believe it is from Cornwall. There are several different versions, some of which go back to the sixteenth century.

This song expresses true Yuletide joy, and is happy and triumphant, even though written in a minor key. The favorite setting was arranged by Sir John Stainer. "God Rest You Merry, Gentlemen" was usually the first carol heard on the streets of London at the holidays; it was popular both in towns and in rural sections, especially on Christmas Eve.

"Good King Wenceslas" is a carol whose content really concerns St. Stephen's Day, December 26 ("Boxing Day" in England). It was a favorite of all who went out to collect alms. This song is based on a story about King (or Duke) Wenceslas, who ruled in Bohemia from 928 to 935. He was very devout and was said to have the power to perform miracles. He showed great liberality to the poor, especially at Christmas and St. Stephen's Day.

The carol is an interesting dialogue between the king and his page; it relates the good deeds of the ruler, how he carries food, drink, and firewood through the dark, snowy night to a peasant's home, and ends with this admonition:

> Therefore, Christian men, be sure,
> Wealth or rank possessing,
> Ye who now will bless the poor,
> Shall yourselves find blessing.

Its tune—that of an old spring carol—was taken from an early Swedish-German hymn collection, *Piae Cantiones,* assembled by Martin Luther, but printed in 1682 after his death. Later, Sir John Stainer harmonized the melody. Some authorities say this carol is rather commonplace; but one believes it "owes its popularity to its delightful tune." (In 1929 Czechoslovakia issued a set of postage stamps, honoring King Wenceslas. The series shows his likeness, his consecration at the Church of St. Vitus, and his martyrdom.)

Besides religious carols, several secular ones also developed. Perhaps the most popular one is "Deck the Halls with Boughs of Holly," a universal favorite in English-speaking lands. It gives a cheery picture of the glowing Yule log in the great hall, with nightly caroling by holiday revelers "in gay apparel." This lively song does not mention Christ's birth, but tells of customs that go back to pagan festivities. We moderns enjoy the gay carol as "Sing we joyous all together." The melody, an old Welsh air, was once used by Mozart as the theme of a composition for violin and piano.

Perhaps the oldest secular carol in existence is the "Boar's Head Carol" with its Latin refrain:

> *Caput apri defero*
> *Reddens laudes Domino.*

This famous song (discussed in Chapter 9) honors a twelfth-century custom; and is still sung at certain Yule celebrations. Another carol with no religious significance is "Christmas Loves Good Drinking."

Songs used with wassail drinking and the expression of good wishes to friends were quite popular. One of these begins with:

> Wassail, Wassail all over the town!
> Our bread it is white and our ale it is brown;
> Our bowl is made of the maple tree,
> With the wassailing bowl, I'll drink to thee.

At each home the revelers sang, drank toasts, and asked their friends to join in these rites.

Children also enjoyed "wassailing" or "gooding" excursions. In the jolly "Here We Come a-Wassailing," they told their hearers they were not beggars, but children they knew well. Then they wished everyone in the household a "Merry Christmas and a Happy New Year!" They appealed to the generosity of the family by singing:

> Good Master and Good Mistress,
> While you're sitting by the fire,
> Pray think of us poor children,
> Who are wandering in the mire.

Such broad hints naturally resulted in their receiving small gifts, so each year the boys and girls looked forward eagerly to their "wassailing" parties and caroling.

As stated before, the fifteenth century was an important epoch in carol development, for it brought "traditional conservative religion up to date," and also "rang up the modern era." It is fortunate for us that a grocer's apprentice of this time, Richard Hill, had a deep interest in Christmas carols. He helped preserve some for us,

149

in an unusual diary, or "commonplace book" that he kept. This was discovered in 1850 behind a bookcase; and now it is kept at the Balliol College Library, in Oxford.

Hill's diary, which has been of great value to scholars, included the years from about 1500 to 1536. In the book, he jotted down miscellaneous things that appealed to him: rules for beer-making, how to break horses, tables of weight, dates of his children's births, religious thoughts, medical and cooking recipes, puzzles, satirical verse, and other items. But to us, the most important thing was his inclusion of traditional carols, including the "Boar's Head Carol," some of which might otherwise have been lost.

In 1521, Wynkyn de Word, an apprentice and afterward the successor of Caxton, the English printer, produced the first printed book of carols. Several decades later, 1562, the Lord Mayor of London gave Thomas Tyndale a license to put into print "certayne goodly caroles to be songe to the glory of God."

Carols, also, were learned in England and widely distributed through printed "broadsides" or "broadsheets" that sold for only one penny. Often they were illustrated with crude woodcuts, showing nativity scenes. Each usually contained three or more carols; they were easy to read; and these quaint sheets helped people get acquainted with Christmas music. Later on, these broadsides proved valuable to scholars who collected them, in their task of preserving our carol heritage.

During the sixteenth century, carols were at their best in England, when such poets as George Wither (1588–1667) and Robert Herrick (1591–1674) were enriching the store of Yuletide poetry. Wither, a soldier-poet, wrote a "rocking hymn," "Sweet Baby Sleep! What Ails Thee Dear?" while Herrick created his "Down with the Rosemary and Bays" and the carol beginning:

> What sweeter music can we bring,
> Than a Carol, for to sing
> The Birth of this our heavenly King?

In an ode, about the holy birth, Herrick described how the Christ Child had been disdained, and ended his carol,

From year to year
We'll make Thee, here,
A Free-born of our City.

While English carols were reaching their height, folk songs were popular on the Continent, too, for Christmas celebrations in France, Spain, Russia, and Poland; and many of these are still in existence, for the troubadours in France and the minnesingers in Germany were developing "song as a vehicle for the expression of emotion apart from religion."

Martin Luther (1483–1546), the noted Reformation leader in Germany, realized the importance of music in men's lives and said, "Music is a half-discipline and school mistress that maketh people more gentle and meek-minded, more modest and understanding." He was always devoted to it; as a boy he sang in the village choir in Eisenach, where Frau Cotta helped him obtain a musical education.

After the establishment of the Lutheran Church, he promoted congregational singing. Edmudstoune Duncan in his *Story of the Carol* says:

> Luther himself set an example, pressing into service such melodies as were sung by the workers in the fields, by the wayside, or indeed, anywhere; and coming from the heart of the people made a fresh appeal when clothed with words of fire and enthusiasm for the the new faith.

The first Protestant hymnal was published in the town of Wittenberg, where Luther had defiantly nailed his theses to the cathedral door in 1517. It contained eight hymns in German, four of them written by Luther himself. Later, with his associates, he made other collections of songs. Some believe that Luther's contribution to church singing helped as much in spreading Protestantism as his preaching and translation of the Bible did.

Martin Luther composed a beautiful carol, *"Vom Himmel Hoch"* ("From Heaven Above I Come to You") for one of his small sons, at Christmas, 1535. It began

151

ALL ABOUT CHRISTMAS

> From Heaven high I come to you
> To bring you tidings, good and true.

He spoke of this carol as "a child's Christmas song, concerning the Child Jesus." Later Johann Sebastian Bach arranged its tune: this has always been a beloved hymn in Germany; and was often heard coming from the church towers.

For a long time, the charming carol and cradle song, "Away in a Manger" has been attributed to Martin Luther, and marked, "Composed by Martin Luther for his children." However, after much research into the origin, some authorities have agreed there is no actual evidence that Luther wrote it. He may have used it with his family; and its flowing melody may have belonged to the early "cradle-rocking" ceremonies.

It is believed that the German Lutherans who settled in Pennsylvania are responsible for its wide use and popularity in the United States. The words of "Away in a Manger" were first printed without a melody at Philadelphia in 1885 in *Little Children's Book: for Schools and Families*. Its most popular tune was composed in 1887 by J. R. Murray (who attributed the words to Luther). The other melody (to which "Flow Gently, Sweet Afton" also is sung) was the work of James E. Spillman.

In Britain, most of the carols, especially those of the narrative type, were produced between 1400 and 1647. During the seventeenth century the Puritans did away with holiday observance, including caroling, for they called Christmas "Superstitious Man's Idol Day" or "The Old Heathen's Feasting Day." Hezekiah Woodward declared that Yuletide celebrations did more harm to religion than any other thing. Some of Cromwell's soldiers ejected Robert Herrick from his parish in 1647. During the "Roundhead" regime carols went underground; but many persons continued to sing them in their homes. Also carol "broadsides" were still printed and sold secretly.

After the restoration of Charles II, caroling came into the open again; and an important book appeared: *The New Carols for the Merry Time of Christmas, to Sundry Pleasant Tunes*. But during the eighteenth century, when religion was cold and formal, carols were looked down upon by sophisticated city dwellers as plebeian and rustic. However, they were still used in the country in some sections. Goldsmith—in 1766—in his *Vicar of Wakefield,* spoke of the fact that some of the parishioners "kept up the Christmas carol."

During this period, there were a few notable additions to Christmas music, including "While Shepherds Watched Their Flocks by Night" by Nahum Tate, Charles Wesley's "Hark! the Herald Angels Sing," and "Christians, Awake, Salute the Happy Morn" by John Byrom. Some new carols were printed in *Poor Robin's Almanack;* but these, according to Percy Dearmer, were "mere eating songs about pork and pudding." During the youth of the author of the *Christmas Carol*—Charles Dickens—carols and caroling had almost disappeared.

Fortunately, certain scholars began to collect and preserve traditional carols. It is because of their efforts that these priceless folk songs were not lost to the world. The first group of this type, *Collection of Christmas Carols,* was published by Davies Gilbert in 1822. *A New Carol Book* (printed in Birmingham about 1830) contained the "Holly and the Ivy," "God Rest You Merry, Gentlemen," and "Hark, the Herald Angels Sing."

Christmas Carols, Ancient and Modern appeared in 1833, the work of William Sandys (an English lawyer who was deeply interested in early music). He asserted that, although caroling still existed in Northern England and the Midlands, it had almost died out in other districts. In his *Christmastide*—1852—William Sandys added more carols to his first collection.

Several of the clergy helped preserve traditional carols by getting words and tunes from individuals who had learned them from parents or grandparents. The Reverend J. M. Neale and the Reverend T. H. Helmore made translations of twelve carols, *Carols for Christmastide* from *Piae Cantiones* (mentioned earlier in connection with Martin Luther). This book was published in 1853 for the benefit of those interested in caroling. Even if most city people, during the nineteenth century, did neglect the early Christmas songs, schools and choirs in villages and rural regions sang and kept them alive.

W. H. Husk, in 1868, in his *Songs of the Nativity,* stated that more hymns than genuine carols were being saved through the broadsheets. But within a decade or so another person said that carol singing was again becoming more prevalent because of the "enormous circulation and sale" of the penny sheets.

The Reverend H. R. Bramley, Fellow of Magdalen College, Oxford, and Dr. John Stainer (organist at that institution) published in 1871 *Christmas Carols Old and New* which contained thirteen traditional carols and twenty-four new hymns; later they increased the number to seventy, twenty-seven being of the older variety. This was an important collection, for it furnished a book for use in churches.

In the last half of the nineteenth century, even though various "poor, so-called carols" were produced, enough of the older kind had been brought to light, so that carols and caroling had again become an important part of the Yuletide celebration, both in churches and homes.

During the present century, traditional carols have become better known; and, in addition, some excellent Christmas hymns have been composed. The almost universal use of Yuletide music helps us "shout the glad tidings" to the world; and the delightful old custom of caroling brings all Christendom more closely together.

> Then let us sing amid our cheer,
> Old Christmas comes but once a year.—Thomas Miller

16

"Good Christian Men, Rejoice"

SINCE OUR CHRISTMAS carols have been produced at several different periods and places, by varied types of individuals, there are interesting stories connected with their composition. Also, it is worth while to know something about the persons who created them, when it is possible to discover the origin of the carols.

One of the earliest ones, and perhaps the carol most universally sung and loved, is "Adeste Fideles" or "O Come, All Ye Faithful." This stirring song has the same tune as the militant hymn, "How Firm a Foundation." "Adeste Fideles" is used both in Protestant and Catholic churches, and has been translated into 120 languages and dialects.

The origin of the Latin text is doubtful, although much research has been done. Some scholars think it was an old carol connected with dancing round the manger; that it might have been used by St. Francis; others claim it stemmed from the thirteenth century, and was the work of a Franciscan friar, St. Bonaventure, an associate of St. Francis. (Born in Tuscany, the former was a learned man, a great teacher, and a writer; he was made Bishop of Albano, later, a cardinal.)

"Adeste Fideles" is known to have been popular, both in France and Germany, as early as the seventeenth century. In France, it was called "The Midnight Mass," for the monks chanted it as they marched in a procession to church on Christmas Eve. Some sources say it may have been used early in the eighteenth century by Catholics, some of whom maintained their own private chapels for worship.

ALL ABOUT CHRISTMAS

The earliest words and melody of "O Come, All Ye Faithful" were found in a manuscript, *Cantus Diversi,* a collection of hymns made in England (about 1750) by John Francis Wade. For several years he lived at a Catholic center in Douay, France, where he copied and sold religious music, besides teaching Latin and singing. One writer says that Wade, for a time, worked as a music transcriber at the home of Nicholas King in Lancashire.

Some sources believe he wrote both the words and music. But Vincent Novello, organist at the chapel of the Portuguese Embassy in London, stated that the melody had been composed by John Reading (1677–1764), organist at Winchester Cathedral, or from a folk tune arranged by him. (This is not accepted by some authorities.)

"Adeste Fideles" is believed to have been printed for the first time in 1782. More than forty different translations of the words have been made; but the one in general use, and preferred by most critics, is the work of Frederick Oakeley (1802–1880). This was printed in *Murray's Hymnal* in 1852. (After taking honors in Latin at Christ Church College, Oxford, Oakeley was a clergyman at All Saints in London. In 1845 he entered the Catholic priesthood; and for several years served as Canon of Westminster.)

"O Come, All Ye Faithful" is often termed the "Portuguese Hymn." It has been credited to Marcos Portugallo (Mark of Portugal, 1762–1830), choirmaster at the Court of Portugal during the first part of the nineteenth century. (He also composed operas in Italy and went to Brazil with King John VI, when the royal house of Braganza was deposed in 1807; Portugallo returned to Italy in 1815 and died there in 1830).

Vincent Novello said that "Adeste Fideles" was named the "Portuguese Hymn" by the Duke of Leeds, when he directed a concert of ancient music late in the eighteenth century—perhaps 1797—in the Portuguese Chapel in London, believing the carol had originally come from Portugal; but this statement has not been proved.

Another hymn with a Latin title, "In Dulci Jubilo" ("In Sweet Shouting" or Jubilation), dates back to the fourteenth century.

This is a "macaronic " hymn, having a mixture of languages in it. "In Dulci Jubilo" contains both Latin and German. The words and melody are in an early manuscript at the University of Leipzig; various forms of the carol appeared in books printed in 1537, in 1550, and also in Luther's *Piae Cantiones* (1582). It was first translated into English about 1540 by John Wedderburn in his *Gude and Godly Ballades.*

An early writer declared that the original words of "In Dulci Jubilo" were sung to a fourteenth-century mystic, named Henry Suso. An angel, with several companions, appeared to him, the legend relates, and told Suso that God had sent them to bring him happiness. The chief angel took him by the hand and bade him join them in a dance and carol, praising the Christ Child and beginning:

> In dulci jubilo
> Now sing with hearts aglow!

During the sixteenth century, this carol was referred to as "an ancient song for Christmas Eve," and was sung widely both in Sweden and Germany. In 1601, a German, Bartholomew Gesius, arranged the melody as we now sing it. The tune has the characteristics of a rhythmic folk song; and this, no doubt, accounts for its popularity and survival.

"In Dulci Jubilo" was translated into English as "Good Christian Men, Rejoice" by Dr. John Mason Neale (1818–1866). After graduating from Trinity College, Oxford, in 1840, he was a chaplain. Because of ill health, he had to give up that position, and he became warden at East Grimstead, Sackville College, where he founded the Sisterhood of St. Margaret.

Fortunately, Dr. Neale had leisure here and could devote much time to delving into old manuscripts; and he used his brilliant talents in translating Greek and Latin hymns. With a fine ear for rhythm, he was able to adapt the English words exceptionally well to the original tunes. His translations were printed in such volumes as *Medieval Hymns and Sequences* and *Hymns of the Eastern Church.* In addition, Dr. Neale wrote more than sixty original hymns, so the world is indebted to him for his exceptional work as a hymnologist. "Good Christian Men, Rejoice" was first published in Dr. Neale's *Carols for Christmastide* in 1853.

"The First Nowell (Noel)" has long been the subject of discussion, as to whether it originated in England or France. The word *"Noël"* is derived from the Latin for "birth," and was applied mainly to the birth of Christ or Christmas. In English the word is spelled "Nowell" or "Nowel," and is defined as "a shout of joy for the birth of the Saviour." It was one of the many French words taken over after the Norman Conquest.

"The First Nowell" is a medieval shepherd song with traditional words and melody. It is noted for its simplicity and sincerity; the poetry and rhythm are not perfect, as was often the case with early folk carols.

The story of the nativity is told to the shepherds by an angel, while the chorus is sung by an angel choir. There are several stanzas; the version we use is considered the best, even though it is not exactly true to the Biblical account. (Luke does not say that the Star appeared to the shepherds.) The last part of "The First Nowell" tells of the coming of the Wise Men," so this carol is also suitable for Epiphany, the Feast of the Three Kings (Twelfth Night), January 6. The song was printed originally in *Christmas Carols, Ancient and Modern,* in 1833.

"Angels We Have Heard on High" is a French-English traditional song (often referred to as the "Westminster Carol"); and it was so named because it was sung at Westminster Chapel at Yuletide. The stanzas tell of the annunciation to the shepherds, and are probably of French origin, as is the tune. But the chorus, the jubilant ringing *"Gloria in Excelsis Deo,"* is the old Latin choral, used in medieval times. This is the "Angels' Song" that Bishop Telesphorus asked worshipers to sing on Christmas, and is said to have been the first Latin hymn sung universally.

Another song from France is the inspiring modern hymn, "Cantique de Noël" ("O Holy Night"), the work of the distinguished French composer, Adolphe Adam (1803–1856). His father, a pianist, taught at the French Conservatory; he did not want his son to be a musician, but a lawyer. At first, the boy taught himself music; and, later, his father allowed him to follow this profession.

Adolphe Adam composed several operas which were produced in his own theater; and he also taught at the Conservatory. His "Cantique de Noël" is noted not only for the beauty of its words and message; but for the melody, with its various beautiful arrangements, that makes this song not only a joy to sing as a carol by a group, but an incomparable solo with its repetition of the phrase, "O Night Divine."

"Bring a Torch, Jeanette, Isabella" is a traditional French carol that comes from the old custom in Provence, in Southern France, of each person's carrying a lighted torch in the procession wending its way to the Midnight Mass in the church where the nativity scene or *crèche* was set up. In one translation, each stanza ends with praise of the Holy Child:

> How lovely is the Son of Mary,
> How lovely is the Child.

Since holiday festivities continue, in some places, until Epiphany, carols honoring the Three Kings are used on their day. In Southern France it was customary to choose three boys to represent the Kings. Dressed in flowing robes, these boys led a procession of children, representing shepherds, angels, etc., along the streets. They sang a carol about the Magi, and continued their ceremonies in the church. A stately French carol, "The March of the Three Kings" is featured in Bizet's "L'Arlésienne Overture," written for a play by Daudet, which took place on Christmas Eve.

Germany has given us several fine carols; perhaps the best one written about the Christmas tree is their beloved "O Tannenbaum! O Tannenbaum!" ("O Christmas Tree! O Christmas Tree!") In it the eternal greenness of the tree is praised; and the idea of the evergreen as a symbol of immortality is stressed. The melody, an old one, is said to have been used in the Middle Ages to accompany a Latin drinking song. This tune is familiar to most Americans; for it is used with the state song, "Maryland, My Maryland," and numerous college songs.

159

ALL ABOUT CHRISTMAS

"O Du Froehliche" (or "O Sanctissima"), meaning "O Thou Joyful Day," has a melody originating from a song sung by Sicilian mariners. On St. Nicholas's Day (December 6), sailors at Bari, Italy, and other ports, used to take his statue from the church out to sea, and return it that same evening.

An old German carol, "How Brightly Beams the Morning Star" ("Wie Herrlich Strahlt der Morgenstern"), was published in 1599, in P. Nicolai's *Freudenspiel*. Its first tune was harmonized by Johann Sebastian Bach; and was often heard chiming from church towers in German cities. Some critics consider this "simple and lovable carol" one of the best of the traditional songs. It ends with these words:

> Sing, ye Heavens, tell the story,
> Of his glory,
> Till his praises
> Flood with light earth's darkest places!

Although the story of "Stille Nacht! Heilige Nacht!" ("Silent Night! Holy Night!") has been told numerous times—and so beautifully by Hertha Pauli in *Song from Heaven*—we shall always be thrilled by the circumstances under which it was written, and by the amazing way it spread from a small Austrian village throughout the world.

There seem to be some slight differences in the accounts as to just when before Christmas, the words, and then the melody, were written; also, about its first use. But from various sources, we are certain that this incomparable hymn was inspired and produced within a very short period of time.

It is true that the composition of the *Messiah* by Handel and of Bach's *Christmas Oratorio* in the eighteenth century had helped instill the Yuletide spirit in many. But there was need for a simple song that could be sung by everyone. This was finally found in "Silent Night!" whose words were written by a village priest and its melody by the church organist. The story goes that these two friends had often discussed the fact that "the perfect Christmas song had not yet been found."

In his youth, Father Josef Mohr (1792–1848) had served as a choir boy; and after his study of theology, he became assistant pastor of the parish church of St. Nicholas in the small town of Oberndorf, near Arnsdorf, in the Austrian Tyrol.

Franz Gruber (the third son of a linen weaver) was born in Upper Austria in 1787. His father had tried to persuade him to follow the same trade. But from the time he was a small child, Franz had been fascinated by music, especially that of the organ. He would slip out secretly and go to his schoolmaster's home, where he learned to play the instrument.

Once, when the teacher was ill, there would have been no music for the church service if Franz (then twelve years old) had not volunteered to take his place. He was allowed to do so, and played the entire service from memory. After this, his father let him take regular music lessons. Franz also completed other studies, including languages, mathematics, and history. And at the age of twenty, he became a teacher and also church organist.

In 1818, it is said that, while Father Mohr was preparing the sermon for the Christmas service, a messenger came, and asked him to go out to bless the newborn babe of a peasant mother. Perhaps seeing the child in her arms reminded the priest of the Virgin Mary and the Holy Babe.

As Father Mohr walked home through the snow and saw the starlit sky, he thought of that first Christmas when the angels sang to the wondering shepherds. He was deeply impressed by the beauty of the scene and the majestic stillness of the wintry night. Then, back home, he thought over the events; and the impulse came to put his feelings into words. It is said that the lines were written rapidly; and soon Josef Mohr had composed the poem that has made his name immortal.

But he had no music for it; and he wanted the composition sung at the Christmas service. Unluckily, the mice had eaten at the organ bellows; because of the deep snows, it was impossible for a man to get there to repair the damage in time for the service.

Therefore, Father Mohr hurried over to see his friend, Franz Gruber, to ask him to furnish the melody for his words. It is reported that the teacher, within an hour or so, had completed the air. Then he took the melody to the priest, who was delighted with it. At the Christmas service in 1818, the two men, singing the tenor and bass, formed a quartet with two women singers (one source tells us), and, to the accompaniment of Father Mohr's Italian guitar, introduced their composition to the world.

Thus one of our most inspiring carols was born. It presents an unforgettable picture of the nativity: the sleeping Infant with his Mother; the light that came down "from Heaven afar"; the announcement to the shepherds that "Christ, the Saviour, is born"; and the glorious song of the angels. The words and music of "Silent Night! Holy Night!" seem especially fitted for each other, for the "beauty and simplicity of the tune are in perfect blending with Mohr's verses," and may be emblematic of the close friendship of the two men.

Not long after the composition of the song, an organ builder, Karl Mauracher, came to repair the church organ. When he had finished the work, Franz Gruber sat down to try the instrument, and drifted into his new Christmas song. Mauracher was delighted with it and asked if he might take it back with him to his valley, the Zillertal. There, when he played and sang it, his hearers were thrilled and called it the "Song from Heaven." (It also became known as the "Folksong from Zillertal.")

In this valley lived four gifted children, with exceptionally good voices, Caroline, Josef, Andreas, and Amalie Strasser. Under the organist's instruction, they learned the song and enjoyed singing it. As their parents were glovemakers, the children went with them each year to the great fair at Leipzig to sell their products. While there, they often sang on the streets. To their great surprise, the General Director of Music, Mr. Pohlenz (who had heard them sing one day), asked them to attend a concert.

At the close of the regular program, the Director announced that four children, with unusual musical ability, were in the audience. Then Mr. Pohlenz invited them to come to the platform and sing before the King and Queen of Saxony. Although the young Strassers were frightened, they rose, went to the front of the hall, and sang several selections, including their favorite "Song from Heaven." Their singing created a sensation; and they were invited to the palace on Christmas Eve, 1832, to sing the carol again before the royal family. Therefore, these children made the song known before it got into print. "Silent Night!" was first published in 1840, in Leipzig, as a Tyrolean Christmas carol; but the names of the poet and composer were not given.

This was the beginning of the spread of the new song throughout Europe and the world. Even though it had now become famous, no one seemed to know who had written the words or the music. When it was published, in a four-part version, it carried the statement, "Author and Composer Unknown." Later, by mistake, the tune was credited to Michael Haydn, brother of the noted musician, Joseph Haydn.

The King of Prussia, Frederick Wilhelm IV, heard "Silent Night!" for the first time in 1854, when it was sung by the entire choir of the Imperial Church in Berlin. He declared that this song should be given first place at all Christmas concerts in his country; he also instructed his court musicians to try to find out the names of the author and composer.

That same year—1854—these men got in touch with the monks of St. Peter's monastery in Salzburg, and inquired whether they had any information about the origin of the song. By a lucky turn of events, a choir boy there, the son of Franz Gruber, heard of the investigation; and he soon convinced the monks that it was his father's music.

At this time Franz Gruber was the choirmaster at Hallein. Here, in 1854, he made an authentic statement about the composition of "Stille Nacht!" which on his autographed copy he called *"Weih-nachtslied"* ("Christmas song"). Even after this discovery, Gruber remained in obscurity, and died in poverty in 1863, before his carol had become famous. Years later (1897), a tablet honoring him was placed on the school where he had taught.

But the world is much richer for this song in which Josef Mohr has given us his incomparable description of that first Christmas night. The "Song from Heaven" has been translated into many different languages. Travelers and missionaries have told of hearing it sung in distant and isolated places: for example, in Hindustani near the mighty Himalayas; also in East Africa and the Sudan. "Silent Night!" is said to have a wider use than any other Christmas carol.

For several years it was sung each Christmas Eve in Hallein at Gruber's home by a choir that was accompanied by a grandson of Franz, playing on the original guitar. Also this rendition was heard around the world by means of radio until 1938, when Austria was overrun.

The carol has been the subject of numerous articles, stories, novels, plays, and a movie. In 1948, on the 130th anniversary of its creation, Austria issued a stamp that included pictures of the author and composer, with the Star of Bethlehem and the words, *"Stille Nacht! Heilige Nacht!"*

It was originally sung in the United States by a group of Tyrolean singers, who made a concert tour through the East and Middle West; and first appeared in an American hymnal in 1871. "Silent Night!" has been sung by almost every famous singer: but it will always be associated with the memory of the beloved Madame Schumann-Heink, who sang it in German on her tours around the world. Also, up to her last years, she sang each Christmas Eve on the radio our favorite carol "Stille Nacht!" first heard in her native land more than a century ago.

17

"There's a Song in the Air"

AT CHRISTMAS, NO carol program is complete without the jubilant, triumphant "Joy to the World." It was written by Isaac Watts (1674–1748), often called the "Father of Hymnody," for he composed more than six hundred songs and hymns. With Charles Wesley, he ranks as one of the most prolific hymn writers of the world. Watts also went a step further, for he made hymn singing a real part of Protestant church services.

Isaac, the oldest of nine children, was the son of a deacon in Southampton, England, who went to prison twice "for his conscience' sake." The mother used to carry Isaac in her arms when she stood at the prison gate to sing hymns to cheer her husband.

At an early age, the boy learned to play the piano, and to the delight of his parents often composed little songs. While just a young boy, Isaac noticed the lack of enthusiasm in congregational singing at their church in Southampton. When his father challenged him to write something better for the people to sing, Isaac, at the age of fifteen, composed his first hymn. Soon afterward he produced several others that were accepted and enjoyed by his father's congregation.

On his twenty-first birthday, Watts preached his first sermon at the Independent Church in Mark Lane, London. When his health failed in 1708, he felt he should resign from the position; but the congregation hired an assistant pastor.

Watts's good friends, Sir Thomas and Lady Abney, invited him to visit them at their estate near London. He accepted with the idea of staying, perhaps, a week. However, he made what is prob-

165

ably the longest known visit in history, for he remained as a guest for thirty-six years until his death in 1748.

During his first years there, the Abney coach took Isaac Watts—whenever he was able to preach—to his church, twelve miles away. He was held in great esteem by the Abneys, who considered it an honor to have him in their home. Once, when Isaac remarked to other visitors about the length of his stay, his gracious hostess declared that his visit was the shortest one they had ever experienced.

During his stay, Watts devoted himself to writing hymns; and by his talents and leadership in this field helped raise the standards of church music. His fifty-two published volumes of hymns have had a strong influence on English hymnody.

In 1719 his collection of paraphrases was printed, *The Psalms of David, in the Language of the New Testament.* Isaac Watts named the hymn based on the Ninety-eighth Psalm "Joy to the World." This Psalm contains the words, "Make a joyful noise unto the Lord, all the earth . . . the world and they that dwell therein"; and it is a song of rejoicing for Israel's salvation from Babylon. But the hymn, "Joy to the World," is concerned with "the redemption of the whole world from sin and sorrow."

At first, this was sung to music composed by a Dr. Hodges (and his tune is still used at times). But later, the present happy and stirring "Antioch," which radiates joy, was adapted rather freely from Handel's *Messiah.* This music seems especially fitted to the triumphant stanzas; and the carol is not only well suited for outdoor singing at Christmas, but is an excellent missionary hymn. The world will always be grateful to Isaac Watts for his contribution of songs; and in Westminster Abbey he is honored by a memorial. This shows him seated at a table, writing hymns, while angels are hovering around him.

> While shepherds watched their flocks by night,
> All seated on the ground,
> The angel of the Lord came down,
> And glory shone around.

This is the opening stanza of a carol, written about 250 years ago, a song still included in most hymnals, and loved both in England and America.

Nahum Tate (1652–1715) wrote the words; he was an Irish playwright, associated with Dryden, and considered one of the best poets of his period. Even though he was Poet Laureate during the reigns of William and Mary, Queen Anne, and George I, Tate's work (written mainly for the stage) is now forgotten. But we shall always remember his inspiring carol, "While Shepherds Watched Their Flocks by Night."

The melody is said to have originated in Hampshire. It was a favorite tune, called "Winchester Old," by Thomas Este, and first appeared in 1592 (about a century before Tate wrote his Christmas hymn) in *The Whole Book of Psalms.*

In collaboration with Nicholas Brady (1659–1726; a country minister, later at Stratford-on-Avon), Nahum Tate published in 1696, *The New Version of the Psalms.* Four years afterward, a supplement to it was printed to be used by the Church of England. This contained sixteen hymns. But today "While Shepherds Watched" is the only one of them still in popular favor with its jubilant closing lines, the song of the angel choir:

> All glory be to God on high.
> And to the earth be peace!
> Good will henceforth from heav'n to men
> Begin and never cease.

"Angels from the Realms of Glory" is considered the finest hymn produced by John Montgomery (1771–1854), who was the creator of over four hundred songs, published in three volumes. His parents were Moravian missionaries. Montgomery was an ardent reformer, who, in trying to bring about social justice, was put in prison twice for his zealous efforts. While there, he devoted much of his leisure to his favorite pastime of writing hymns.

His Christmas song, beginning:

> Angels, from the realms of glory,
> Wing your flight o'er all the earth;
> Ye who sang creation's story
> Now proclaim Messiah's birth.

appeared in Montgomery's newspaper, *Iris* (published in Sheffield, England) on December 24, 1816, with the title, "Good Tidings of Great Joy to All People." It was also published in *The Christmas Box,* 1825, as one of "Three New Carols."

"Angels from the Realms of Glory" was set to the tune of an old French carol. But in most collections of Christmas songs, it is used to the melody "Regent Street" (named from the location of St. Philip's Church), composed by Henry Smart (1813–1879). He was blind, a noted musician who played the organ at St. Philip's, and wrote many popular hymn tunes.

"Hark! the Herald Angels Sing," written by Charles Wesley (1707–1788), is the only hymn by this author to be included in the *English Book of Common Prayer.* It is still one of the most widely sung of all Christmas songs, and is considered one of the ten favorites in English hymnals. Charles Wesley (brother of the founder of Methodism, John Wesley) has often been called the "Poet Laureate of Methodism" and the "Prince of Hymn Writers."

In his youth, Charles had decided to become a minister; and with John made a voyage to America to preach their new doctrines. However, because of ill health, he had to return to England. While on shipboard, he enjoyed hearing some Moravians singing hymns; and this is said to have imbued him with the idea of composing such music.

During his lifetime, Charles wrote more than sixty-five hundred hymns. John Wesley also loved music and composed sacred songs. While the brothers were still living, twenty-five hundred of their works appeared in print. For many years, Charles was organist at St. George's Church in Hanover Square. When he went riding on his pony the story goes that he often took papers from his pockets and jotted down words for hymns as they came to mind. One day when the pony stumbled and fell on him, Charles wrote in his diary that he had sprained his hand. As a result, the accident "spoiled my hymn writing for that day."

"Hark! the Herald Angels Sing" was written in 1739 and later revised. (The first lines—so one authority states—were changed by the Reverend Martin Madan; also the next three stanzas were "modified" by him, while John Wesley added the fifth.)

The carol was inspired, it is said, when Charles Wesley was walking to church one Christmas Day and was thrilled by the joyous chiming of the church bells in London. He composed "Hark! the Herald Angels Sing" as a companion piece to his beautiful Easter hymn, "Christ, the Lord, Is Risen Today." At first both were set to one tune. The Christmas piece was also sung to the same melody as that of "See the Conquering Hero Comes."

But the version we prefer today was adapted in 1855 by Dr. W. H. Cummings (1831–1915), organist at Waltham Abbey in England. In 1840, Felix Mendelssohn had composed a cantata, *Festgesang (Festival Song)* to be used to honor the anniversary of printing. This music was sung at a great celebration in Leipzig.

Dr. Cummings took part of the section, "Gott Ist Licht" ("God Is Light"), "a noble and spirited choral," and fitted the words of Charles Wesley's "Hark! the Herald Angels Sing" to it. Then he arranged the composition for his choir to sing on Christmas Day. When the hymn was printed with this tune, called "Mendelssohn," it was so well received that it soon became the favored version.

Once Mendelssohn had told the printers that he felt the original words for this part of the cantata, *Festgesang,* were not too well suited to the music. He believed that perhaps something of a martial nature should be used instead. No doubt the composer would be surprised and delighted to realize how well his melody fits the words of one of our favorite holiday carols and processionals, "Hark! the Herald Angels Sing."

"Once in Royal David's City" is a beautifully told story of the Saviour's birth. The words were written by Mrs. Cecil Frances Alexander (born in 1823 in Ireland), wife of the Bishop of Derry, later Primate of all Ireland. Mrs. Alexander, who is said to have been a retiring person, wrote her poems for certain special occasions, and had no idea that they would ever appear in print and bring her acclaim. Her eight books of hymns, including the favorites, "There Is a Green Hill Far Away" and "Jesus Calls Us O'er the Tumult," contain about four hundred songs.

169

Her Christmas hymn, "Once in Royal David's City," was first published in 1848 in *Hymns for Little Children*. According to one authority, the song was written by Mrs. Alexander for her god-children, for they "complained that their Bible lessons were dreary." The melody was written by Henry J. Gauntlett (an organist at his father's church in Olney, England) who produced several pieces of church music.

In the five stanzas of the carol, Mrs. Alexander tells the story simply, so children may understand the event. She also wanted them to realize what His coming meant to them; and in her fourth stanza tells them:

> For He is our childhood's pattern,
> Day by day like us He grew;
> He was little, weak, and helpless,
> Tears and smiles like us He knew;
> And He feeleth for our sadness,
> And He shareth in our gladness.

Although many of our Christmas carols are of foreign origin, the United States has produced several hymns of high rank. They include one of the earliest American songs, the inspiring "It Came Upon the Midnight Clear," written by the Reverend Edmund H. Sears (1810–1876) when he was a minister at Wayland. He was a native of Sandisfield, Massachusetts, a graduate of Harvard Theological School, and an excellent minister and scholar. Although affiliated with the Unitarian Church, Dr. Sears had a firm faith in the divinity of Christ. He died at Weston, where he held his last pastorate.

It was on a cold wintry day in December, 1849, as Dr. Sears sat by the fire in his study, and watched the snow coming down, that the words of "It Came Upon the Midnight Clear" came to him. He believed that real "good will toward men" could cause people to rise above petty, earthly things; and that sometime "the new Heaven and earth" would recognize Christ as King.

After completing the stanzas, Dr. Sears sent them to his friend, Dr. Morrison, editor of the *Christian Register* in Boston. Morrison was so impressed by the poem that he used "It Came Upon the Midnight Clear" at Christmas programs; and the next year—1850—he published it in his magazine.

A friend of the author insisted that the poem be set to music, so Dr. Sears asked Richard S. Willis (1819–1910) of Boston to compose a melody for it. (Willis after his graduation from Yale, studied music in Germany where he and Mendelssohn were friends.) When Willis read the poem, he was thrilled by its beauty, and completed the musical setting in a short time as it was to be used at a Christmas service. This tune is named "Carol." Later, Sir Arthur Sullivan, also impressed by the content of the poem, made a setting for it, which he adapted from a folk melody.

As one writer stated, Dr. Sears "has enriched hymnody with his glorious lyric" and its "note of good cheer." Dr. Morrison once said that no matter how mediocre he felt his Christmas sermon to be, the singing of his friend's incomparable hymn made up for any deficiencies in his own message. Also, "It Came Upon the Midnight Clear," although written a century ago, is truly "a carol-like hymn that stresses the social message of Christmas"; and its theme still has the same implication for modern times, for we have many among us today who "bend beneath life's crushing load," and who long for the time when "the whole world" will "send back the song, which now the angels sing."

Edmund H. Sears also wrote another Christmas song, "Calm on the Listening Ear of Night," which has been somewhat neglected. Dr. Oliver Wendell Holmes praised it as one of the most beautiful poems ever written. Dr. Sears created his first version in 1834, when he was only twenty-four years old, just after he had completed his work at the divinity school. Later, in 1851, he revised it. The hymn has sometimes been sung to the same tune as "It Came Upon the Midnight Clear," and also to "Varina." Dr. Ninde, an authority on hymnody, declares these two songs of Dr. Sears are worthy to take their places "with the choicest nativity lyrics in English hymnody."

Our country is proud of an outstanding carol which has the visit of the Magi as its theme; and it has been termed the first all-

ALL ABOUT CHRISTMAS

American carol by some critics. This song, "We Three Kings of Orient Are," is distinctive, for both the words and music were written by the same person, an Episcopalian rector, the Reverend John Henry Hopkins, Jr. (1820–1891), ordained in 1850. He wrote this composition in 1857, while serving at Christ Church in Williamsport, Pennsylvania. It was first printed in 1859; and its popularity grew rapidly. The carol was widely praised long before it was included in regular hymnals.

Dr. Hopkins's *Carols, Hymns, and Songs* appeared in a volume in 1862; and in 1883 his verses were collected and published as *Poems by the Wayside Written More Than Forty Years Ago.* Several of these have also been set to music. The Reverend Mr. Hopkins died at Troy, New York, in 1891.

"We Three Kings of Orient Are" is considered by critics as one of the most successful of all modern carols. Its stanzas, like those of "Good King Wenceslas," are arranged for dramatic production. All three monarchs join in the first stanza and tell of their following the Star. Then in turn each sings alone—Melchior, Kaspar, and Balthasar—telling of his special gift to the King, and what it symbolizes. Finally the three reunite in singing the fifth stanza. Such a rendition makes a very stately and impressive performance.

And certainly, no one has given us a more impressive description of the Star of Bethlehem than has the author in his distinctive refrain:

> O Star of wonder, star of night,
> Star with royal beauty bright,
> Westward leading, still proceeding,
> Guide us to the perfect light.

Although several of Henry Wadsworth Longfellow's poems are of a religious nature, not many of them have been given a musical setting. One noticeable exception is his reverie, the Christmas hymn, "I Heard the Bells on Christmas Day."

This was written on December 25, 1863, just six months after the Battle of Gettysburg, when the Civil War was at its height. Longfellow, one of our most beloved poets, was saddened by the horrors of this conflict, for "hate seemed overstrong at the moment." Also, his own son, while serving in the Army of the Potomac, had been wounded.

When Longfellow heard the Christmas bells chiming out, he came to the realization, from the depths of his despair, as the bells rang "more loud and deep; 'God is not dead, nor doth He sleep!'" He believed that God *is* powerful enough to overcome the world's strife, and to bring peace and good will to earth. In ending each stanza, the poet stresses this idea with the phrase, "Of peace on earth, good-will to men!" The words of this Christmas hymn are doubly worthy of our thoughtful consideration today, almost a hundred years after they were written. And this carol should be sung prayerfully by us each time the holidays return.

The tune is pleasing and appropriate; it was written by an English organist and composer, John Baptiste Calkin. The bass notes sound like the ringing of a bell, while the last four measures originated in an old "Amen."

Other American Christmas songs that have won favor include the Negro spirituals, "Rise Up, Shepherd, an' Foller," arranged by J. B. Herbert and "Go Tell It on the Mountains" that "our Jesus Christ is born."

A charming modern carol, "There's a Song in the Air," was written by Josiah G. Holland in 1872. He was born in Massachusetts in 1819, and died in 1881. He graduated from medical college, was a teacher, lecturer, and editor. His column (in the Springfield, Massachusetts *Republican*), called "Timothy Titcomb's Letters," was later made into a book. Dr. Holland also wrote the novel, *Arthur Bonnicastle,* and several volumes of poems. In 1870, he became the founder and editor of *Scribner's Monthly*.

His Christmas poem, "There's a Song in the Air," at once made a strong hit with Sunday School members especially. When a new Methodist hymnal was being prepared for publication in 1905, three noted composers submitted melodies for "There's a Song in the Air." Since they were all excellent, the three were printed in the new collection. However, the one composed by Karl Harrington (a professor of Latin at Wesleyan University, also one of the musical editors on the new hymnal) seems to be preferred. This carol has been heard all over the world, in homes, churches, and at missionary stations.

Probably the best-known American carol, and in the opinion of many our favorite one, is "O Little Town of Bethlehem." The author, Bishop Phillips Brooks (1835–1893), one of the most eloquent American preachers of the nineteenth century, first served as rector at the Holy Trinity Church in Philadelphia. Later, he preached at Old Trinity Church, Boston. In front of this building, you can see his statue—"a very speaking likeness"—in bronze, created by the famous sculptor, Saint-Gaudens.

Phillips Brooks came from an intellectual and musical family, and even as a child was always singing. By the time he was sixteen, he knew two hundred songs by heart. After he entered the ministry, he was especially interested in Sunday School music. He loved to hear the children sing, so it is not surprising that he wrote his best song for them.

Late in the summer of 1865, when Dr. Brooks was just thirty years of age, he told his congregation he was going abroad for a year. Naturally his parishioners were saddened by his leaving; but they knew he would use his time well and gain much inspiration for his future work.

His travels in the Holy Land were a wonderful experience for him. In his letters home, he related what it meant to him to visit the region associated with the life of Christ. He added that every place "seemed marked with His footprints. There were the walks He walked, the shores where he taught, the mountains where he prayed." Everywhere Phillips Brooks went, he could visualize the Saviour and His disciples in those same places.

On Christmas Eve, 1865, he rode out to Bethlehem, saw the shepherds in the fields, and below him in the starlight "the little town of Bethlehem," looking much as it did the night that Christ was born. This scene was stamped upon his memory, never to be forgotten. Then, from ten until three A.M., Dr. Brooks attended the service at the Church of the Nativity. This was one of the most inspiring events of his whole life.

He wrote home: "I remember especially Christmas Eve . . . when the whole church was ringing with the splendid hymns of praise to God. It seemed as if I could hear voices . . . telling each other of the 'Wonderful Night' of the Saviour's birth."

Phillips Brooks did not write the song that made him famous—the song of the small Judean town and the wondrous event that happened there—until two or three years after his return. No doubt he often pictured the memorable scene in his mind, for in "O Little Town of Bethlehem" he has given us a vivid description of the first Christmas in the Holy Land.

After his return, he became a greater minister than ever before. Because of his religious experiences abroad, he continued his deep interest in the children of his church. Just before Christmas, 1868, when they were preparing for the annual Sunday School program, he wrote his song, "O Little Town of Bethlehem" for the boys and girls to sing.

Dr. Brooks asked his friend, the choir director and organist, Lewis H. Redner (1831–1908) to furnish a simple tune to go with his poem. The week before Christmas passed; and still Mr. Redner had not been able to write the melody he wanted for it. On Saturday night, he went to bed, thinking about the beautiful lines. And the story goes that at midnight he suddenly awoke; a melody had finally come to him. So he got up, jotted down the tune, and next morning completed the harmony. Mr. Redner declared that it "was a gift from Heaven." (This melody has been given the rather inappropriate name of "St. Louis.")

That Sunday, "O Little Town of Bethlehem" was sung for the first time by the Sunday School of Holy Trinity Church in Philadelphia. Phillips Brooks, sitting in the back of the room, was thrilled by this experience of hearing the boys and girls sing his song. (It is interesting to note that neither he nor Mr. Redner had children of their own.)

The song delighted all who heard it; but it did not come into wide use until about 1890. Two years later it was published in a hymnal of Dr. Brooks's denomination. At first he did not have his name attached to it; but later the author was revealed.

ALL ABOUT CHRISTMAS

Phillips Brooks also created other Christmas poems, including his inspiring "Everywhere, Everywhere, Christmas Tonight!" He was loved by all who came in contact with him. One writer tells that, when a mother told her little girl that Dr. Brooks had gone to heaven, the child exclaimed, "How happy the angels will be!"

Nowadays, "O Little Town of Bethlehem" has been given its just acclaim; it appeals to both young and old; it is simple and yet we feel the greatness of the soul that could write:

> How silently, how silently
> The wondrous gift is given!
> So God imparts to human hearts
> The blessings of His heaven.

18

"O Come, All Ye Faithful"

> Then came the merrymakers in,
> And carols roared with blithesome din,
> If unmelodious was the song,
> It was a hearty note and strong.
> —Sir Walter Scott, in *Marmion*

SINCE WE HAVE such a rich heritage of inspiring Christmas carols—the products of different periods, of varied nationalities, and countries—caroling is one of the oldest folk customs still enjoyed at the winter holidays. From the days of the early Christians, encouraged by such men as St. Francis of Assisi, people began to sing songs in the vernacular, instead of the formal Latin hymns. They enjoyed singing them, for they were more suited to untrained voices, and gave everyone a chance to express his emotions.

Caroling, in several forms, was indulged in throughout Europe; and even bishops and other church officials (according to Durandus) sang carols on the night of the nativity. Martin Luther relates that he and his young friends "at the time of the festival of Christ's birth" used to go from house to house in various villages, singing Yuletide songs "in four-part harmony." After he married Katharina von Bora, they had a family of six children; and they enjoyed many happy hours together in singing. For several weeks before Christmas, the Luthers practiced their carols; then, when the great day arrived, the family and some close friends gathered around their Christmas tree. Martin Luther led the caroling and played an accompaniment on his lute. In 1866 an artist, named Spangenberger, painted a picture (which hung in the gallery at Leipzig) that showed the great Reformer singing with his wife and children.

Many other German families also sang around their lighted trees such favorites as "O Tannenbaum! O Tannenbaum!" and "Stille Nacht! Heilige Nacht!" In the Tyrol, carolers always went out under the star-studded heavens to serenade their friends and relatives by singing beloved old carols.

French peasants enjoyed singing their Christmas songs or *Noëls* at their homes around the nativity scenes in churches, outdoors, or in inns and taverns. The group of carolers carried a lantern at their head; and whenever they saw a lighted candle in a window, they would stop and sing, for this light was the signal for them to serenade the household. Often small coins or other gifts were thrown to them from the windows.

In some parts of France, boys and girls dressed as shepherds and shepherdesses played drums and other instruments, as torchbearers lighted the way to church on Christmas Eve. At home, members of French families always celebrated the holy season by caroling around their *crèches;* and these replicas gave them a vivid picture of the circumstances that surrounded the birth of the Christ Child.

Nowadays, in Paris and other large cities in the country, there are impressive midnight services at such great cathedrals as Notre-Dame or the Madeleine, which is patterned after the Parthenon at Athens. Just as the clock strikes twelve midnight, a great organ "thunders out a welcome"; and the large choir sings the old, yet ever new "Adeste Fideles," accompanied by such instruments as the harp and flute. This carol invites all to take part in the adoration of the Holy Infant; *"Venite adoremus,"* for now the centuries-old prophecy has been fulfilled and "Unto us a Child is born, unto us a Son is given."

To attend such a service is indeed inspiring; and our American author, Washington Irving, felt this thrill which he has so well expressed: "I do not know of a grander effect of music on the moral feelings than to hear the full choir and the pealing organ performing a Christmas anthem in a cathedral, and filling every part of the vast pile with triumphant harmony."

In Spain and Italy, members of many households gather around the *presepe,* or *nacimiento,* to sing carols honoring the season. In 1833 William Sandys (a British collector of carols) described how the Spanish celebrated at their manger scenes, each evening, during Christmas week. After reciting parts of old plays, called *relaciones,* they danced and sang songs to the accompaniment of the *zambomba.* This instrument was made by stretching parchment across the mouth of an earthen jar, "with a slender reed fixed in the center." Sandys said the sound was like that of "a tambourine rubbed by the fingers."

At one church in Naples, San Domenico's at the Christmas service, a woman places an image of the Baby Jesus, the *Bambino,* in the priest's arms. Then, in a procession, all the attendants march to a grotto, where he lays the figure in the "Crusader's Crib" (which is made of stones brought from Bethlehem by the Crusaders). Everyone kneels around the manger and they sing together an old carol, a lullaby to the Christ Child.

Italy was long noted for her holiday musicians, the "Pipers of Rome" or *Pifferai.* These men were shepherds who came down from the mountains, chiefly of Abruzzi and Umbria. Sometimes they were dressed in sheepskins; or perhaps they appeared in coats of blue linen, red vests, and wore broad-brimmed hats adorned with feathers and tassels. They came to town on St. Catherine's Eve, November 25, and went around in threes; one performed on the bagpipes, while the other two played pipes of the clarinet or flageolet type, before the street shrines dedicated to the Virgin Mary.

Many people invited these musicians into their homes where they played and sang old folk songs and carols. The "Pifferai" always carried large leather bags with them, in which they put the gifts received for their caroling. Then just before Christmas, they returned to their homes in the hills to enjoy the food they had gathered on their yearly expedition.

In other European countries, too, caroling was popular. Russian school children, for instance, or members of the church choirs, sang traditional carols under the windows of the well-to-do citizens, and received small coins for their efforts. The Christmas singers in

179

Russia often wore grotesque animal heads on these holiday expeditions.

Christmas carols in Poland are called *kolendy;* on Christmas Eve, members of the family join hands, walk around their lighted trees, and sing together. They repeat this each evening until Epiphany, and, in some places, until Candlemas.

"Blowing in the Yule," with horns and caroling, has been spoken of in connection with Denmark and Jacob Riis in Chapter Twelve. The children of Scandinavian lands have a special candlelight service at four P.M. on Christmas Eve in their churches. There they sing Christmas carols which have been handed down for generations. When their singing ends, the boys and girls receive a treat of fruits and candies. That evening, at their homes, the children join with their elders in singing dance carols around the trees.

For several centuries, caroling has been a popular holiday pastime in England. During the Middle Ages, when the morality and mystery plays were given, carols often were sung between the acts. Sometimes the chorus would leave the stage singing, and then would continue their music on the street. Someone has suggested that this may have been the origin of English outdoor singing at Yuletide. Since caroling was customary, the people called the Christmas of 1525, "Still Christmas"; that year, because of the serious illness of Henry VIII, there was a decree prohibiting "carols, bells, or merry music."

In many British homes, Advent wreaths, made of fir, holly, or laurel, hung from the ceiling with the four candles, one for each Advent Sunday. Parents and children stood under the wreaths and sang traditional music, just as the Germans gathered around their trees.

Bringing in the Yule log in Britain was always the occasion for caroling. Each member sat down on it and sang a song, before the great brand was placed in the wide fireplace. Singing Yule music was the custom, too, when the steaming bowl of wassail was passed from one person to another. Whenever the merry crowds of holiday revelers went out on Twelfth Night to "wassail" the fruit trees to insure abundant production, they sang special carols during the ceremonies.

Today, when we hear well-trained choirs sing the traditional carols, it seems a far cry from the days when ancient minstrels went from castle to castle singing Christmas songs to entertain guests during the long drawn-out holiday feasts. One such old singer, who appeared before Queen Elizabeth in 1575, was described by Percy as dressed in a long gown, with voluminous sleeves, red socks, and black shoes. After bowing three times before his sovereign, the minstrel cleared his throat, stroked his harp as a prelude, and went into his song.

During the Elizabethan period, it was customary for citizens to gather at Whitehall in London for caroling. They also engaged in dancing and various "revels" on these occasions. When the "Ancient Master of the Revels" called on someone to sing a carol, he could ask others to sing with him. This musical evening was interspersed with food, especially hot cakes, that were washed down with great flagons of cider or ale. It was also a custom to have carols sung from church towers in London; and instead of the usual Psalms at the afternoon services, the attendants sang Christmas songs. At the end of the singing, the church clerk wished each one a "Merry Christmas!"

Before the Reformation, and later, during the reign of Henry VIII's daughter, Queen Mary, the priests in their canonical robes, formed a procession, and carried lights around the steeple of St. Paul's, while the city singers or "waits" sang well-known Christmas carols.

One source tells us that these waits originated from boy choirs that went out caroling just before the holidays. But others assert they were watchmen, at first hired to protect the homes of wealthy citizens. With the bellman, who called out the hours, the waits patrolled the streets. Often the waits "sang out," or played hautboys (oboes) to indicate the time of day or night.

Then, the bellman and the waits "gradually assumed an ornamental function" and were hired to play and sing for weddings and other social affairs. In the towns, waits often had special patrons whom they visited regularly. Some places had their own uniformed bands of waits that furnished music for such events as the inauguration of the Lord Mayor. At Newcastle there was a "Waits' Tower" where the community musicians used to meet to practice.

In rural districts, these singers had a certain social standing. On frosty nights during the holidays they would tramp around in the snow, carrying lanterns, festooned with greenery, on long poles. Often their leader held aloft a Christmas tree. At isolated farms, the people looked forward each season to the visit of the waits, who always received a royal welcome. They sang lustily their ancient melodies, and often combined sacred carols with others that praised the joys of drinking and merrymaking. The visitors received food and drink, and could warm themselves before the glowing Yule logs.

At the homes of the gentry, the rustic singers were invited to enter and sing for the family and their guests. Then "the old halls of castles and manor houses resounded with the harp and the Christmas carol." In his poem, "The Norman Baron," Longfellow writes:

> In the hall, the serf and vassal
> Held that night their Christmas wassail.
> Many a carol, old and saintly,
> Sang the minstrels and the waits.

After our early American writer, Washington Irving, had spent Christmas, 1820, in Yorkshire, England, as a guest at Bracebridge Hall, he wrote in his famous *Sketch Book:*

> I had scarcely got into bed when a strain of music seemed to break forth in the air, just below the window. I listened and found it proceeded from a band, which I concluded to be the waits from some neighboring village. They went around the house playing under the windows. The sounds, as they receded, became more soft and aerial, and seemed to accord with quiet and moonlight.

Irving also commented on their singing in these words:

> Even the sounds of the waits, rude as may be their min-

strelsy, breaks upon the midwatches of a winter night with the effect of perfect harmony, as I have been awakened by them in that still and solemn hour "when deep sleep falleth upon man." I have listened with hushed delight, and connecting them with the sacred and joyous occasion, have almost fancied them into another celestial choir, announcing peace and good-will to mankind.

On Christmas morning, at Bracebridge Hall, Irving heard the patter of children's feet outside his bedroom door; and "presently a choir of small voices chanted forth an old Christmas carol, the burden of which was,

> 'Rejoice our Saviour He was born
> On Christmas Day in the morning.' "

When he opened his door, there stood three little children, a boy and two girls, "lovely as seraphs." They were going around, singing at each chamber door; but as soon as they saw the author, they scampered away along the gallery.

Later, that day, after supper, when one of the bachelor relatives, Master Simon, was called upon to sing "a good old Christmas song," he responded with this quaint carol:

> Now Christmas is come,
> Let us beat up the drum,
> And call all the neighbors together,
> And when they appear,
> Let us make them such cheer,
> As will keep out the wind and the weather.

Even though, for many decades, the waits were a national tradition in Britain, as early as the eighteenth century, some persons complained that their sleep was disturbed by the nightly performances of these local musicians. (Of course, the main object of their playing and singing was to collect money in the Christmas boxes which they carried from house to house.) Gradually the waits fell into disrepute; and a law was passed by which "minstrels wandering abroad" were classed with vagabonds, rogues, and beggars. In the nineteenth century Stainer and Barret declared: "At the present day the Waits are the detached bodies of impromptu musicians, who make night hideous for three weeks before Christmas with wretched performances of indifferent melodies."

According to Michael Harrison, such singers existed in Westminster until recent years. They were required to obtain licenses to perform on the streets, and to collect contributions in their Christmas boxes. It is said that such permits were issued as late as 1871. But from time to time waits were arrested for performing without licenses.

Nowadays, in England, their places have been taken by other singing groups; and all through the country and in the great churches of London, like St. Paul's and Westminster Abbey, holiday celebrants gather to enjoy inspiring concerts of Christmas carols.

In Wales, singing is an important part of everyday living; and the Welsh have long been famous for their excellent group performances. There carolers often go around at four or five o'clock on Christmas morning to sing at the homes. When their serenade is completed, they are asked to come in and are given refreshments of hot broth.

Formerly, on the Isle of Man this custom was observed: the young people who thought they had talent for writing Christmas carols composed their stanzas and recited them in church, as George Borrow has related. The ones selected by the clergy as best and most suitable were sung at the church services; and also used for caroling in the neighborhood.

Everyone took his own candle to light the church for the evening caroling where the church clerk was in charge. Often the singing kept up until quite late with some of the songs of a rather "riotous nature." On the way home, the churchgoers stopped to sing at taverns and to imbibe something to quench their thirst.

For many decades, caroling has been a great source of comfort, especially in times of depressions or war. Then "all sorts and conditions of men" join in small village churches or in great cathedrals to keep up their courage and morale by singing beloved and familiar carols. This was the case in England during some of their blackouts. On battlefields, also, at different periods, Christmas carols have been sung, showing that in spite of human conflict, men still remember and cherish the truly worth-while things of life.

One story tells us that, on Christmas Eve in 1870, during the Franco-Prussian War, when Paris was besieged, the French and Germans faced each other in trenches before the city. Suddenly, a young Frenchman jumped out of his trench, and in a beautiful singing voice astonished the Germans with Adolphe Adam's incomparable "Cantique de Noël" ("O Holy Night"). The men on the opposite side seemed awestruck by his performance; and not a shot was fired in his direction. When the French singer had finished the carol, a tall German responded. He came out of his trench to sing, in his own language, Luther's beloved Christmas hymn, "Von Himmel Hoch" ("From Heaven Above I Come to You").

A similar event happened in World War I in the Argonne Forest when German troops in their trenches sang "O Du Froehliche! O Du Selige!" which the French answered with their own carol, "Noël! Noël!" Afterward the men exchanged gifts of chocolate and other small presents; and to honor Christmas Day the guns were silent for several hours.

During this same war, one nurse wrote home about caroling at a base hospital in France. Each nurse, dressed in her long blue coat, overseas cap, and rubber boots, carried a lighted candle and joined in a procession with her fellow workers. Early on Christmas Day, 1918, they went around the hospital singing "Silent Night" and other familiar carols to bring their patients a bit of home and holiday spirit.

The Christmas days that came around during the years of World War II found our American soldiers in many different parts of the world. And they showed much ingenuity in preparing their holiday celebrations in out-of-the-way places. One soldier wrote from an island in the South Pacific that he had helped the chaplain prepare for the Christmas service by decorating a tree and setting up an impromptu altar. For tree lights he used flashlight bulbs, dipped in bright paint. Colored floodlights were created by tinting the headlights of a jeep with red and violet paint. "It was really beautiful," he added, "to hear the familiar Christmas carols ringing out through the thick jungle."

In 1920 a group of Los Angeles teachers placed a monument at the grave of Franz Gruber in Hallein, Austria, with this inscription:

FRANZ GRUBER
In Reverent Commemoration
of a Teacher
for His World Message
of Peace and Brotherly Love

Pilgrimages are often made here, during the holidays, and also to the tomb of Father Josef Mohr, to honor these two friends who gave the world an unforgettable carol.

An incident that those who took part in it will always remember occurred at Hallein, on Christmas Eve, 1946, following World War II. A group of American soldiers and WAC's met at Franz Gruber's grave to pay him tribute. All joined in singing "Silent Night! Holy Night!" They were accompanied by Karl Adler of Salzburg on the same guitar used at the Christmas service of 1818, when, for the first time, the world heard the song.

It's a long way from Austria to far-off Australia, where, instead of observing Christmas amid snow and ice, the people, "down under," are having their summer season. The Australians often enjoy their holiday dinners outdoors on the beaches or in the woods. Even though their climatic conditions are very different from those of the northern parts of Europe and the United States, the Australians enjoy caroling as a tribute to the day when Christ was born.

In fact, in Melbourne, a unique way of singing carols has developed that has become known all over the world—the inspiring "Carols by Candlelight" program. This impressive open-air ceremony has spread throughout their continent, and to other parts of the world, Johannesburg, South Africa, for example. Also the special candle holders have been sent to small villages in England, such as Salford, Chipping Norton, so their people could hold similar festivals.

It was back in 1937 that Norman Banks, then a radio announcer at 3KZ, in Melbourne, conceived this worth-while idea. On Christmas Eve, he saw a small, white-haired woman (incurably ill) sitting at an open window with a lighted candle in her hand. She was softly singing Christmas carols to the accompaniment of the music from her radio. It is too bad that she died without knowing that her simple act of Christmas worship would inspire Norman Banks to start a movement that has brought together thousands of individuals of different religious beliefs to sing Christmas carols.

At once he began to plan "Carols by Candlelight" for the following Christmas. At his request, several thousand citizens, with lighted candles, gathered around a small platform at Alexandra Gardens along the river. There, under his leadership, they sang together Yuletide songs that are universally loved. Within a short time the idea became so popular that now, each year, about 300,000 gather for this annual carol festival, with its simple, but dramatic, lighting effects.

Mr. Banks stressed the use of the candles; and now the orders for them and the holders are often placed as early in the year as March. More than two thousand individuals help plan the extensive affair; distinguished visitors, such as the Lord Mayor of London and the Mayor of New York, have been present; and noted musicians have sung at this festival.

Persons of every type, rich and poor, young and old, join in the celebration that takes place at ten P.M. on Christmas Eve, ending with all joining in singing "Auld Lang Syne." This program, since 1950, has been broadcast to all parts of the world, including Mexico, India, the Yukon, China, South Sea Islands, Europe, and Tibet. In 1949, it was heard in the United States through 519 stations.

Not only do the citizens of Melbourne enjoy singing together on this special occasion, but Norman Banks linked "Carols by Candlelight" with a fine project for helping sick and disabled youngsters. Several years before the first caroling—in 1933—after seeing a little girl with infantile paralysis in a local hospital, he had made an appeal for help for these victims. So Mr. Banks started "the world's first one-day radio appeal for a charitable cause."

The response, at first, was small, but each year more money has been given; and in recent years a new hospital unit for children, costing 300,000 pounds, was completed, "the only hospital in the world built by a radio appeal." Thus the citizens of Melbourne have combined two wonderful operations—the pleasure of caroling together in democratic fashion and the greater joy of aiding the unfortunate.

Although Norman Banks is no longer with Station 3KZ (in 1952 John Ford and Phillip Gibbs had charge of the festival), his work lives on. The world will not forget the project he sponsored—after hearing a little old lady singing carols—and his dream of permanent world peace among all the nations of the globe.

Here, in the New World, the first Christmas celebration took place off the coast of Maine on St. Croix Island in 1604, when the settlers enjoyed themselves "with true French gaiety and feasting," as one writer tells us. And they, no doubt, joined lustily in singing the *noëls* of their native France.

Since the Puritans in England, in 1652, forbade Christmas caroling, it was only natural that the colonists of the same faith in Massachusetts should follow suit a few years later in 1659. Cotton Mather was one of the leaders in this movement. However, early in Boston, "broadsides" were peddled on the streets; one of the sheets was adorned with drawings illustrating the carols "The Holly and the Ivy" and "I Saw Three Ships a-Sailing."

In other American settlements carols were sung, notably in French New Orleans, by the Dutch in New Amsterdam, and by the Episcopalian settlers in Virginia.

The Moravians, who founded Bethlehem, Pennsylvania, in 1741, brought with them both stringed and wind instruments and "cultivated music as an enrichment of their worship and as a recreation." They published the first American hymnbook, *Hirtenlieder von Bethlehem* (*Shepherd Songs of Bethlehem*) which Christopher Saut of Morgantown printed for them in 1742. Benjamin Franklin in his noted *Autobiography* tells of hearing good "musick" at Bethlehem, played by an orchestra with instruments that included an organ, violins, hautboys (oboes), clarinets, and flutes.

At their Yuletide observance, the Moravians celebrated with

"merry music," both instrumental and vocal. As this colony was made up of religious refugees from several countries, they sang together, in 1745, the Christmas hymn, "In Dulci Jubilo," in thirteen languages.

There's an interesting story that, at one Christmas, during the 1750's, a band of unfriendly Indians was lurking in a near-by forest, and intended to attack the Moravian settlement. Suddenly, at dawn, on Christmas Day, the savages heard a loud, blaring noise, something entirely new to them, as their only musical instruments were tom-toms. This was the sound of the trombone choir, announcing from the Brethren's House that the day of Christ's birth had come.

As this strange music re-echoed through the woods, the Indians fled in terror. So today, as each Christmas Day dawns, the outstanding trombone choir at Bethlehem, Pennsylvania, plays the old traditional German Christmas carol "How Brightly Beams the Morning Star," from the tower of the Moravian Church, reminding the townspeople that their settlement was saved on Christmas Day about two centuries ago.

Gradually in New England, music was accepted at the holidays; and late in the eighteenth century the ban on caroling was done away with; also music became a part of church services. In 1815 the first Christmas concert was held in Boston by the Handel and Haydn Society, at famous old King's Chapel.

During the nineteenth century, caroling was fostered by schools and churches, at their annual Christmas "entertainments" with their "treats" and the usual visits from "Good Old St. Nick." There were long programs of "pieces" and carols, and these affairs helped make caroling the popular holiday pastime it is today.

And nowadays young people all over our country unselfishly bring happiness to shut-ins and the sick in hospitals by their group caroling. In some places—Memphis, Tennessee, for example—they go around in trucks; a street car, gaily festooned with evergreens, in Washington, D.C., has carried the singers; while in 1950, at Canoga Park, California, a group of riders did their caroling on horseback.

Philadelphia, too, has a unique event; at dawn on Christmas Day, men dressed as shepherds, with a piper or flute player, sing holiday greetings. At the same time, out on the old Plaza in Los Angeles, little girls with lighted candles sing Spanish carols as they walk from quaint Olvera Street to the church, Our Lady of the Angels, that has stood there for over a century.

Across the continent, at Lake Wales, Florida, carols float out from the famous Bok Singing Tower, while the people of Seattle hear them sung by a civic chorus. The musicians are on a lighted boat that moves over the lake and brings pleasure to many listeners.

A similar event happens in Naples and Alamitos Bay, suburbs of Long Beach, California. Naples has winding canals crossed by picturesque bridges; and at the holidays, homes along the banks are gaily decorated inside and out with glittering trees, manger scenes, and Santa with his reindeer. Often you hear carols coming from hidden loudspeakers. Just before Christmas there is a mile-long parade through the canals and along the bay. Thousands of spectators come to see the beautifully lighted and decorated boats, which are filled with singers from churches, clubs, or schools. It is inspiring to hear the familar carols come floating over the waters.

Hot Springs, Arkansas, has sponsored an interesting holiday celebration that features caroling. Here the story of the nativity is presented on a green slope in Hot Springs National Park. While the audience waits quietly, at a distance they hear the faint sound of singing. Then two hundred carolers, dressed in choir robes, and carrying candles, move slowly down the incline. The faces of the singers are lighted up, but as they reach the stage, they snuff the candles. Then a narrator tells the old story of that first Christmas; the choir sings traditional carols; and the impressive scene ends with all the participants kneeling before the manger of the Baby Jesus.

Years ago, during the Gold Rush, Cornish miners went to California; now, at Grass Valley, a mining town, descendants of the original workers continue their well-known choir, which was organized over seventy years ago. Many visitors go to the town each year to hear the caroling. This singing has been broadcast from coast to coast at times; in 1940, for example, the program originated in the Idaho-Maryland mine, two thousand feet below the earth's surface.

Caroling around community Christmas trees has become a tradition with us in our towns and cities, from Maine to California, and from Washington state to Florida. "Joy to the World," "Hark! the Herald Angels Sing," or "O Little Town of Bethlehem" sound out joyously as persons of all ages sing together. Sometimes the caroling is led by high-school glee clubs, church choirs or other community groups. One authority believes this custom started from the ancient street festivals of Spain and Italy.

At the White House lawn, in our national capital, crowds gather to see the lights go on our "National Community Tree." Then spectators, from every walk of life, including disabled veterans from near-by hospitals, join in caroling, just as another group does around the distinctive tree at Radio City in New York; and a third choir of carolers sings under the mighty redwood, our "National Christmas Tree" in Central California.

All over America, caroling goes on; we pause, in the midst of our holiday shopping, in a great department store to hear a chorus of employees singing from a balcony. On the streets music comes from loudspeakers; and members of the Salvation Army add their share of holiday carols.

At home, families get out the old carol books and sing around the piano. Some share their music with their neighbors or the passers-by. One group, the Boyers of Pueblo, Colorado, play their electric organ and sing on the porch. Even when touring the West in a trailer, they continued this yearly practice of sharing their carols, which are chosen to suit all tastes, and range from "Ave Maria" to "Rudolph, the Red-nosed Reindeer."

Many persons sing to radio accompaniment or with records; and excellent records have been made by outstanding artists and choral groups. Thousands of these are sold each year and are enjoyed by individuals who don't have pianos. Also through records, in recent years, we have become acquainted with certain carols, not so familiar, such as "The Twelve Days of Christmas," a welcome addition to the better-known ones.

ALL ABOUT CHRISTMAS

At our educational institutions, from the little red schoolhouse to great universities, caroling is an important part of pre-holiday festivities. In some schools, carols sound from upper windows to greet students as they arrive; in others, carolers go through the halls, and those in classrooms join with them in the old traditional favorites.

There are artistically staged pageants, both at churches and schools, with visualizations of nativity scenes, including the announcement to the shepherds and the adoration of the Magi. These are given with suitable carols as an accompaniment, and usually end with the unforgettable scene—Mary with the Infant Jesus—while a chorus softly sings the carol, "Sleep, Holy Babe."

Therefore, of all our holiday traditions, caroling, perhaps, like the holly, "bears the crown," for this universal Christmas custom unites all Christendom in songs that emphasize the real reason for the celebration—the birth of Christ. As we join in "O Come, All Ye Faithful," may we have faith that right will finally prevail and that "peace on earth" will be a reality.

> And they who do their souls no wrong,
> But keep at eve the faith of morn,
> Shall daily hear the Angel song,
> "Today the Prince of Peace is born."
>
> —James Russell Lowell.

Bibliography

Books

AULD, WILLIAM M., *Christmas Tidings*. New York, Macmillan Company, 1931

AULD, WILLIAM M., *Christmas Traditions*. New York, Macmillan Company, 1933

BAILEY, OLIVE, *Christmas with the Washingtons*. Richmond, Va., Dietz Press, 1948

BAYARD, L. R., *When the Star Shone*. Los Angeles, Pageant Publishing Co., 1921

BECKER, MAY L., *Home Book of Christmas*. New York, Dodd, Mead & Co., 1941

BECKER, MAY L., *Christmas Is Coming*. Boston, Houghton Mifflin Co., 1939

BONSALL, ELIZABETH H., *Famous Hymns*. Philadelphia, Union Press, 1923

BRADY, AGNES M., *Christmastide*. Dallas, Upshaw Co., 1927.

BRAZELTON, JULIAN, *Uncle Toby's Christmas Book*. New York, Harper & Brothers, 1936

BROWN, THERON, and BUTTERWORTH, HEZEKIAH, *Story of the Hymns and Tunes*. New York, George H. Doran, 1905

BRYANT, EDWARD A., *Yuletide Cheer*. New York, Thomas Y. Crowell Co., 1912

BUDAY, GEORGE, *Story of the Christmas Card*. London, Odhams Press, Ltd., no date

BUGBEE, WILLIS N., *Tiptop Christmas*. Syracuse, N. Y., 1870

BULLEN, A. H., *Christmas Garland*. London, J. C. Nimmo, 1887

CAMPBELL, R. J., *Story of Christmas*. New York, Macmillan Company, 1935

CARTER, ELSIE H., *Christmas Candles*. New York, H. Hoyt & Co., 1915

CHAMBERS, E. (Editor), *Book of Days*, Vol. 2. London and Edinburgh, W. & R. Chambers, 1863

COUNT, E. W., *Four Thousand Years of Christmas*. New York, Henry Schuman, 1948

CRANE, FRANK, *Christmas and the Year Round*. New York, John Lane Co., 1917

CRIPPEN, T. G., *Christmas & Christmas Lore*. New York, Dodge Co., 1928

CROTHERS, L. M., *By the Christmas Tree*. New York, Houghton Mifflin Co., 1908

DAHLGISH, ALICE, *Christmas*. New York, Charles Scribner's Sons, 1934

DEARMER, P., WILLIAMS, R. V., SHAW, M., *Oxford Book of Carols*. London, Oxford University Press, 1928

DIER, J. C., *Children's Book of Christmas*. New York, Macmillan Co., 1936

DOUGLAS, G. W., *American Book of Days*. New York, H. W. Wilson, 1937

DUFFIELD, S. W., *English Hymns, Their Authors & History*. New York, Funk and Wagnalls Co., 1886

DUNCAN, W. E., *Carols*. New York, Charles Scribner's Sons, 1911

EATON, ANNIE T., *Animals' Christmas*. New York, Viking Press, 1944

EICHLER, LILLIAN, *The Customs of Mankind*. Garden City, Doubleday & Co., 1924

FIELD, RACHEL, *Christmas Time*. New York, Macmillan Company, 1941

FOOTE, H. W., *Three Centuries of American Hymnody*. Cambridge, Mass., Harvard University Press, 1940

FORD, LAUREN, *Ageless Story*. New York, Dodd, Mead & Co., 1939

FROST, LESLEY, *Come Christmas*. New York, Coward-McCann, Inc., 1935

GARDNER, H. J., *Let's Celebrate Christmas*. New York, A. S. Barnes, 1940

GAYLEY, C. M., *Classic Myths*. Boston, Ginn and Co., 1900

GRAHAM, ELEANOR, *Welcome Christmas*. New York, E. P. Dutton & Co., Inc., 1932

GRIBBLE, L. R., *Christmas Treasury*. New York, Macmillan Co., 1929

HADFIELD, JOHN, *Christmas Companion*. New York, E. P. Dutton & Co., Inc., 1929

HARRISON, MICHAEL, *Story of Christmas,* Long Acre, London, Odhams Press, no date

HAUGEN, R. E., *Christmas* (Edited by Haugen) Vol. XX, Minneapolis, Augsburg Pub. House, 1950

HAYES, A. M., *Wreath of Christmas.* Norfolk, Conn., 1942

HENNIKER, ROSE H., *Perfect Christmas.* New York, E. P. Dutton & Co., Inc., 1933.

HORDER, G. G., *Hymn Lover.* London, J. Curwen & Sons, 1909

HOTTES, A. C. *1,001 Christmas Facts and Fancies.* New York, A. T. de la Mare Co., Inc., 1937

HUTCHINS, CHARLES L., *Carols, Old and New.* Boston, The Parish Choir, 1916

IRVING, WASHINGTON, *Sketch Book.* New York, Thomas Y. Crowell Company

KENT, C. A., *Fifty Great Songs of the Church.* Chicago, Morgan-Dillon & Co., 1942

KIRKLAND, WINIFRED, *Where the Star Still Shines.* New York, Fleming H. Revell Co., 1924

KVAMME, T. O., *Christmas Carolers' Book.* Chicago, Hall & McCreary Co., 1935

LEWIS, B. W., *Christmas Book: Anthology for Moderns.* New York, E. P. Dutton & Co., Inc., 1928.

LINCOLN, J. C., *Christmas Days.* New York, Coward-McCann, Inc., 1938

MABIE, H. W., *Christmas Story.* New York, Dodd, Mead & Co., 1908

MARKS, H. B., *Rise and Growth of English Hymnody,* New York, Fleming H. Revell Co., 1937

McKNIGHT, G. H., *St. Nicholas.* New York, G. P. Putnam's Sons, 1947

McSPADDEN, J. W., *Book of Holidays.* New York, Thomas Y. Crowell Co., 1927

MILES, C. A., *Christmas in Ritual and Tradition.* London, Unwin, 1912

MORRIS, ERNEST, *Legends o' the Bells.* London, Sampson, Low, Marston & Co., Ltd., 1949

MORRISON, GOUVERNEUR (Editor), *Bells, Their History and Romance.* Santa Barbara, Calif., J. F. Rowny Press, 1932

MOTTINGER, A. H. (Editor), *Christmas.* New York, Schirmer, 1948

NICHOLS, J. R., *Bells thro' the Ages.* London, Chapman & Hall, Ltd. 1928

NINDE, E. S., *Story of the American Hymn.* New York, Abingdon, 1921

OBERNDORFER, ANNE S., *Noels.* Chicago, Fitzsimmons Co., 1932

PATTEN, HELEN P., *The Year's Festivals.* Boston, The L. C. Page & Co., 1903

PAULI, HERTHA, *St. Nicholas's Travels.* Boston, Houghton Mifflin, 1945

PRINGLE, MARY P., *Yuletide in Many Lands*. Boston, Lothrop, Lee, and Shepard, 1916

RICKERT, EDITH, *Ancient English Carols*. New York, Duffield & Co., 1910

RUDIN, CECILIA M., *Stories of Hymns We Love*. Chicago, John Rudin & Co., 1936

SCHAUFFLER, R. H., *Christmas*. New York, Dodd, Mead & Co., 1928

SCOTT, TEMPLE, *Christmas Treasury*. New York, Baker & Taylor, 1910

SECHRIST, ELIZABETH H., *Christmas Everywhere*. Philadelphia, Macrae-Smith Co., 1936

SECHRIST, ELIZABETH H., *Red Letter Days*. Philadelphia, Macrae-Smith Co., 1940

SMITH, ELVA, *Christmas in Legend and Story*. Boston, Lothrop, Lee, and Shepard Co., 1915

SMITH, H. A., *Lyric Religion, the Romance of Immortal Hymns*. London & Edinburgh, Fleming H. Revell Co., 1931

SPICER, DOROTHY G., *Book of Festivals*. New York, Women's Press, 1937

THEN, J. N., *Christmas*. Milwaukee, Wisc., Bruce Pub. Co., 1934

THEN, J. N., *Christmas Comes Again*. Milwaukee, Wisc., Bruce Pub. Co., 1940

THOMPSON, DOROTHY, *Once on a Christmas*. New York, Oxford University Press, 1938

VAN LOON, H. W., *Christmas Carols*. New York, Simon and Schuster, Inc., 1937

VITZETELLY, HENRY, *Christmas with the Poets*. London, D. Bogue, 1951

WALTERS, H. B., *Church Bells of England*. London, Oxford University Press, 1912

WASNAR, FRANZ (Editor and arranger), *Trapp Family Book of Christmas Carols*. New York, Pantheon Books, 1950

WATERFIELD, C. H., *Road to Christmas*. New York, Abingdon Press, 1925

WELLS, A. R., *A Treasure of Hymns*. Boston, Chicago, United Society of Christian Endeavor, 1914

WENDTE, C. W., *At Christmas Time*. Boston, Beacon Press, 1917

WERNECKE, H. H., *Christmas*. Webster Grove, Mo., Orchard Book Shop, 1936

WERTSNER, ANNE, *Make Your Own Merry Christmas*. New York, M. Barrows & Co., 1946

WHEELER, OPAL, *Sing for Christmas*. New York, E. P. Dutton & Co., Inc., 1943.

ENCYCLOPEDIAS

Encyclopedia Americana. New York, Americana Corp., 1952
New International. New York, Dodd, Mead & Co., 1914

MAGAZINES

AGAY, FENES, "Sing a Song of Christmas!" *Everywoman,* December, 1952

ANDERSON, DOROTHY M., "Holly . . . Mistletoe," *American Home,* December, 1949

ARTHUR, JULIETTA, "Century of Christmas Cards," *American Home,* December, 1946

BASKETTE, FLOYD, "Signs of the Times," *Classmate,* December 3, 1950

BENGSTEN, BENNIE, "Father of the Christmas Seal," *Classmate,* December 16, 1951

BENGSTEN, BENNIE, "Phillips Brooks," *Classmate,* December 24, 1950

BEST, KATHERINE, and HILLYER, KATHERINE, "Town of the Month," "Palmer Lake, Colorado," *Good Housekeeping,* December, 1951

CAREW, DOROTHY, and ROSAPEPE, JOSEPH, "The Truth about Santa Claus," *Saturday Evening Post,* December 13, 1952

CORNELL, GEORGE W., "Church Bells Are Coming Back," *Los Angeles Examiner,* September 20, 1953

DAVIS, PHIL, "Santa Claus Land," *Buick Magazine,* December, 1948

DIBBKE, GLADYS G., "Sharing the Greens," *American Home,* December, 1952

DOWDEY, CLIFFORD, "World's Highest Paid Santa Claus," *Saturday Evening Post,* December 22, 1951

EDWARDS, VINCENT, "America's First Christmas," *Classmate,* December 13, 1946

EDWARDS, VINCENT, "Story of a Famous Christmas Carol," *Christian Herald,* December, 1946

FEUER, S. CLARE, "One Candle Kindles Many Others," *Classmate,* December 14, 1947

FOSTER, EUNICE W., "Christmas Music," *Classmate,* December 14, 1947

HADLEY, PAUL, "Mistletoe, Our Christmas Parasite," *Christian Advocate,* December, 1950

ALL ABOUT CHRISTMAS

HODESH, ROBERT, "At Home with Santa Claus," *Ford Times*, December, 1952

JEFFERSON, HELEN G., "Grass Valley Choir," *Christian Advocate*, December 22, 1949

KECK, WENDELL M., "Dr. Watts's Christianized Psalms," *Christian Advocate*, March 23, 1947

KERIGAN, FLORENCE, "Christmas City," *Classmate*, December 17, 1950

KING, A. J., "Where Christmas Comes Alive," *Classmate*, December, 1949

LAKE, H. C., "Christmas Music," *Classmate*, December, 1948

LeBUFFEM, THE REV. FRANCIS P., "When Is Christmas?" *American Weekly*, December 19, 1948

LOCKE, ZELMA G., "Christmas Carol Broadsides," *Classmate*, December 18, 1949

LOCKE, ZELMA G., "Poinsett and Poinsettia," *Classmate*, December 14, 1947

MAJORS, H. K., "Santa's Family Tree," *Christian Advocate*, December 14, 1950

MAREK, GEORGE, "Christmas Music," *Good Housekeeping*, December, 1952

MAREK, GEORGE, "Musical December 25," *Good Housekeeping*, December, 1951

MARSHALL, ELEANOR M., "He Is America's Santa Claus," *Christian Advocate*, December 15, 1950

MARTIN, REBECCA, "Greek Cross Day," *Classmate*, January 1, 1950

McCUTCHAN, R. G., "Good Tidings," *Christian Advocate*, December 16, 1943

NEAL, HELEN S., "Carols Enchant Us," *Christian Home*, December, 1952

OFFERGELD, ROBERT, "The Christmas Crib," *Mademoiselle*, December, 1948.

OSTLER, FRED J., "Father of the Christmas Seal," *Coronet*, November, 1947

PAULI, HERTHA, "Our First Christmas Tree" (Condensation) *Coronet*, December, 1944

PAULI, HERTHA, "Song from Heaven" (Condensation) *Coronet*, November, 1943

PEATTIE, D. C., "Golden Bough of Christmas," *Country Gentleman*, December, 1952

SALISBURY, DOROTHY C., "Christmas Trees to Burn," *Family Circle,* January, 1948

SANDERS, P. S., "Christmas Tide and Epiphany," *Christian Advocate,* December 25, 1947

SCHONBERG, H. O., "I Want a Christmas Story," *Etude,* December, 1950

SCOTT, WINIFRED, "Santa's Father," *P.E.O. Record,* December, 1949

SWEET, W. W., "Five Shillings Christmas Fine," *Christian Advocate,* December 21, 1950

TODD, MARTHA, "Tea Time Chat," *Christian Herald,* December, 1946 and January, 1947

TOOKER, DOROTHY, "Narcissus and Holly for December," *Classmate,* December 10, 1950

TREADWELL, LYNN, "Star Over Bethlehem," *Ford Times,* December, 1946

WALLER, PHOEBE, "Christmas Tree," *Classmate,* December 21, 1947

WILKIE, KATHERINE E., "High Days and Holidays of Israel," *Classmate,* March 26, 1950

WINTERS, FRANKLIN, "First Christmas Tree in America," *Christian Advocate,* December, 1949

WOODSON, W. D., "Fifteenth Century Wreaths," *Classmate,* December 10, 1950

———, "Christmas Customs Round the World," *Better Living,* December, 1952

———, "Christmas in an Envelope" (Hallmark advertisement), *Coronet,* December, 1952

———, "Deck the Halls," *Young People,* December 25, 1949

———, "Santa Claus Lives Here," *McCall's,* December, 1952

———, "There Were Three Kings," *Collier's,* December 27, 1952

PAMPHLETS

———, *Christmas Trees, the Tradition and Trade,* Agricultural Information Bulletin, No. 24, U.S. Dept. of Agriculture, Washington, D.C.

———, "America's Christmas City," reprint by Bethlehem, Pa. Chamber of Commerce

Also many newspaper clippings from various parts of the United States, also from Melbourne, Australia.

Index

Abney, Sir Thomas, and Lady, 165, 166
Abolition of Christmas, 7
Adam, Adolphe, 158, 185
"Adeste Fideles" ("O Come, All Ye Faithful") ("Portuguese Hymn"), 155, 156, 178, 192
Advent wreath, 180
Albert, Prince, 38, 64, 65, 133
Alexander, Mrs. Cecil F., 169
"All-Father." See Woden
Alter, Dr., 124
Amahl and the Night Visitors, 22, 23
American Artists' group, 135
American Forests Products Company, 69
American Red Cross, 139, 141
"America's Christmas City." See Bethlehem, Pennsylvania
"Ancient Master of the Revels," 181
Anderson, Mrs. Eugenie, 142
"Angels from the Realms of Glory," 167, 168
"Angels We Have Heard on High" ("Westminster Carol"), 158
Animals at Christmas, 44, 87, 108
Argonne Forest, 185
Arnsdorf, 161
Arthur Bonnicastle, 173
"Apple Florentine," 105
"Ave Maria," 191
"Away in a Manger," 152

Babouschka. See Befana
Bach, J. S., 151, 160
Bailey, Olive, 109
Balls, three, 28

Balthasar, 13, 14, 172
Bambino, 179
Banks, Norman, 186–188
Bari, Italy, 27
Bart, Barry, 141
Bay (laurel), 46
Bayberry candles, 114
Bede, The Venerable, 127
Been, Holland, 128
Befana, 16
Bells, Christmas, 124–130: antiquity of bells, 125; first use on Christian churches, 125; early English church bells, 125; their inscriptions, 125, 126; baptism, 126; early use of Christmas bells, 126; in Scandinavia, Italy, Spain, 126; "Blowing in the Yule," 126, 180; in Australia, 127; in British Isles, 127, 128; "Berkeley's Bell" ("pudding bell"), 127; "Tolling (Ringing) the Devil's Knell" ("The Old Lad's Passing"), 127, 128; superstitions about bells, 128; Christmas bells, inspiration to poets, 128, 129; Christmas bells in the United States, 129, 130; revival of church bells, 130
Bennett, Ernest, 137
"Berkeley's Bell," 127
"Bethlehem" (nativity scene), 90, 91
Bethlehem, in Holy Land, 14, 174
Bethlehem, Pennsylvania ("America's Christmas City"), 71, 90, 92–94, 108, 118, 122, 123
"Bethlehem Star Lane," Van Nuys, California, 122
Bissell, Emily, 139, 140, 142

"Blessing of the Waters," 17

"Blowing in the Yule," 126, 180

"Boar's Head in Hand Bring I," 100–102, 148–150

Bok Tower, Florida, caroling, 190

Bonaventure, St., 86, 87

Boxing Day (St. Stephen's Day), 38

"Boy Bishops," 27, 28

Bracebridge dinner, 106, 107

Bradley, Rev. Edward, 132

Brady, Nicholas, 167

Bramley, Rev. H. R., 154

Brandywine Sanitarium, 139

Brasier, Virginia, 73

"Bring a Torch, Jeanette, Isabella," 159

"Broadsides" ("broadsheets"), 150, 152, 154, 188

Brooks, Phillips, 174–176

Buday, George, cited, 133

Byrom, John, 153

Cake of the Three Kings (Twelfth Night cake), 20

Calkin, J. B., 173

"Calm on the Listening Ear of Night," 171

Candles, Christmas, 113–119: early use at winter feasts, 113; at Jewish Feast of Lights, 113; candles, symbolic of Christ, "Light of the World," 113; establishment of Candlemas, change of date, Blessing of the Candles, 113; Luther and Christmas tree candles, 114; candles for the Christ Child, 114, 115; candle customs, 116, 117; Advent candle, 117; American candlelight services, 118; candles in homes, 118, 119; luminarios, 119; number of candles used, 119; our Christmas, a "Feast of Lights," 119

"Cantique de Noël." See "O Holy Night"

Cantus Diversi, 156

Cards, Christmas, 131–137: number used in the United States, 131; origin and importance, 131, 132; four claimants to first card (Rev. Edward Bradley, W. A. Dobson, William Egley, John Calcott Horsley), 132, 133; early English publishers (Goodall and Son, Raphael Tuck and Sons, Marcus Card Company) and prize contests, 133, 134; in America, Louis Prang's cards, 134; decline in artistry of greetings, 135; revival of interest in good cards, 135; various types, 136, 137; selection and display, 137; cards during wartime, 137; importance of holiday greetings, 137

"Carols by Candlelight," 186–188

Carols, Christmas, 144–176: first carol, 144; popularity, 144; origin of "carol," 144; characteristics, 145; St. Francis, "Father of the Christmas Carol," 145; development of carols, 145, 146; subjects, 146–149; Richard Hill's diary, 149, 150; first printed carols, 150; "broadsides" ("broadsheets"), 150; carols by Wither and Herrick, 150, 151; folk songs on continent, 151; Luther and carols, 151, 152; carols in England, 152–154; Puritan opposition, 152; collection and preservation of carols, 152–154; stories of individual carols, 155–176

Carols for Christmastide, 158

Carols for Christmas Time, 153, 154

Carols, Hymns, Songs, 172

Caroling, joy of, 144; early practice, 144, 145, 148, 149, 152–154, 192;

popularity, 177; Luther and caroling in Germany, 177, 178; in France, 178; in Spain and Italy, 178, 179; in Russia, 179, 180; in Poland, Scandinavia, 180; Great Britain, 180–184; in Elizabethan times, 181; before and after Restoration, 181; waits, 181–184; origin, 181; in rural districts, 182, 183; Longfellow and waits, 182; Irving and waits, 182, 183; caroling in Wales, 184; on Isle of Man, 184; in wartime, 184–186; in Australia, "Caroling by candlelight," 186–188; in America, 188–192; in New England, New York, Virginia, 188, 189; by Moravians, 188, 189; modern caroling, 189–192; in Memphis, Washington, D.C., Canoga Park, California, 189; Philadelphia, 190; Los Angeles, Bok Tower, F l o r i d a, Long Beach, California, Hot Springs, Arkansas, 190; Grass Valley, California, 190, 191; around various community trees, 191

Caspar. *See* Kaspar
"Cherry Tree Carol," 146
"Children's Christmas Tree," 70
Christ, "The Light of the World," 119
"Christ, the Lord, Is Risen Today," 169
Christmas, celebration of, in Europe, 2–8; opposed by early church fathers, 2; first observance at Rome, 2; celebrated on different days, 2; December 25 set by Pope Julius I, 2; reasons for choice, 2, 3; merging of pagan and Christian rites, 3, 4; English Christmases under King Arthur, the Anglo-Saxons, Alfred the Great, Normans, Tudors, Stuarts, 5–7; opposed by Puritans, 7; after the Restoration, 8

Christmas, celebration of, in America, a composite one, 4, 12; observed by Columbus, 4; at St. Croix Island, 188; opposition of Pilgrims at Plymouth, 8; celebration legalized in Massachusetts, 9; observance in New Amsterdam, 9; in Virginia, 10; Moravian customs, 10; Spanish observance in our Southwest, 11

Christmas, names, 1; origin, 1–11
Christmas Box, 186
"Christmas brand." *See* Yule log
Christmas Carols, Ancient a n d Modern, 153, 158
Christmas Carols, Old and New, 154
Christmas, Florida, 10
"Christmas Flower." *See* poinsettia
"Christmas Gardens," Baltimore, 95, 96
Christmastide, 154
"Christmas Tree Lane," 72, 73
"Christmas Stamp, The," 139
"Christmas Village" (Torrington, Connecticut), 35
Christmas with the Washingtons, 109
Churchill, Winston, 136
Church of the Nativity, 174
Cleland, Thomas M., 141
"Cock Crow Mass," 126
Cole, Sir Henry, 132
Coles, R. C., 124
Collection of Christmas Carols, 153
Comet, Halley's, 123
Constantine, Emperor, 2
Cornelius, Peter, 64
Cornell, G. W., 130
"Coventry Carol," 146
Crèche, 90, 159, 178
Cross of Lorraine, 141

"Crusader's Crib," 179
Cummings, Dr. W. H., 169

Darling, Tom, 141
"Deck the Halls," 148
Dickens, Charles, 8, 106, 132, 153
Dies Solis Invicti Nati, 3
Dobson, W. A., 132
Dohanos, Steve, 141
Druids, 46, 52, 54, 55
Durandus, 113, 177

Ecke, Albert, 58
Ecke, Paul, 58
Egley, William, 132
Encinitas, California, "Poinsettia Capital of the World," 58
Engleman, Vernon, 95, 96
English Book of Common Prayer, 168
Epiphany (Feast of the Three Kings) (Twelfth Night), 16–22; meaning of "Epiphany," 16; first mention, 16; combination of heathen and pagan rites, 77; "Blessing of the Waters," 17; "Greek Cross Day" at Tarpon Springs, Florida, 17; at Long Beach, California, 18; Epiphany, at Milan, 19; "Star Boys," 19; gift day for Spanish children, 19; at Rome, 20; in England, burning of Christmas trees, 21; in South America, 21; in Mexico, and Los Angeles, 21, 22
Este, Thomas, 167
"Everywhere, Everywhere, Christmas Tonight," 175

"Father Christmas," 31, 38, 134
"Father of the Christmas Carol." *See* St. Francis
"Father of the Christmas Stamp." *See* Einar Holboell

"Father of Hymnody." *See* Isaac Watts
"Feast of All Mankind," 4
Feast of the Three Kings. *See* Epiphany
Festgesang (Festival Song), 169
Firearms, fireworks, use at Christmas, 10
"First Christmas Tree," by Van Dyke, 62
"First Nowell," 146, 158
Florentin, St., 65
Follen, Charles, 66, 67
"Folksong from Zillertal," 102
Foods, Christmas, 96–112; importance, 97; in "Merrie England," 97–107; at holiday feasts of King Alfred, 97; Henry II, 97, 98; Edward I, 98; Richard II, 98; Henry IV, 98; Henry V, 98; Henry VI, 98; Henry VII, 97, 98; "subtleties," 99; feasts of Henry VIII, 99; Elizabeth I, 99; boar's head custom, 100, 101; banned by Cromwell, 100; restoration, 101; peacock, as holiday dish, 97, 98, 101, 102; mince (mutton) pies, 102, 103; "wayfarers' pies," 103; origin and symbolism of mince pies, 103; Sir Henry Grey's pie, 103; large modern pie, at Salt Lake City, 103; plum pudding (pottage), 103, 104; Mrs. Fraser's recipe, 104; Christmas cakes, 104, 108; Puritans' opposition to holiday feasting, 104, 105; wassail, 104, 105; superstitions connected with Christmas foods, 105; "Apple Florentine," 105; Pepys's dinners, 105, 106; Sir Roger de Coverley's, 106; Dickens and food, 106; Irving's Bracebridge dinner, 106, 107; continental foods, 107; fish, 107; turkeys, 107, 108; breads,

107, 108; rice pudding, 108, 110; cookies, 108–110; *Pfefferkuchen,* 108; sharing food with poor, 108; with Christ Child, and Mary, 108; Christmas foods in early Virginia days, 109; at the Washingtons', 109; cranberries, 110; menu of 1897, 110, 111; Bracebridge dinners at Yosemite, 111, 112; at Victoria, B.C., 111
Ford, John, 188
Fowler, Mrs. Margaret, 58, 59
Francis, St., 96, 145, 147, 155, 177
Franklin, Benjamin, 188
"Friendship Tree," 137
"Frumante" ("furmety"). *See* Christmas foods

Gauntlett, H. J., 170
Gelasius, Pope, 113
Geoffrey of Lorraine, 141
Gibbs, Philip, 188
Gifts, Christmas, 36–44; gifts of Three Kings, 36; of early Romans, 36, 37; in Egypt, 37; during Middle Ages in England, 37, 38; on Boxing Day, 38; Swift's complaint, 39; St. Nicholas, as chief gift-bringer, 39, 40; gifts in Germany, Switzerland, 41; in France, 41, 42; in Spain, Italy, Russia, 42; Scandinavia, Hungary, Mexico, 43; on New Year's Day, 42; to animals, 44; modern giving, 44; gifts, a tribute to the "Giver of Perfect Gifts," 44
Glastonbury thorn tree, 47
"Gloria in Excelsis Deo," 145
"Glutton mass celebration," 98
"Go, Tell It on the Mountains," 173
"God Rest You Merry, Gentlemen," 147, 148
Goethe, 88, 89
"Golden Bough." *See* mistletoe

"Good Christian Men, Rejoice." *See* "In Dulci Jubilo"
"Good King Wenceslas," 148, 172
Goodall and Son, 133, 134
"Grandfather Frost," 42, 43
Grant tree, the General ("Nation's Christmas Tree"), 74, 75
Grass Valley, California, 90, 91
Greccio, Italy, 85
"Greek Cross Day." *See* Epiphany
Greenery, Christmas, 45–60: early winter use by Jews, Romans, Teutons, etc., 45, 46; importance in Britain, 46; bay (laurel), 46; rosemary, 46, 47; legends, 47; taking down greens, 47; holly, name, kinds, 48, 49; in the United States, 49; beliefs about holly, 49–51; symbol of Mary, 50; Christ's crown of thorns, 50; holly in churches, 50; praise of holly, 50, 51; "he" and "she" types, 51; bringing in the holly, 51; making peace under its branches, 51; Mackay's lines, 51; mistletoe, 51–56; name, origin, 51; called "Golden Bough," 52; connection with Druids, 52, 54; Greek myth, 52; Aeneas, 52; in Norse legends, 52–54; at York Minster, 55; beliefs about mistletoe, 55, 56; use as medicine, 52, 54, 55; a parasite, 52, 53; in California, 53; Scott's lines, 55, 56; Shakespeare's, 56; kissing under mistletoe, 56; poinsettia (the "Christmas Flower"), 57, 58; its discoverer, Dr. Poinsett, 57; Della Robbia wreaths, 58, 59; description, origin, created by Mrs. Margaret Fowler, 58, 59; number made, 59; use of funds, 59; "Sharing of the Greens," 59; "Hanging of the Greens," 59, 60

Gregory, Pope, 3
Grey, Sir Henry, 103
Gruber, Franz X., 161–164, 186
Gude and Godly Ballades, 157

Hallein, 163, 164, 186
Handel, 160, 166
"Hanging of the Greens," 59, 60
"Hark! the Herald Angels Sing,"
    129, 153, 168, 169
Harrington, Karl, 173
Harrison, President Benjamin, 68
Harrison, Michael, cited, 132, 133,
    184
Haver, James, 132
Helmore, Rev. T. H., 153
Herbert, J. B., 173
"Here We Come a-Wassailing," 149
Herford, Oliver, 56
Herod, 14, 19
Herrick, Robert, 103, 150, 152
Hessian Christmas trees, 66
Hill, Richard, diary, 149, 150
Hodges, Leigh M., 140, 141
Holboell, Einar, 138, 139, 142, 143
Holland, J. J., 173
Holly, 48–51
"Holly and the Ivy," 147, 148, 153,
    188
Holmes, O. W., 105, 171
"Holy Supper," 44
Honorius III, Pope, 86
Hopkins, Rev. J. H., 172
Horsley, J. C., 132, 133
Hot Springs, Ark., caroling, 190
"How Brightly Beams the Morning
    Star," 160, 189
Hunter, Eleanor, 130
Husk, W. H., 154
Hymns for Little Children, 170
Hymns of the Eastern Church, 157

"I Heard the Bells on Christmas
    Day," 172, 173
Imgard, August, 67

"In Memoriam," 129
"In Dulci Jubilo" ("Good Christian
    Men, Rejoice"), 156–158, 189
Irving, Washington, 106, 107, 111,
    112, 178, 182, 183
"Isle of Bells" (Britain), 127
Isle of Man, caroling, 184
"It Came Upon the Midnight Clear,"
    170, 171

"Joy to the World," 165, 166, 191

Kaspar (Caspar), 14, 111, 112
Keble, John, 130
Kent, Rockwell, 141
"Kindle the Christmas Brand," 78,
    79
Kings, the Three (Magi) (Wise
    Men), 13–23; adoration of
    Christ Child, 13; visit reported
    only by St. Matthew, 13; journey
    to Bethlehem, 14; meeting with
    Herod, 14; "Star of Bethlehem,"
    14, 15; later life, martyrs, burial,
    16; tomb at Cologne, 16; well
    named for them, 16; meeting
    with Befana, 16; date of visit to
    Christ Child, 16; celebration of
    their feast day, 16–23; *Amahl
    and the Night Visitors,* 22, 23
King's Canyon National Park, 75
"Kissing Ring (Bough)," 54, 57, 92
Kissing under mistletoe, 51, 56
Krippe, 90
Kristkindl, das, 40, 41
"Kümmelbrod," 109, 110

Lamb, Charles, 76
"Largest Living Tree," 70, 71
Leeds, Duke of, 156
Libanus, 37
"Lights, Feast of," 113, 119
Lights, special holiday effects, 119
*Little Child's Book: for Schools and
    Families,* 152

Lochen, Holland, 128
Long Beach, California, "Greek Cross Day," 17, 18; caroling on canals, 190
Longfellow, H. W., 172, 173, 182
Los Angeles, California, 21, 22, 71, 190
"Louis, St.," 175
Louise, Queen, 139
Lowell, James R., 192
Lucia, St., 41, 115, 116
Luminarios, 119
Luther, Martin, 114, 148, 151–153, 157, 177, 178

Macaronic hymns, 157
Mackay, Charles, 51
Macy, Evalena, 84
Madonna della Grazie, 88
Magi. *See* Three Kings
"March of the Three Kings," 147, 159
Marcus Card Company, 134
Massinger, description of a peacock, 101, 102
Mauracher, Karl, 162
Mayer, Christian, 96
Mayers, Herbert, 141
McGarrigle, Jimmy, 32
Medieval Hymns and Sequences, 157
Melbourne, Australia. *See* "Carols by Candlelight"
Melchior. *See* Three Kings
Mendelssohn, 169, 171
Messer John of Greccio, 86
Messiah, 160, 166
Miller, Dorothy Green, 94, 95
Miller, Thomas, 154
Mince pies, 102, 103
"Misrule, Lord of," 5, 99, 112
Missouri, University of, Wayside Manger, 195
Mistletoe, 51–56
"Mistletoe Bough," 56
Mithraism, 2

Mohr, Father Josef, 161–163, 186
Montgomery, John, 167, 168
Moore, Dr. Clement C., 30, 129
Moravians, 10, 92–95, 108, 188, 189
Morrison, Dr., 170, 171
Moses, G., 136
"Most Famous Christmas Crib in the World," 89, 90
Murray's Hymnal, 156
Murray, J. R., 152
Mutton pies. *See* mince pies.

Nacimiento, 90, 179
Nast, Thomas, 30
"National Living Christmas Tree," 73, 74
National Tuberculosis Association, 140–142
"Nation's Christmas Tree," 74, 75, 191
"Nation's Christmas Tree Festival," 75
"Nation's Community Tree," 73, 74, 191
Nativity scenes, 85–96; old custom, 85; popularity in the United States, 85; originated by St. Francis, 85–87; miracles, 87; spread of idea, 87, 92; simplicity of early scenes, 87; elaborate ones, 87, 88; artistry, 88; Madonna della Grazie, 88; scene at Naples, 88, 89; groups in museums, 89; created by Lang family of Oberammergau, 89; "Most Famous Christmas Crib in the World," 89, 90; use of scenes in homes in various lands, 91, 92; heirloom figures, markets, 92; popularity of nativity scenes in the United States, 92; at Bethlehem, Pennsylvania, (Putz), 92, 93; at Salem, North Carolina, 92; "Putz-visiting," 93, 94, 108; community "Putz," 93;

significance of groups, 96; collecting "Putz" figures, 94, 95; Mrs. Dorothy G. Miller's collection, 94, 95; Vernon Engleman's "Garden," 95, 96; Christian Mayer's, 96; commercial window displays, 96

Neale, Rev. J. M., 153, 157

New Carols for the Merry Time of Christmas to Sundry Pleasant Tunes, 152

New Version of the Psalms, 167

Nicholas, St. (Santa Claus), 24–35; different names, 24; a real person, 24–27; chosen Bishop, 24; visit to Holy Land, 25; imprisonment, 25; miracles, 25, 26; generosity, 26; gifts to three daughters, 26; death of, 26, 27; burial at Myra, 27; removal of remains to Bari, 27; his celebration there, 27; Boy Bishops, 27, 28; insignia of St. Nicholas (three balls), 28; patron saint, 28, 29; churches named for him, 29; St. Nicholas and Dutch in America, 29; his feast day merged with Christmas, 29; St. Nicholas Society, 30; the saint, pictured by Thomas Nast, 30, 31; modern "St. Nicks," 31; in England, "Father Christmas," 31; Bill Strother, 32; Jimmy McGarrigle, 32; "St. Nick's" transportation, 32, 33; his parades, 33

"Noël! Noël!" 185

Noëls, 144, 178

"North Pole" (Santa's Workshop), 34

Novello, Vincent, 156

"O Come, All Ye Faithful." *See* "Adeste Fideles"

"O Du Froehliche! O Du Selige!" ("O Sanctissima"), 160, 185

"O Holy Night," 158, 159, 185

"O Little Town of Bethlehem," 174–176, 191

"O Tannenbaum! O Tannenbaum!" ("O Christmas Tree! O Christmas Tree!"), 159, 178

Oakeley, Frederick, 156

Oberndorf, 161

"Old Heathen's Feasting Day," 152

Olvera Street, Los Angeles, 11, 12

"Once in Royal David's City," 169, 170

Oratorio, Christmas, 160

Origin and development of modern American Christmas, 1–12

Oxford Book of Carols, 144

Pagan winter feasts, 1

Palmer Lake, Colorado, Yule Log Hunt, 83, 84; Star, 122

Pantomimes, Christmas, 8

Pastores, Los, 11

Pauli, Hertha, 166

Peacock. *See* Christmas foods

Pfefferkuchen, 108

Pepys's Christmas dinners, 105, 106

Pfuetz, Douglas, 142

Philadelphia, 70, 190

Piae Cantiones, 148, 153, 157

Pierce, President, 68

Pifferai, 129

Pinata, 12

Pinchot, Gifford, 68

Pipers, Roman. *See Pifferai*

Planetariums, Griffith, Hayden, 123, 124

Plays, Christmas, beginning of English stage, 6

Plum pottage. *See* Christmas foods

Poems by the Wayside, 172

"Poet Laureate of Methodism." *See* Charles Wesley

Poinsett, Dr. Joel, 57

Poinsettia ("Christmas Flower"), 57, 58
"Poinsettia Belt," 57, 58
"Poinsettia City" (Encinitas, California), 58
"Poinsettia Fiesta," 58
Portugallo, Marcus, 156
Portuguese Chapel, 156
"Portuguese Hymn." *See* "Adeste Fideles"
Posadas, Las, 11, 12
Psalms of David, 166
Praesepio (presepe). See nativity scenes
Protestant hymnal, first, 151
Prang, Louis, 134, 135
"Prince of Hymn Writers." *See* Charles Wesley
"Pudding Bell." *See* "Berkeley's Bell"
Puritans, 7, 104, 105, 152, 188
Putz, 92–95
"Putz-visiting," 93, 94, 108

Reading, John, 156
Redner, L. H., 175
"Regent Street," 168
Register, Christian, 170
Rich, Edmund, 8
Richardson, Dr. R. S., 123
Riis, Jacob, 126, 139, 180
"Rise Up, Shepherds, an' Foller," 173
Rockefeller Center, 71, 72
Rockwell, Norman, 136
Roosevelt, F. D., 69
Roosevelt, Theodore, 68
Rosemary, 46, 47
"Rudolph, the Red-nosed Reindeer," 191

Salem, North Carolina, 92
Salt Lake City mince pie, 103
Salzburg, 163, 164
Sandys, William, 153, 154, 158, 179
Santa Claus. *See* St. Nicholas
Santa Claus, Indiana, 33, 34

Santa's Helpers, 31
"Santa's Workshop." *See* "North Pole"
Santóns, 91
Saturnalia, 3, 37
Schumann-Heink, Madame, 67
Scott, Percy C., 142
Scott, Sir Walter, 101, 177
Scribner's Monthly, 173
Seals, Christmas, 138–143; wide use, 138, 143; carry message of hope, 138; originated by Danish Einar Holboell, 138; first seal, 138, 139; spread of custom, 139; article by Jacob Riis, 139; Emily Bissell's idea, 139, 140; first American seal, 140; first sale, 140; national co-operation, 140; sales supported by Red Cross and National Tuberculosis Association, 140, 141; Cross of Lorraine, 141; seal collections, 141; seals, designed by artists, 141; results of use of seals (decline in death rate), 142; preventive work, 142; our debt to Denmark, 142; importance of Holboell's idea, 142, 143; seals carry health message, 143
Sears, Rev. E. H., 170, 171
"Sharing of the Greens," 59
Shepherd Songs of Bethlehem (Hirtenlieder von Bethlehem), 188
Siege of Paris, caroling, 185
"Silent Night! Holy Night!" ("Stille Nacht! Heilige Nacht!") 160–164, 178, 185
Singers, Tyrolean, 164
"Sleep, Holy Babe!" 192
Smart, Henry, 168
"Song of Heaven," 160, 162
Songs of the Nativity, 154
Spangenberger, 177, 178
Stainer, Sir John, 147, 148, 154

Star, Christmas ("Star of Bethlehem"), 120–124; man's reverence for stars, 120; songs about the Christmas star, 120; star, as holiday decoration, 120, 121; "Star-singing," 121, 122; "Star Man," 122; community stars, 122, 123; "Christmas sky," at planetariums, 123; theories about star, 123, 124
"Star Boys," 19
"Star of Bethlehem" (Christmas Star), 14, 15, 120, 164, 172
Stephen's, St. Day, 38
"Still Christmas," 180
Stocking-hanging custom, 26
"Strassburg Tree," 62
Strasser children, 162, 163
Strother, Bill, 32
"Subtleties," 99
Suckling, Sir John, 106
Sullivan, Sir Arthur, 171
Suso, Henry, 157
Swift, Jonathan, 39

Tarpon Springs, Florida, "Greek Cross Day." See Epiphany
Tate, Nahum, 153, 166, 167
Telesphorus, Bishop, 145, 158
"There's a Song in the Air," 173, 174
Theriot, La., 10
"Tolling (Ringing) the Devil's Knell." See "Old Lad's Passing"
Torrington, Conn. See "Christmas Village"
Trees, Christmas, 61–75: pagan use changed to Christian custom, 62; "First Christmas Tree," by Van Dyke, 62; early use of trees or branches in homes, 62; spread of custom, 63–65; Luther's tree, 63; German trees, 63, 64; "Christmas Tree," by Peter Cornelius, 64; English trees, 64;

brought by Prince Albert, 64, 65; St. Florentin's tree, 65; Christ Child's gift of tree, 65; tinsel as decoration, 65, 66; legend of trees at Bethlehem, 66; "Tree of Life," 66; Hessian trees, 66; Charles Follen's tree, 66, 67; August Imgard's, 67; simple decorations, 67; Pastor Schwan's tree, 67; opposition to trees, 67, 68; growth in popularity, 67, 68; use in New England, 68; President Pierce's tree, 68; President Benjamin Harrison's tree, 68; Theodore Roosevelt's objection, 68; overruled by Gifford Pinchot, 68; report of American Forests Products Company, 69; trees, now "Big Business," 69; where obtained, 69; F. D. Roosevelt's Christmas tree farm, 69; types of trees used, 69; German decorations, 70; American ones, 70; "Tree of Light," 70; community trees, 70; "Largest Living Tree," 70–72; "Christmas Tree Lane," 12, 13; "Nation's Christmas Tree" (The General Grant), 74, 75; Nation's Christmas Tree Festival," Sanger, California, 75; "Tree of Universe" (Yggdrasil), 77; burning trees on Twelfth Night, 22
"Twelve Days of Christmas," 191
Twelfth Night. See Epiphany
Tuck, Raphael and Sons, 134
Tyndale, Thomas, 150

"Urn of Fate," 42

Van Nuys, California, 122
"Varina," 171
"Visit from St. Nicholas, A," 30, 129
"Vom Himmel Hoch," 151, 152, 185

Von Bora, Katharina, 177

Wade, J. F., 184
Waits, 181–184
"Waits" Tower, 182
Wassail, 104, 105
"Wassail! Wassail!" 149
Wassailing, 21, 149, 180, 181
Watts, Isaac, 165, 166
"Wayfarers' pies," 103
Wedderbrun, John, 157
Weihnachtslied ("Christmas Song"), 163
Welsh caroling, 184
Wesley, Charles, 129, 153, 168
Wesley, John, 168
"We Three Kings of Orient Are," 23, 120, 171, 172
"While Shepherds Watched Their Flocks by Night," 153, 166, 167
Whole Book of Psalms, 167
"Wie Herrlich Strahl der Morgenstern." *See* "How Brightly Beams the Morning Star"
"Wiegenlieder," 144
Willis, R. S., 171
"Winchester Old," 167
Wise Men. *See* Three Kings
Wither, George, 45, 150

Woden (Odin) ("All-Father"), 2
Woodbury, F. J., 72, 73
Woodward, Hezekiah, 152
Wreaths, Della Robbia, 58, 59

Yggdrasil ("Tree of Universe"), 77
Yule log, 76–84; fire, a symbol of home and safety, 76; use of fire in early ceremonies, 76, 77; Yggdrasil, old pagan log replaced by "Christmas Brand," 77; Yule log in England, 77–79; how chosen and brought in, 77, 78; beliefs about it, 77; songs, ceremonies, 78, 79; Herrick's "Kindle the Christmas Brand," 78, 79; friendship, games, snapdragon, story-telling near log, 79; logs in different countries, 79–82; superstitions regarding the brand, 82; symbol of Christ, the "Light of the World," 82; modern logs, 82, 83; Yule Log Hunt, Palmer Lake, Colorado, 83, 84; description of fire, from *Snowbound,* 84; caroling near log, 180

Zillertal, 162

Set in Linotype Granjon
Format by Edwin H. Kaplin
Manufactured by The Haddon Craftsmen, Inc.
Published by HARPER & BROTHERS, *New York*